YOU RAISED US – NOW WORK WITH US

YOU RAISED US – NOW WORK WITH US

Millennials, Career Success, and Building Strong Workplace Teams

LAUREN STILLER RIKLEEN

Cover design by Elmarie Jara/ABA Publishing.

Printed in the United States of America.

18 17 16 15 14 5 4 3 2 1

Library of Congress Cataloging-in-Publication data on file.

978-1-62722-585-4

Discounts are available for books ordered in bulk. Special consideration is given to state bars, CLE programs, and other bar-related organizations. Inquire at Book Publishing, ABA Publishing, American Bar Association, 321 N. Clark Street, Chicago, Illinois 60654-7598.

www.ShopABA.org

Dedication

To our Millennial children, Alex and Ilyse,

with the hope that this book will help

their generation and ours find the best of

each other in the workplace, and to my

husband, Sander, for his constant support

and unfailing wisdom.

Contents

Acknowledgments

In a book about the Millennial generation, it is appropriate that much of my gratitude is directed to Millennials. Throughout the research and writing process, Millennials were at the ready, helping me think through ideas and offer suggestions.

Much of this book is based on a survey that was developed by Jae Ho Kim, then a student intern from Babson College, now a young professional living in South Korea. Jae Ho's assistance developing the questions in each of the subject areas covered in the survey helped ensure that the voice of the Millennials is heard in each of the chapters.

I am also deeply grateful to the gifted cadre of Boston College students who worked with me. I feel fortunate that Natalie Sileno sought me out after a presentation I made at a BC event, and hope she did not come to regret her kind offer to undertake a summer internship with me which extended into her senior year (just prior to beginning her adventures at our soon to be shared alma mater, Boston College Law School).

The English Department at Boston College must be doing extraordinary work, as this book has benefitted from three amazing English majors. Evelyn Garrity provided dedicated and insightful analysis and research assistance, all with a maturity far beyond her Millennial years. The fact that her devotion to this project extended to prompt and enthusiastic responses to email questions while she was experiencing her semester in Europe increases my gratitude beyond words can express.

Allison Rottman stepped forward when Evelyn went abroad with the expectation that her assistance would only be needed through the first month of her senior year. I so appreciate that she stayed through the entire semester, helping me complete the manuscript by providing valuable assistance with endnotes and my multiple revisions of text.

I am also grateful to Marie McGrath for her detailed review of the manuscript, her insightful comments, and her related editorial and research assistance. It is a better book because of her comments and detailed copy edit.

Laura Faulkner has been of tremendous help since she was a student at our beloved Clark University. Her continued support, even as her career has taken her to different geographies, is always appreciated.

The process of developing the best name for this book involved a village of suggestions, but in the end, it was a Millennial who proposed the title. For more than a year, I complained to anyone who would listen about my nameless book and received a number of interesting suggestions, but none had full support from the multiple generations I am trying to reach with this book. None that is, until Leslie Nachbar said: "How about *You Raised Us, Now Work With Us.*" I am also grateful to Leslie for taking the time to read an early draft and provide detailed, thoughtful comments.

Others who read and commented on drafts at various stages involved a range of generations. In particular, I want to thank Beth Parsons, who, in addition to being a sharp editor, is a great sounding board, a wise advisor, and a wonderful niece. Also in the "I am so lucky to have them as a relative category" is Rachel Spitzer Rikleen, whose early comments shaped subsequent revisions, and who has the additional roles of being a brilliant lawyer and perfect sister-in-law. I am also grateful to Alice Richmond for her thoughtful suggestions and Scott L'Heureux for his review and ongoing interest and commentary on the topic.

The survey could not have reached as many people as it did without the help of everyone on my mailing list who took the time to forward a link to their Millennial friends and relatives. The large response to the survey helped supplement all the other research incorporated into this book. As important, I am so grateful to the many Millennials who took the time to offer thoughtful comments and anecdotes on their survey responses. Their unattributed comments bring the research to life and their insights enrich every issue discussed in the book.

This manuscript underwent a journey on the way to publication. Along that road, I was fortunate to encounter Joelle Delbourgo and Lisa Ball, and hope that our paths will cross again in the future.

Active engagement in bar associations has long been an important part of my life as a lawyer. I am currently privileged to have several leadership roles in the American Bar Association and remain a steadfast admirer of all that the ABA accomplishes through the efforts of thousands of volunteers and an incredibly dedicated staff. I am proud that the ABA is the publisher of this book.

For most of the time that I have been writing this book, I have had the opportunity to be serving as Executive-in-Residence at the Boston College Center for Work & Family in the Carroll School of Management. My delight in having connected with this remarkable group of people is exceeded by how fortunate Boston College is to have within it a Center that is recognized around the world for its cutting edge research and sophisticated synthesis of global studies on work-life issues and employee engagement. It is an honor to be working daily with colleagues who care so deeply about their work, who are making such an important contribution to workplaces in all sectors, and who are such an inspiration to be around.

The writing of this book got its start and was completed at the White Stallion Ranch in Tucson, a place which has been a vacation spot and a refuge for our family for years. There is no better place to write—or, for that matter, to avoid writing—than this beautiful and incredibly well-run oasis in the Sonoran Desert. May the True family legacy continue for generations to follow.

Book-writing is always an invasive species for families. Although fodder for interesting conversations, it can also be an annoyance and an interference with other priorities. My husband, Sander, gave new meaning to the word "flexibility," as he calmly shifted priorities to help and never complained about the complex rearranging that he so kindly did to support this endeavor—as he does all endeavors in our life together. The weekend he spent devoted to his extraordinarily helpful edits to the manuscript demonstrated once again his brilliant eye for detail and showed why his clients are lucky to have him as their lawyer.

My Millennial children, Alex and Ilyse, have played a role as inspirations for this book, as sounding boards for my ideas, and as additional proof that Millennial parents generally love to be around their kids and are enriched by their company.

Being part of a loving extended family helps make the otherwise difficult process of writing a book much easier, and makes life more precious. My thanks and love to each of you.

Introduction: Why Another Book about the Millennial Generation Now?

"They are entitled." "They are coddled by overbearing parents." "They do not want to work hard." "They are not loyal to their employers." As the Millennial generation moves into the workplace in increasing numbers, this evolving narrative is now becoming a fixed description. These descriptions form the themes that the media seizes upon and that employers use when frustrated by behaviors they do not understand.

These are also unfair characterizations that miss the mark and negatively impact a multi-generational workforce. When leaders in the workplace adopt this view without further analysis, they lose opportunities to develop the extraordinary potential of a generation that, as a result of current demographics, will be thrust into leadership roles at a younger age than their predecessors. They also miss important research about ways to engage this generation of future workplace leaders.[1]

During the years I have researched this book, I have often felt as though I straddled two worlds. My own view of the generation is partly shaped by my role as a mother of two Millennials. In my role as mom, I was chief dessert-maker to a home frequently filled with my kids and their smart, talented, and funny friends. Yet, in my professional capacity, I was often speaking before audiences where I fielded questions from Boomers and Gen Xers who were unhappy with many of the workplace behaviors they observed in their youngest colleagues.

These experiences highlighted for me that there are two views of Millennials—one from the vantage point of their parents and the other from the perspective of workplace leaders. But writing this book has made clear how easy it is to miss a third critical view of Millennials: how they see themselves. We can only truly strengthen intergenerational relationships by understanding the roots of each of these perspectives as a foundation for change.

You Raised Us, Now Work with Us seeks to bridge the generational divide by separating the myths from reality in the behaviors ascribed to Millennials. In doing so, it is helpful to be mindful of one key distinction: the generational lens is most frequently used by older generations when criticizing behaviors of younger people. That is, the reputation of Millennials has developed from older adults attributing observed characteristics to the generation as a whole. As a result, a generational reputation has taken hold.

Millennials, however, do not necessarily place their interactions with older adults in a generational context. In fact, it is more likely that you will hear someone born during the Millennials' birth years resist being referred to as a Millennial altogether.

I recall a meeting in which generational issues were being discussed. The sole Millennial in the group stated that she does not know anyone her age who liked being called a Millennial because the term had developed too many negative connotations after years of articles stereotyping so many aspects of their behaviors. It struck me that generational disconnects begin with the characterization of individual behaviors as representative of an entire generation. When this happens, older generations risk losing opportunities to develop stronger bonds with their Millennial work colleagues.

The goal of this book is to help the generations understand each other better, recognize the impact of their respective behaviors on the workplace, and provide specific strategies that can be employed to develop a better and more effective work environment.

The Generational Lens

The selected birth years that are ascribed to generations provide a framework for studying the impact of events on patterns of behaviors. Major experiences that occur during those selected formative years of a generation offer a context for analyzing the footprints each generation leaves behind. This book relies on the following commonly accepted dates as the relevant time frames: for Baby Boomers, birth years between 1946 and 1964; for Gen X, birth years between 1965 and 1978; and for Millennials, birth years between 1978 and 2000. It should be noted that there is some variation among researchers when identifying the birth years applicable to the Millennials, with ranges in the early years from approximately 1978 to 1982, and in the later years from approximately 1997 to the early 2000's.

Millennials are also often referred to as Gen Y, a name that took hold because they are the generation that followed Gen X. Both are used interchangeably and, particularly with respect to responses to the author's survey, both terms are used in this book.

Exploring Nuances, Strengthening Ties

Three generations comprise the overwhelming majority of today's work force: Baby Boomers, Generation X, and Millennials.[2] Numerous books and articles have described in detail the characteristics of each of these generations and the shared cultural experiences that have contributed to their values and behaviors. This book relies on that prior research as background, but its primary focus is Millennials' relationships with other generations.

This book has four goals. The first is to analyze and build upon other research about the Millennials with independent data, and to provide new insights into how Millennials view work as they begin their careers in the midst of an economic crisis. The second is to help Boomers and Gen X better meet the opportunities and challenges that Millennials bring into the workplace by providing practical recommendations for strengthening intergenerational teamwork and relationships. Third, the book is intended to help Millennials navigate their way through the complexities of today's work environment. And fourth, the book highlights the opportunity available to all generations to make needed changes in the workplace that will benefit everyone.

Each of these goals is threaded throughout the three parts of this book. Part One describes the key behaviors attributed to Millennials as well as Millennials' reactions to what other generations say about them. It also provides a cultural and familial context to what is observed. Part Two details the impacts of these behaviors on the workplace, including the ways in which disinterested leadership styles, inflexible work practices, and ineffective management can play into Millennials' reputation at work. Finally, Part Three focuses on the adaptations that are needed in the workplace to adjust to changing demographics while offering advice to Millennials as they learn to navigate their career.

The Survey

A foundational element for this book is the author's survey of Millennials.[3] The survey questions were designed to build upon studies, books, and media analyses of Millennials, and to seek their own views of how they have been portrayed. The survey asked Millennials about communications and technology in the workplace, their relationship with their families, their reputation as "entitled" and whether they believe it is a fair description, their intention to balance career aspirations with their family responsibilities and personal interests, and their expectations with respect to what they owe the workplace—and what they think the workplace owes them.

Of the more than 1,000 Millennials who responded, nearly 40% were students, evenly split between undergraduate and graduate school, with less than 4% in high school. More than 80% of the respondents described themselves as in the workforce, of which nearly 3/4 were employed full-time (note that some employed full-time were also attending college or graduate school programs). Respondents worked in a wide variety of occupations, such as law, teaching, healthcare, social services, financial services, marketing and public relations, retail, information technology, the sciences, and government.

The survey asked the respondents to identify their age range according to the following categories: under 18; 18–22; 23–25; or 26–31. This provided an opportunity to look for differences within the Millennials, to determine if the views of older Millennials differed from their younger cohorts. Approximately half of the respondents were in the 26–31 age range, and approximately 80% were female. Respondents came from all regions of the United States, with 90% of the 50 states represented, and a few from other countries.

The first wave of Millennials in the workplace has come of age during extremely difficult economic conditions, resulting in an unexpectedly harsh introduction into the world of work. The survey was first distributed in 2009 and held open for the next few years, during the height of the economic crisis, providing extraordinary insight into how members of this generation view the impact of the economy on their own career choices and opportunities. Their responses reveal a far more nuanced view of the world than the media coverage and much of the other information written about them suggests. These responses, combined with the significant other body of data that is developing about Millennials, offer an opportunity to understand their talents, their aspirations, and their challenges.

As is the case whenever significant differences among age groups are observed, questions arise. Are Millennials actually different from their Boomer and Gen X predecessors? Or is the workplace simply feeling the effects of a large number of young people making their presence known? The answers are explored in this book.

Cautionary Notes

This book addresses generational trends and the reputation that has developed regarding Millennials as a generation. It is not about individuals, a distinction that is critical.

When reading or writing about any analysis of generational patterns of behavior, several cautionary notes must be kept in mind. First, the birth years that identify each generation are artificial boundaries used to frame an understanding of a group that includes millions of people. They are themes that give coherence to observed patterns, but in no way do they describe everyone within the group. Birth years provide a helpful way to understand a generation that, by virtue of when they were born, has shared certain key societal events and cultural experiences at a particularly impressionable time. No generalized description can ever depict an entire demographic.

Moreover, age is but one variable of many that affect behaviors. The Sloan Center on Aging at Work at Boston College has identified a "prism of age" which looks beyond the impact of chronological years. Their study identifies an alternative framework for analyzing age diversity that takes into account such factors as career stage, physical-cognitive age, and life-events age. The prism of age offers another way for generations to understand each other.[4]

It is also important to emphasize that the complexities of characterizing a generation through shared experiences at particular points in time are further complicated by considerations of race, ethnicity, economic circumstances, geography, family circumstances, and a variety of other factors that differentiate how individuals respond to various events and opportunities. Researchers on this topic have noted the selective pool of Millennials that frames much of the data generated. One author stated that "most research on [Millennials] has focused on people who are from middle-class backgrounds and are more affluent."[5] Another commented that "much of what we know about the twenty-something years comes down to selective, basically narrow frames of reference," usually "able-bodied middle-class Americans."[6]

A fascinating book by Keli Goff provides an important perspective on the multi-layered generational lens that should be applied to these issues. Goff wrote about the seismic shift taking place among young black Americans whose age places them within Gen X, but whose own life experiences warrant an independent analysis, particularly with respect to their evolving political affiliations. As the offspring of parents who fought to end segregation and to pass laws to provide equal rights, members of this post-civil rights generation—named the Hip-Hop Generation by Bakari Kitwana—are staking out their own social and political identities, based on experiences that are distinct from their white Gen X counterparts.[7] Goff's important analysis of the differences within the Hip-Hop Generation provides insight into the caution needed whenever generational generalizations are made.

The impact of September 11, 2001, is another important example of major life events having different impacts within a generation with the long time span that is applied to the Millennials. Millennials born before approximately the mid-1990s may be the last remaining part of a generation to remember a time before fear of domestic terrorism altered how we travel and our access to buildings, creating a new normal of life.

A further cautionary note is warranted when describing the way Millennials communicate and use technology, as there are significant differences in the technology available to those born in the 1990s and those born earlier. The oldest Millennials were unlikely to have had cellphones before they graduated from high school; the youngest Millennials have been provided with phones as early as elementary school. A college email address was required to participate in Facebook when it was created in 2004; within just a few years, Facebook was so popular it became a verb as well as a noun. Older Millennials likely transitioned from the paper encyclopedia to the Britannica on-line while in high school, at a time when bloggers were rare and the medium little understood. Younger Millennials grew up with constant access to a far more sophisticated internet, where Google answered their questions and blogs were ubiquitous.[8]

The music-sharing database Napster is another example of the widely differing experiences between older and younger Millennials. Napster was a cultural phenomenon, driven by older Millennials, which revolutionized the way the world listens to music. Younger Millennials only know iTunes, and may not even be aware Napster existed, let alone recognize its historical significance to the way music is accessed online.

The speed at which technology changes has profound societal impacts and leads to the question of whether the number of years encompassing a particular generation should be reviewed.[9] This book leaves it to future demographers to determine if the rapidity of change warrants a shortened designation of future generational timeframes.

PART ONE

Chapter 1

On the Cusp

When "Anything is Possible" Meets Reality

Of all the negative characteristics used to describe Millennials, perhaps none has stuck more firmly than the notion of "entitled." This term, which is the subject of a later chapter, permeates much of the commentary about Millennials, regardless of economic background or education levels. Closer analysis reveals a wide gulf between how others use this term and how Millennials view this description.

When Millennials speak about the opportunities they have been given and share their fears about the choices ahead, it becomes clear that they enter their adult years wondering just how far the accomplishments of their childhood can take them in a workplace reeling from a prolonged economic downturn. They similarly worry about what it means to have been told all their lives to study hard and follow their passions and dreams, only to feel overwhelmed by choices, buried in historically high student loan debt, and thwarted by an outdated workplace structure.

In the midst of these concerns, they continue to push forward, sorting out their goals and aspirations. A conversation with one young Millennial illustrates these issues.

> *Jill, a rising college senior, was describing the conflicts she experienced over the past year regarding her career path. She began by explaining that when she was in 6th grade, her best friend was*

diagnosed with a brain tumor. Although she was only in middle school, she remembers being inspired by the surgeon that operated on her friend, noting: "Somewhere he made a decision to become a doctor and gave my best friend back to me." She was struck by the realization that: "This doctor had followed his passion and did something great with it. It made me much more academically focused."

Once Jill began college, she was certain that she was on a path to medical school and a career specializing in neuroscience. But she began to question that career goal when she took a course during her freshman year on the craft of teaching. She loved the course and was so impacted by what she was learning that she became a Teaching Assistant during her sophomore and junior years.

Early in her junior year, as she tried to sort out whether to pursue her long-held dream of becoming a doctor or her passion for teaching science, Jill felt discouraged by the substantial negative reactions she was finding on all fronts. At every opportunity, she sought career advice from doctors who only complained about how the profession has changed and how difficult their lives had become. They then invariably stated that they would never recommend the medical profession to a young person today.

When she spoke with people about whether to pursue her love for teaching science to high school students, she faced a different type of reaction, one steeped in assumptions: "You did not need to attend this university to become a high school teacher." She found these reactions disheartening: "I hate that the philosophy exists that the incentive for attending a 'better school' is to open doors to do things you could not otherwise have done at a different school."

As she struggled with her career decision, a chance conversation with a family friend led to an introduction to a pediatric surgeon involved in public health, particularly injury prevention. That meeting resulted in an opportunity to shadow him, which even included observing some surgeries. Watching a senior physician dedicated to his patients and to public health issues rejuvenated Jill's passion for medicine. She decided to pursue her dream of becoming a doctor: "I ultimately decided that I loved science too much to not go forward."

She also felt that her pursuit of a medical degree would provide her with greater opportunities to be a change agent.

Still, Jill felt she was not ready to apply to medical school for admission immediately following college. She recognized that she was exhausted from her grueling academic schedule and needed a break: "I feel too tired now. I worked crazy-hard in high school and through college, and don't feel ready to go right into the difficulty of medical school. I want to do the normal have-a-crappy-apartment-in-the-city thing."

During her hiatus, she hopes to work as a science teacher. She is excited by the idea of teaching human physiology or even starting a neuroscience program, stating: "There aren't enough great science course options in high school."

As Jill and her college friends enter their senior year, she is struck by how difficult a time this is in their lives. She observed that many of her fellow seniors got into college by having multiple areas of interest, but they have not yet developed a passion for any one thing. As a result, they feel anxious about choosing a particular direction: "If everything is an option for you and nothing stands out, that is stressful."

She noted that financial concerns also weigh heavily on their minds. As college students throughout a period of economic crisis, they are frequently reminded that they will be graduating at a time of diminished job prospects. Many students even find it hard to obtain volunteer internships, and feel torn about following advice that tells them what jobs they are "supposed" to seek in this economy, such as in the high tech industry.

As a peer advisor to incoming freshman, Jill recalled a session in which a student leader asked other peer advisors to identify one thing they wish they had known as an incoming freshman. Jill's answer revealed the heavy societal expectations that she and many of her colleagues feel: "When I came here, I thought everything was open and anything was possible. But being here made me feel that my options have narrowed. It is easy to fall into the trap of responding to what you are 'supposed' to do."

Jill is a smart, insightful, and talented young woman. But she is not unique in her desire to pursue her dreams, and her willingness to work hard to achieve them. Her candid assessment of her experiences to date and hopes for the future demonstrated a clear-eyed introspection and a sophisticated understanding of the difficulties that many in her generation face as they grapple with whether they, in fact, have a world of options available as they have always been told. Jill maintains, however, a drive to achieve and a passion to contribute to the world around her that remains undaunted by negative advice. It is that optimism, the desire to tap into her passions, and the goal to find meaning in her work that best exemplifies so many others in her generation.

Jill is part of a large generation that has been the focus of books, blogs, articles, media analyses, and debates, even though the oldest members are only in their early 30s. The media offers a continuous narrative of accomplished Millennials who have already made profoundly important contributions to the world. Children from immigrant families, inner-city neighborhoods, and wealthy communities alike have excelled in the classroom and beyond. Some are technology entrepreneurs who have made a fortune on the sale of companies that have taken their seedling of an idea into widespread application. Extraordinarily young athletes have made record-breaking contributions to their sports—either through team performance or individual accomplishments. And many are trying to find their way in a world where they are told of their boundless opportunities, but the job market is weak, loan repayments loom large, and options feel limited. Jill is but one example of an accomplished young person faced with making decisions about the choices she has been told await her, worried about what it means to finally choose and concerned about what will really happen once the road starts to narrow.

Millennials are now entering the workforce in large numbers. To those generations already there, the integration of the Millennials into their workplace culture has not been easy. Senior generations frequently misread their younger colleagues' self-confidence, their inquisitive nature, and their need for ongoing feedback, seeing instead entitled behaviors and an excessive need for praise. They can also be resistant to—or even threatened by—the technology which Millennials have seemingly mastered since birth.

This clash of generational patterns has its roots in misperceptions and misunderstandings. If these negative perceptions can be eliminated and the generations can see each other in the positive light they deserve, the results can be transformative for the workplace.

Chapter 2

Generations in Transition— Searching for the New Normal

The Long Workplace Shadow

The parents of the Baby Boomers, and many Gen Xers, were from the generation described as "Traditionalists" whose formative life experiences were marked by World War II and a severe and prolonged global depression. Scarred by childhood and young adult years rooted in war and deprivation, Traditionalists tackled work with a sense of duty and an innate caution towards any behaviors that could result in unemployment. Their drive to build a life of economic security for their families resulted in significant conformance at work.

This conformance included workplace norms that developed at a time when women typically did not work outside the home. The structure of the workplace assumed that all family needs would be addressed by a spouse at home who filled the traditional roles of wife and mother, while men put in long hours at work. This resulted in a workplace that became defined by rigid office hours, face-time demands, inflexible work arrangements, and both formal and informal opportunities that favor men without outside responsibilities. This structure became embedded as workplace culture, and has proven to be a formidable opponent of those seeking greater flexibility and equal opportunities at work.

It Used to be All About Us: the Baby Boomers

The Baby Boomers number approximately 80 million in the United States, and continue to be actively engaged at work and in the home, in stark contrast to early predictions about when the Boomers would be retiring.[10] Research demonstrates that Boomers are working nine years longer than they originally planned.[11]

One survey of Boomers revealed that almost half of the respondents who were still in the workforce planned to continue working into their 70s. Further, 67% said they were likely to consider working at least part-time once they retired. When asked about their reasons for delaying retirement, their top reasons were consistent with what would be expected from a generation known for its prodigious energy: 68% said they want to "stay busy"; 66% reported they wish to "stay intellectually engaged"; and almost half said they "want the sense of fulfillment" they get from working.[12]

With the benefit of hindsight, it is easy to see why the predictions that Boomers would enter retirement similar to the way their parents did were so off the mark. As the largest generation in history, Boomers have been at the vortex of tremendous societal change since their early years. At every stage of their lives, they have created a new blueprint. In their adolescence and early 20s, they were on the front lines of a breath-taking array of social changes and a powerful anti-war movement. One author commented that Boomers should take their place in history " . . . as a generation that fought a great cultural war to expand and advance liberty", contributing to a society that is vastly different than the world into which they were born.[13]

As a result, there should have been no reason to expect that they would retire in conformance with the "traditional" retirement age of the past. It is no surprise that they would choose to stay busy, intellectually engaged, and seek continued fulfillment from their work.

Their role in bringing about tremendous societal change, however, did not extend into their role at work. The Boomers' earlier contributions as pioneers who helped shape a cultural revolution are in significant danger of being overshadowed by their less effective role as leaders and supervisors in the traditional workplace structure they inherited. It is in this workplace that the Baby Boomers have thrived, finding opportunities to build on the middle class comforts provided by their Traditionalist parents and, in many cases, gaining significant wealth. The Boomers' current influence on our economy is pervasive. For example, in the United States, Baby Boomers control 50% of overall assets and 70% of disposable income.[14]

Their focus on wealth creation, however, left little time to think about the workplace norms they were perpetuating—and the new ones they were creating—for the next generation. Boomers worked long hours in the office and expected that those around them do so as well.

Today, most work environments are dominated by Boomers whose youthful energy morphed into a killer combination of workaholic habits and competitive instincts. As will be discussed in greater detail, Millennials primarily interact with Boomers in the workplace in an employee-boss relationship. In this light the Boomers' legacy at the center of cultural change is an historic artifact. The Boomers impact on the workplace is far more relevant to what Millennials are experiencing today.

Does Anyone Know We Are Here? Generation X

At only slightly more than half the size of the Baby Boomers, Gen X has had less of a societal impact than its predecessor generation. Lacking the more seismic descriptions which identify the Boomers, Gen X is frequently described as independent and resourceful.[15] These characteristics emerged partly as a result of a skyrocketing divorce rate that occurred during their childhood. According to U.S. Department of Commerce research: "Between the late 1960's and 1980, the divorce rate doubled, reaching a level where at least 1 out of 2 marriages was expected to end in divorce . . . "[16]

In addition, Gen X grew up at a time when more women returned to the workforce. Over time, the narrative evolved of Gen X as "latch key kids" who would return from school, letting themselves into an empty house.[17] They became identified as members of a generation that had to learn to take care of themselves, contributing to their independence at work: "On the job, Generation Xers tend to be self-reliant. Of those with divorced parents, many lived in two different neighborhoods every week, and they learned to thrive in the midst of chaos and change."[18]

Gen Xers entered into a workplace dominated by two older generations. Traditionalists and their Boomer offspring may have clashed as parents and adolescents, but, together, they created a workplace culture marked by rigidity and overwork. The pervasive—some would say smothering—influence of the Boomers' competitive ways and workaholic tendencies significantly impacted Gen X as they settled into their jobs. Early media commentary had posited the theory that Gen X would be influential in creating a more family friendly work environment based on the generation's own early childhood experiences. A 2000 study from the Radcliffe Public Policy Center reported that: "This survey . . . supports the notion that so-called Generation Xers do indeed have different priorities than the Baby Boomers who preceded them into the workplace."[19]

But something happened along Gen X's road to change. They adapted. By the time members of Gen X were old enough for full-time employment, the culture of the workplace overpowered the hopes they may have had for a life more balanced than the homes in which they grew up.

As a result of its small size, Gen X's adaption was a practical necessity.

The structure of the workplace continues to be built around a long-obsolete notion that a spouse is at home taking care of family obligations. Gen Xers, for the most part, have made themselves fit into that existing structure, rather than be a change agent for a workplace redesign. As will be described, they are seen by Millennials as united with Boomers in maintaining the status quo and resistance to rethinking how and when work is conducted.

For many Xers, expectations of moving into leadership positions have been delayed by the slow pace of Boomer retirements. With Boomers staying active in the workforce longer than predicted, many members of Gen X have been left wondering if they will ever have an opportunity for senior leadership roles before being passed by ambitious Millennials.

Some commentators have questioned whether either post-Boomer generation is ready for leadership roles. For example, a Human Resources director at Florida Metropolitan University-Melbourne noted that many of the Gen X and Y workers projected to replace retiring Boomers are not yet adequately prepared for management.[20] Comments like these suggest the importance of Boomers' becoming more invested in leadership succession and the preparation of younger generations for greater responsibilities at work.

Enter Millennials

The population of Millennials in the United States is estimated at 86 million and is the largest cohort in history—7% larger than the Baby-Boomers.[21] And that number is expected to grow to 88.5 million by 2020 as a result of immigration.[22] Globally, the population of Millennials is estimated at 2.5 billion.[23] In the U.S., approximately 60% of the Millennials are now old enough to be in the workforce.[24] Overall, Millennials are expected to comprise 75% of the global workforce by 2025.[25]

From a very young age, Millennials have already had a generational impact. As authors Howe and Strauss noted more than a decade ago: "As a group, Millennials are unlike any other youth generation in living memory. They are more numerous, more affluent, better educated, and more ethnically diverse."[26]

As will be discussed in greater detail throughout this book, Millennials have an opportunity to use their collective power to change the workplace. Based on their childhood years, the expectations for their future success are as high as the demands for their early achievements.

Chapter 3

Uphill Both Ways—The Millennials' View of their Generational Legacy

The survey developed for this book provided respondents with opportunities to comment on their relationships with, and observations of, senior generations. Millennials expressed strong opinions about the ways in which Boomers and Gen Xers have impacted the world and their lives, offering a nuanced perspective that recognizes both the achievements and the missed opportunities of their predecessor generations. The survey responses also provide significant insight into some of the underlying qualities that Boomers and Gen Xers misjudge in Millennials, leading to negative generalizations.

A Different Generational Lens

There is a startling distinction between how Millennials feel about many of the adults in their own lives and the way Boomers, in particular, interacted with adults during their formative years. As adolescents, the mantra of the Baby Boomers was "Don't trust anyone over thirty." A Google search of that statement results in millions of hits, many of which provide insight into the pervasive generational distrust that existed at the time.

This type of generational discord is not prevalent with Millennials. Unlike Boomers who have always been conscious of generational differences, Millennials are far less likely to view their experiences through a generational lens, likely because there has never been a reason to do so. Millennials' generally trust their parents, mentors, and other influential adults in their lives. If they experience conflict with someone older at work, they will more likely focus on the specific point of disagreement and not necessarily the generational difference between them. Research has shown that Millennials generally enjoy working with older generations and value opportunities to be mentored by them. Many worry, however, that senior management does not necessarily relate to them, and that their personal drive can be intimidating.[27]

Many survey respondents acknowledged that their path has been made easier as a result of the work and sacrifices of those who came before them. For example, a respondent in the design field noted the easier journey for her generation:

> *I think my generation is so used to having everything handed to them rather than working for it. The older generations, in my opinion, had to work much harder to succeed.*

Similarly, another respondent expressed concern that Millennials were embarking on a career path with less initiative then prior generations did because of their more comfortable upbringing:

> *My parents and grandparents had to earn everything, often start- ing at a young age. Our generation did not have to earn things in the same way. As a result, we learned to expect the privileges of doing and receiving things without having to earn them.*

Some expressed concern about the fragility of the gains made by prior generations. One respondent's comment highlighted this worry:

> *Although there are some of us who appreciate the struggles of the past, I believe overall there is a short-term memory problem in that we forget how recently inequalities existed and how easily they could re-assert themselves.*

An interesting generational conflict emerges, however, when Millennials express their perspective on the contributions of prior generations. Survey responses show that Millennials recognize the historic significance of the Boomers' efforts—their fight for racial equality during the Civil Rights Movement, women's equality during the Women's Rights Movement, their demonstrations to end the Viet Nam War, and other major social reforms in which Boomers played a prominent role. Many respondents tempered their appreciation of these accomplishments by noting that Boomers need to move past the contributions of their younger years and address the issues that currently threaten the well-being of future generations.

Millennials point to world problems and workplace inequities that negatively impact their lives today and give rise to fears for their future. They see themselves as the recipients of a legacy of failures that includes an environment threatened by global climate change and political leaders that they feel are out-of-touch with the tremendous challenges ahead. They also noted that older generations have imposed enormous pressures upon Millennials to succeed in college, graduate school, and beyond, without taking responsibility for their own contributions to the soft job market, the declining economy, and the tremendous national debt burden that is left for future generations to address.

Overall, the survey comments shed light on the prism through which Millennials view the contributions, sacrifices, and, at times, the hypocrisy of prior generations. These responses should also help Boomers and Gen Xers understand that it is unrealistic to expect that Millennials will emulate their work habits, and in fact, such a belief is counterproductive to developing an effective corps of future leaders.

Appreciating the Legacy of Education

The Pew Research Center reports that, when compared with past generations at comparable ages, Millennials are more highly educated.[28] More Millennials are graduating high school, attending college, and going to graduate school. A comparison of 1970 data (when Baby Boomers were in their prime education years) with 2010 data (capturing the Millennials) demonstrates this increase. The percent of 14 to 18 year-olds enrolled in school rose from 89% to 93% from 1970 to 2010, and the percent of 18 to 24 year-olds enrolled rose from 32% to 52%. Not only did the *percent* of enrollment increased, but the *total* enrollment dramatically increased. In 1970, there were 7 million college and graduate students, compared to 18.9 million college and graduate students in 2010.[29]

Among respondents who have been the beneficiaries of parents focused on their education, there was a shared appreciation of that important legacy. Respondents understood the important role that education has played in their own lives, and recognized that the desire to educate the next generation is enduring. For example, a respondent in the public relations field stated:

> *I think that every generation of parents wants more for their children. Along with other improvements in education, it is more common for children to go to college and learn more about what opportunities are available when that may or may not have been the case (or as common) in earlier generations.*

Another respondent in the administrative field acknowledged the educational opportunities available today that were not so easily accessible to earlier generations:

> *College was a priority for me . . . as opposed to [my parents'] experience, where college was not allowed for my mom.*

Similarly, a graduate student stated:

> *My parents were much more successful than my grandparents. I think about this especially in terms of gender equality and the accessibility I have to education.*

Can We Move On?

Layered within many of the responses acknowledging the hard work of generations who came before is a sense that this appreciation is accompanied by a quietly muttered "get over it already". For many respondents, the difficulties and limited opportunities endured by prior generations were seen more as interesting socio-economic history than instructional models to follow. They did not interpret stories of their ancestors as guidelines for present behaviors; rather, they saw them as providing a foundation which should help Millennials move faster towards their own goals.

This perspective can significantly impact the way in which generations interact with one another at work. Millennials expect that they should benefit from—and be able to build upon—the gains made by other generations to improve the workplace. They find it frustrating and nonsensical when senior generations at work seem to want Millennials to experience the same difficult path they traveled. One respondent observed:

> I think that older people are irritated that the standard of living has increased since the Great Depression, and that young people have an expectation that things will go their way.

This concern is at the heart of a significant generational disconnect present in the workplace today. Millennials do not believe that the desire to benefit from the efforts of prior generations should reflect negatively on their own work ethic or their own plans to contribute positively to the world, as summarized by this respondent:

> Every generation has its quirks and characterizations. True, 'The Greatest Generation' probably has sacrificed more than we will ever know, but you can't blame us for being brought up in a particularly affluent period of American history. I think, if anything, affluence has helped shaped many people's world view and shown them, even more so than growing up in poverty does, that most of the world's population is in need some way or another, and because of the available resources, they are able to do more than ever to help.

One respondent in the engineering field wryly captured both an appreciation for the accomplishments of those who came before, and the universal desire to take credit for those efforts:

> *I suppose . . . our generation [is viewed as entitled because it] enjoys things that earlier generations had to work for, and when those things require work, we are indignant. I think this is true in many aspects (female equality in the workplace, availability of education, technology advancements . . .). On the other hand, these were not achieved with a solitary contribution and I would not agree with a single person of an earlier generation beating his own drum. That nonsense has probably been going on since the beginning of time. I can't wait to complain about it.*

Respondents also displayed a healthy recognition of their own place within the rhythms of the generations, as noted by this respondent:

> *Pardon me while I lol. LOL. I understand what they're saying, I honestly do. . . . I know I've been brought up to understand the cost of luxuries. We don't have extended cable in our house because the monthly charges are off the wall. But we do have video game systems and computers because they're worth the money. We pay our bills like good hard-working Americans. Every generation thinks the next generation is a bunch of spoiled brats, but they forget that they've been working to make things better for us.*
>
> *They shouldn't begrudge us the very fruits of their labor. Our task is saving the planet for OUR kids now, and no doubt we'll soon be sitting on a front porch grumbling about how those kids think that they can plug their electric car in ANYWHERE. I look forward to it.*

These comments indicate that there is a rhythm to generational transitions. Each generation leaves a legacy of accomplishments and mistakes. How successive generations build upon these accomplishments and learn from the mistakes remains an ongoing challenge.

The Haze of Hindsight

Every generation tends to see itself through its own "up by the boot-straps" prism. It is a long-held caricature that older generations believe young people have it too easy. They enjoy describing the hardships of their life, for example, the difficulties of walking to school "uphill both ways". Perhaps it is the haze of hindsight that allows each generation to take pride in its own history of sacrifice, while viewing those who are younger as less worthy and insufficiently appreciative. Understanding this tendency, however, could be key to solving intergenerational communication challenges.

If each generation views itself through rose-colored glasses, the way in which they express pride in their accomplishments may convey—subtly or otherwise—a lack of respect for the very real challenges that the Millennials are facing. In this respect, Millennials reported receiving no shortage of advice or criticism. Noted one respondent:

> *My 4 grandparents who are all in their mid-80s and all collecting social security benefits love to tell me how lazy my generation is; they conveniently forget that I work 60–70 hours per week and pay nearly 40% of my income in taxes so they can receive their entitlements.*

As this quote suggests, older generations may not even think about the fact that Millennials face the circumstances of paying into entitlements that they fear will be unavailable to them in the future. Many respondents also felt that Boomers and Gen Xers lack sufficient insight into their generations' responsibility for the economic crisis. As one respondent stated:

> *America lacks business ethics which is the fundamental problem with the current economy. People care too little about others and who they have to ruin to get where they want to go. If you look at the current financial crisis, most of the actions that set us on the path of job loss and foreclosure were done by people in older generations. Millennials did not defraud investors. Millennials did not participate in predatory lending. . . .*

Evolving societal expectations also have an impact on the attitudes generations express towards themselves and one another. Each generation is likely to act in accordance with the prevailing customs and traditions of their time, as noted by this respondent in the social service sector:

> *Older generations had different loyalties and priorities and lived more cautiously. Society also had different expectations, particularly of women. It was just a different time and so that approach is not necessarily more noble.*

The Complexity of Choice

Millennials are more likely to have experienced far greater physical comfort in their formative years than their parents or grandparents could have imagined. Respondents appreciated this greater comfort, but it was tempered by a perception that other generations fail to appreciate that the modern world's complexity can be as daunting.

Millennials have grown up in a culture of unprecedented consumer choices and commercial spending. Since their childhood, Millennials have been the target of retailers who saw them as beneficiaries of parents who would respond to their children's clamor for the latest "must have" item. Howe and Strauss reported, for example, that spending on advertising directed at Millennials as children rose from $100 million in 1986 to $2 billion in 1996.[30]

Overwhelming choices have consequences. Millennials have long been expected to navigate a faster-paced, media-saturated, technology-driven, highly-pressured environment with a dizzying array of options in every facet of life. Several respondents expressed concern that, just as they are expected to appreciate the hardships endured by prior generations, those same generations should recognize the difficulties Millennials face as they try to navigate the complexities of their own world. For example:

> *Older generations always view their lives as being 'harder' than younger ones. They tend to focus on elements of life that were more*

difficult in their youth, but they completely discount elements that are far more difficult/complex in today's world.

Another respondent similarly noted that having more physical comforts does not mean that life is now easy:

. . . [W]e are considered 'soft' by the older generations because we grew up in times of great prosperity in America. Many have never needed to engage in manual labor which, supposedly, builds 'character.' Traditional definitions of 'character' are antiquated and need to be adjusted to fit the contemporary world we live in today.

Generations, Gender, and Rejecting the Cost of Emulation

Even when respondents articulated respect for the sacrifice and hard work of prior generations, Millennials were less willing to view Boomers and Xers as positive role models. Respondents expressed frustration with the "do as I did" mantra that prior generations repeat as they urge Millennials to succeed by their methods.

This "advice" from more senior colleagues is seen as reflecting a lack of insight into the real costs of that approach, as this respondent noted:

They think that because they had to kill themselves to get ahead then we have to do the same. I think often we don't want the same things; it doesn't seem worth it to be at the top if you are exhausted and stressed the whole time.

This perspective emerged with a particular vehemence when female respondents spoke of their relationships with senior women at work. These respondents described a gendered generational divide with deep roots. They felt unfairly judged by more senior women on a variety of topics.[31] Moreover, young women consistently reported a strong desire for senior female role models, but just as consistently lamented that such role models do not exist in their workplace. Workplace data starkly reflects these concerns. For example, one study reported that: " . . . only 14 percent of the college-educated Millennial women and 16 percent of the college-educated

Millennial men surveyed are currently working at a job with a woman in a leadership role whose career they wish to emulate."[32]

Throughout the survey responses—and in my own countless discussions with Millennials—younger women spoke of rejection when seeking support from senior female colleagues and a wistful hope that it will eventually improve. Respondents described conversations in which older female colleagues insistently advised younger women that, to succeed, they must endure the same difficult path of long hours at the office and significant familial sacrifices at home.

Respondents saw such advice as out of touch with today's modern work environment. They identified the power of technology to provide greater flexibility to attend to family responsibilities without career penalty. Young women poignantly described how they felt insufficiently supported by older women in the workplace, even as they articulated a desire for female role models and sponsors to assist in their career advancement. For these younger women seeking mentoring support, there was a clear need for supportive female leadership in the workplace.

Several female respondents reported that senior women colleagues seemed angry at Millennials for not sufficiently appreciating the sacrifices they had to make to succeed in the workplace. These respondents, however, disagreed with the notion that Millennial women were unaware of the sacrifices that the pioneers of their gender had to make. Rather, the respondents resented when senior women seemed unwilling to help younger generations navigate greater opportunities for flexibility without having to sacrifice career success. They were pained by advice that failed to acknowledge alternative paths. For example, one respondent stated:

> *This is an area where the generation gap becomes the most apparent. To many of the first- and second-wave women with whom I work, "work life balance" means having the ability to hire a nanny and otherwise contract out the family/personal part of one's life, whereas my generation seems more focused on a hands-on approach to childrearing and family responsibilities. At the end of the day, while we're all using the same term—"work/life balance"—the term has very different meanings depending on who is using it.*

Another respondent differentiated between her feelings of appreciation for women who have broken through barriers that she does not have to, and her desire to make her own life choices:

> *I work for an older woman attorney that had to struggle to break the glass ceiling. I am very appreciative of those women for allowing my generation to have equal status in many respects. I do find a very large disconnect between the generations, however. While she gave up her personal life to work (she has 3 children but I suspect she didn't have very much time for them) my family will always come first. I feel that my generation has the attitude of "work to live" not "live to work."*

One respondent observed that the natural order of progress is to build upon the gains of prior generations and then to take those gains for granted:

> *I think to some extent the working mothers in the previous generation felt like they really had to struggle, and occasionally feel that our generation is expecting the benefits they fought for, without 'paying dues.' . . . That's the nature of progress—that successive generations take certain improvements for granted. Previous generations were probably considered 'entitled' because they grew up with electricity and indoor plumbing . . . :)*

Facing Work in a Troubled Economy

The Millennials' strong relationships with their Boomer parents do not extend to a similarly positive opinion of the Boomers' impact on the world in their adult years. Baby Boomers were the target of significant criticism for stepping away from the activism and idealism of their youth, and accepting and perpetuating the status quo of a regressive work environment. In addition to attributing the cause of the economic crisis to earlier generations, respondents frequently expressed fears about the economic burdens they face in the future. Noted one graduate student:

While we have had advances in technology and a better standard of living, our parents also had that compared to their parents, but they have since used their positions of power to burden our generation with a huge global debt. Our generation is trying to make up for the mistakes which our parents have made, while not over-looking their advances. Our generation also realizes that we may not have social security or job security like our parents have, so we are trying to deal with those issues.

Many respondents also described both Boomers and Gen Xers as mired in a way of doing business that negatively impacts the workplace. For example, and as will be discussed in later chapters, respondents stated that they felt thwarted by managers who neither communicate nor value teamwork—two qualities that are an integral part of Millennials' own generational DNA.

The tension between team versus individual efforts can be seen in one study which reported that 49% of employers believed that individual goals would drive better performance for Millennials, and felt that Millennials perceived team goals negatively. The Millennials' responses, however, did not match the employers' views: although 75% of Millennials saw individualized goals as inspiring better performance, they also viewed group goals positively, contrary to their employers' predictions. Moreover, about 20% of employer respondents said they "did not know what drives performance" in Millennials. These findings supported Millennials' concerns that Boomers often misjudge their values in the workplace.[33] A global study reported that: "Millennials place a high priority on workplace culture and desire a work environment that emphasizes teamwork and a sense of community. They also value transparency (especially as it relates to decisions about their careers, compensation, and rewards)."[34]

The disconnect between what Millennials value, and what senior executives *think* Millennials value can lead to miscommunication and distrust. Noted one Millennial worker in the health care field:

I do feel that the older generation doesn't feel comfortable interacting with younger people. . . . [M]y Board doesn't feel comfortable sharing information and working together. They claim we have a generation gap that leads to misunderstanding and communication issues.

As will be further described, the challenges posed by the economic crisis and the seeming unwillingness of the workplace to understand what drives Millennials at work emerged as an ongoing theme throughout the survey responses.

Intra-Generational Differences and the Commonality of Confidence

In addition to the strong opinions Millennials expressed about other generations, they also demonstrated an intra-generational divide that appeared consistently throughout the survey responses. Respondents at the upper end of the Millennial age-range criticized their younger cohorts for behaviors similar to criticisms levied by senior generations.

This recurring theme raises an interesting question. Is the disapproval that older generations express towards younger generations simply a rite of passage that, with Millennials, occurs earlier because of the wide age span and vastly different experiences that existed between those born in the 1980s and those born in the 1990s?

Many survey respondents expressed annoyance that younger Millennials took too much for granted—a criticism that might sound familiar to senior generations. For example, a respondent in the marketing field noted:

I think there is a significant difference between the 25–31 Generation Y versus the 18–24 year old half of Generation Y. I don't know if this half was coddled more, or given less responsibility growing up, but I see a clear difference in the accountability and responsibility of many of the young people that come to work for me. As a 30 year old woman, I do believe there was a difference in the luxuries and access to technology that I was afforded versus others in this group and that may present the difference in work ethic.

A college student who worked part-time seemed bemused that the annoyance older generations express towards today's youth may be similar to feelings that "older" Millennials may harbor towards their younger cohorts:

> [Older generations think] we expect things to be easy for us, and we don't show proper gratitude when our lives are made easy by others. I generally ignore it as 'up the hill both ways' syndrome. I think that older generations are offended by the fact that younger generations take so much for granted about how quickly we get things done because of the innovation of those before us.
>
> I fall prey to this as well, even with the youngest members of my own generation. I did not grow up with a computer in my house, nor did I have a computer of my own or a mobile phone until I was an adult, etc. You spoiled brat to think you are entitled to one! How unfair for me.

This good-humored response is emblematic of two defining qualities that emerge in many of the responses and much of the research about Millennials: they exude a fundamental self-confidence and optimism that fuels their motivation to succeed on their own terms. This confidence and positive outlook keeps them moving forward along their own inner-guided path, but also impacts how they are perceived by older generations who often misinterpret these characteristics.

These are the qualities that have helped them achieve so many early successes. But such successes did not come without a village of support. At the center of that support network are over-achieving parents whose presence loomed large in the formative years of these young adults.

Chapter 4

Ground Control to Major Tom— Send in the Helicopter

Since Millennials first entered grade school and as they have moved into college and beyond, school administrators, deans, college presidents, and older workplace colleagues have had to grapple on a regular basis with something they had not previously encountered in their daily lives: parents who are always ready to swoop in and help their offspring through every challenge. No problem seems too big or too small for a parental intervention to occur. As a pre-college Millennial wryly observed:

[O]ur generation of parents are very involved in our life and try to help us become better—whether we want/need it or not . . .

The media is replete with stories—both alarming and humorous—about parents who have challenged grades, sports' player selections, admissions choices, teaching methods, and even hiring decisions and compensation levels. As interesting—and shocking—as these anecdotes can be, they also over-simplify the emotional ties that exist between Millennials and their parents. The image of hovering "helicopter" parents who over-indulged and over-protected their children makes great fodder for jokes and complaints, but the stories fail to provide the context that is foundational to understanding the relationship between Millennials and their parents.

The Millennial-parent bond has significantly impacted how Millennials are adapting to the workforce. This chapter explores these ties and the varied and complicated ways Millennials view the influence of their parents in their lives. All generations can benefit by moving beyond the stereotypes to understand both the positive and negative aspects of Millennials' relationships with their families. Ultimately, such understanding should lead to greater workplace effectiveness as employers grapple with the influence of parents in the lives of their employees and the occasional presence of parents as chief negotiators for their children's salary.

Boomers as Adolescents: Bringing Activism Home

Most Millennials who are part of the first large wave to enter the workforce were raised by Baby Boomers who generally employed a parenting style markedly different from the way in which Boomers themselves were raised. Parent-child tensions were a hallmark of the Boomers' teen-aged years. As the Boomers emerged into adolescence, they blamed their parents' generation for a segregated nation, narrowly-defined sex roles, even more rigid views about sexuality, and what they saw as an inexplicable and unwinnable war in Viet Nam. The Boomers responded strongly to these injustices with demonstrations, sit-ins, walk-outs, and sometimes violence.

With Boomers feeling empowered to challenge so much of the world they were inheriting from their parents, it was difficult for peace to then reign within the home. Most of the Boomers' parents had grown up in families hit hard by the Depression and a brutal World War. When the war ended, returning veterans finally felt free to settle down and raise a family. Having lived through decades of deprivation and war, fighting social injustice was not necessarily high on their agenda. After all the pain, suffering, and tumultuousness that permeated their formative years, many of the Boomers' parents likely found peace within the status quo.

That inward focus, however, proved to be a catalyst for the family upheaval that ultimately followed. As Boomers responded to the significant societal injustices around them, they also challenged their parents' complacency, resulting in conflict at home as their parents grew increasingly bewildered by the generation gap they were experiencing with their children. Many young Boomers could not understand how their parents were not more actively engaged in eliminating racial inequality or responding more aggressively to a war in Viet Nam that seemed to have no purpose. Their parents, on the other hand, could not fathom why their kids did not appreciate how lucky they were to grow up free of the deprivations that marked their own childhood years.

Stranger Danger and Other Fears

When Boomers became parents, they developed different terms of engagement with their children. They actively worked to become parents who would be "cooler" and more in touch than they felt their own parents were. And these lessons were equally learned by the oldest of Gen X as they, too, became parents.

The parents of Millennials threw themselves into their parental role by reading expert advice on child-rearing and embracing new theories about early development. Where prior generations had limited guidance from their family doctors—many of whom had rigid beliefs about strictly timed feedings and letting infants cry—Boomers could rely on a plethora of experts who vied for their rapt attention. The earliest and arguably the most influential was Dr. Spock, whose child-centered approach helped parents around the world learn to tap into their own instincts as they raised their children. By the time Millennials were filling nurseries, their parents were turning to post-Spock experts on child-care who offered a wide range of advice on pregnancy, delivery, breast-feeding, infant development, toddler behaviors, early childhood education, and teen-age discipline.

As author Jean Twenge noted, the children born following the reliability of birth control, the availability of legalized abortion, and the cultural shift toward parenthood as a choice were "the most *wanted* generation of children in American history."[35] Other reasons for the intense parental attention showered on Millennials include their position in a family's birth order, smaller family size, and the higher level of education achieved by Millennial parents. Authors Howe and Strauss report that: (1) Millennials

have grown up in smaller families with fewer siblings than prior generations; (2) a historically high percent of Millennials are first-born, which
researchers correlate with higher achievement and greater identity with
parental authority; and (3) the parents of Millennials are more educated
than parents in previous generations. As a result of these demographic
shifts, parents have more time and resources available for their children.[36]

In addition, events taking place in the Millennials' early years also had
a profound impact on how they were raised. The Millennial-parent bond
may have emerged from a desire to be close, but it was solidified by a
confluence of circumstances resulting in an aggressive attention to safety
and a hyper-focus on the Millennials' well-being. This attention—perhaps
even obsession—with infant and early childhood safety has roots in several
incidents involving child abuse and murders that were the focus of intense
media scrutiny and which led to widespread public fears.

In the toddler years of the oldest Millennials, the nation was riveted by
a series of highly publicized and sensationalized pre-school sexual abuse
cases which terrified parents and undermined trust in day care providers.[37]
The first of these was in 1983 in Manhattan Beach, California, where the
administrator and teachers at the McMartin Preschool were accused of
sexual abuse acts that were described as including satanic rituals and ani-
mal mutilations. The following year, horrific allegations were made against
the Fells Acre Day School in Massachusetts, which included suggestions
of a "magic room" where abusive acts took place. Other alleged incidents
which garnered national attention occurred in Bakersfield, California, Dade
County, Florida and Maplewood, New Jersey, fueling widespread fears that
children needed increased levels of protection and parents needed to provide a heightened level of vigilance for their safety. The veracity of many of
these claims has since come under scrutiny, however, the terror at the time
substantially influenced the way that Millennials were raised.

Parental fears of danger lurking behind every door were further exacerbated by several tragic child abductions and murders in the late 1970s and
1980s. The circumstances of these abductions and the gruesome details surrounding the children's deaths went beyond the kidnap-for-ransom cases
that captured global headlines in prior generations, such as the kidnapping of Charles Lindbergh's child. As one researcher wrote: "By the 1980s,

as a result of the publicity surrounding a series of kidnappings of young boys—Adam Walsh, Etan Patz, Kevin White, and Jacob Wetterling; children who lived in all parts of the country and in communities large and small—Americans began to register intense fears about child abductions as sexual crimes. . . . The fears rapidly altered child rearing patterns. . . . Increasingly, whenever they could do so, parents kept their children under tight supervision, walking or driving them to school, and restricting a once more casual attitude toward informal play."[38]

The Structure of Play

As neighborhood streets seemed unsafe from predators, parents became increasingly vigilant and protective. In many communities, the days of unsupervised time outdoors ended. Play could no longer be considered the creative domain of childhood; rather, it became the structured world that parents planned and implemented. Boredom—once alleviated only through imagination and made-up games—was sacrificed to scheduled recreation.

Once many Millennials entered first grade, their after-school time was filled with budding resume-building activities. Organized clubs and early programs devoted to youth sports grew into a cottage industry that created a feeder system into the next level of structured programs.

With so much time accounted for by lessons and teams, Millennials were molded into accomplished adolescents. Their parents became general contractors, subcontracting aspects of their children's development to coaches, tutors, instructors, supervised play dates, and other structured activities—and in doing so, also felt they were insulating their kids from stranger danger.

Boston College Professor Peter Gray's research describes the loss of free and unstructured play that has evolved over the past decades. His work looks at the impact of this on creative development and, particularly relevant to how Millennials are faring in the workplace, problem-solving skills: "Free play and exploration are, historically, the means by which children learn to solve their own problems, control their own lives, develop their own interests, and become competent in pursuit of their own interests. . . . By depriving children of opportunities to play on their own, away from direct adult supervision and control, we are depriving them of opportunities to learn how to take control of their own lives."[39]

Boomers as Parents—Coach, Advisor, and Best Friend

As a generation that grew up believing they had all the answers, Boomers were eager to transfer that wisdom to their children. And as competitive overachievers in most aspects of their lives, Boomer parents had strong opinions about how to raise their children to be successful. In doing so, Boomers also tied their children's achievements to their own self-image as parents. In their competitive world-view, the more accomplished the child, the more successful the parent.

Boomer parents saw themselves as friend and teacher, the hip tutor for their eager young children who would be their pupils. And teach they did. Parenting became one more place for Boomers to focus their prodigious energies. Boomer parents started teaching while their children were in utero. They sang, read, and played music to pregnant tummies, preparing for the emergence of infants who would be prepped for their life of accomplishments even before birth.

If a generation could be perfected by applying all the latest ways of thinking about childhood and adolescence, than Millennials would surely be the best ever. As authors Howe and Strauss observed, "No generation has been tended with such care through pregnancy." In noting the dramatic rise in birthing classes, use of prenatal vitamins, increased attention to diet and exercise, and decreased smoking and alcohol use during pregnancy, the authors further observed that expectant mothers "even worry about their worrying—and train themselves to avoid stress."[40]

These lessons in parenting were well learned by Boomer protégés, the Gen X parents. Gen Xers both emulated and perfected the Boomers' intense parenting approach. Whatever the obstacle, parents of Millennials helped clear the path and serve as advocate-in-chief for their offspring.

As a result, Millennials have been guided, directed, cajoled, begged, and occasionally even ordered to work hard, study, participate, excel, attend, speak up, compete, and succeed. They have also been told to be fair, be inclusive, express themselves directly, play nice, and share their candy and toys. These messages may not always have been consistent, but they were earnest and offered in the Millennials' best interests—or at least in their best interests as perceived by their parents.

Millennials have relied upon their parents even through their teen years, ages when prior generations experienced far greater intergenerational tension. One article, reporting on a study comparing the assistance provided by parents to their children in 2008 with assistance provided in 1988 noted: Eighty-six percent said they had provided advice in the previous month; less than half had done so in 1988. Two out of three parents had given a son or daughter practical assistance in the previous month; in 1988, only one in three had."[41]

Howe and Strauss reported on a 1999 survey of 12 to 14 year olds; when asked who they most looked up to, the young respondents resoundingly chose their parents.[42] They then compared this data with similar survey questions asked of young Boomers in 1974. The data showed two-thirds of Millennial teenagers: " . . . say their parents are 'in touch' with their lives, and six in ten say it's 'easy' to talk with parents about sex, drugs, and alcohol." The 1974 survey reported that a majority of teenagers felt unable to comfortably talk to their parents about personal concerns and 40% stated that they would be better off if they did not live with them.[43]

Other data further corroborates the bonds between Millennials and their parents. A study by the Pew Research Center reported parents stating that they were "having fewer serious arguments with their children in their late teens and early 20s than they recall having with their own parents when they were that age."[44] In a Clark University Poll of Emerging Adults, 55% of the respondents (between the ages of 18 and 29) reported "that they have contact with their parents via texting, email, phone, or in person every day or almost every day, and an additional 24% keep in contact at least a few times per week."[45]

In a fascinating twist on the view that Millennials always seek parental advice, articles also report on the increased role Millennials play in providing their parents with advice. One article noted: "Many parents—who have shed their status as fogy untouchables and become pals with their progeny—are treating their offspring as worldly equals. They think of their computer-savvy, plugged-in children as confidants, and so they look to them for advice on life decisions, as well as major purchases: cars, computers, vacation packages, real estate, home décor."[46]

Consistent with this other data, survey respondents reported similarly close relationships. When asked how they would characterize their relationship with their families, more than 73% reported "very close", nearly 23% reported "close"; and fewer than 4% reported "not close". More than 85% of the respondents reported that their relationship with their family was "quite important" and more than 13% said it was "somewhat important". Less than 1% characterized this relationship as "not important". As one respondent stated:

> *My parents are very supportive and typically trust my judgment. They are always there if I have questions and let me talk through my concerns. They also raise important questions that I might not think of.*

Another noted:

> *My parents have always been there for me whenever I needed anything, whether it was money or just a hug. We may not always get along with one another but we stick together.*

Many respondents were likely to see the process of seeking advice from their parents as a logical, well-considered opportunity to benefit from the wisdom of trusted advisors who are the ones most capable of providing help. Nearly 84% reported that they "frequently" or "sometimes" sought both career and personal advice from their parents. Although more respondents reported that they "frequently" seek career advice, the percentage reporting that they "never" seek career or personal advice was about the same relatively low 16%, respectively. In general, respondents viewed their parents as the wise figures that Boomers and Gen Xers, in fact, worked so hard to become.

This reliance on and comfort with parental guidance permeated many of the responses. A college student stated:

My mother always provides the best advice and I'm willing to ask her opinion on anything.

A public sector worker described a methodology for seeking advice:

When making a big life decision (like moving jobs, going to grad school, considering marriage, etc.), I always consult my family, more than I do my friends. They don't provide specific advice on my chosen career path, etc., but help me answer my own questions by walking through my thought process with me.

Another young respondent highlighted the role of parents as confidants:

I use my parents for advice on personal and professional matters. I find that my parents are my most loyal advisors and understand my needs the best.

A respondent in the sciences field spoke with deep gratitude for her family's advice:

I would have a lot of difficulty following through on a decision that my immediate family didn't understand or support. Although I only see them once a year, I call them often and inform them of my day, my opportunities and my plans for the future. I like to run my ideas by them . . . They have supported my full growth and development thus far and I am happy to keep them active and present going forward.

A social service worker expressed similar appreciation:

My family are my closest friends. I am so very lucky to have them in my life. They are the ones I go to first with problems, and they listen and give great advice. They are my rock.

As noted, in any good friendship, giving and receiving advice can be a mutual benefit of the relationship, and it is no different for many respondents and their parents. This represents a departure from the more traditional expectation that parents provide and children receive advice. Respondents saw the advice flowing comfortably in both directions. As one college student stated:

> *I still live with my parents while in college and we have a very close relationship and I am always seeking advice from them. They give me relationship advice, career advice, college advice and just overall practical advice. I give them a lot of advice as well. We respect each other a lot and therefore we respect each other's opinions . . . .*

Even though most respondents reported close family relationships, not all depended upon their parents for advice. Several respondents stated that their parents had a more hands-off approach, for example:

> *My parents have always encouraged me to make my own decisions/mistakes and learn from them, so they don't offer up advice unless I ask for it.*

And some responses suggest that, at least for some members of this generation, a bit of youthful obstinacy remains alive and well:

> *I'm pretty independent. I tell them about things in my life, but I never "seek advice." That doesn't stop them from giving it though . . . and that always makes me want to do the opposite. ;)*

Whether expressed in a light-hearted or appreciative tone, respondents reinforced what other data makes clear—Millennials have an unabashed closeness with their families that profoundly influences the decisions they make in most aspects of their lives.

The Role of Siblings

The respondent's reliance on their parents as confidant in various aspects of their lives extended, although to a lesser extent, to their siblings. In general, respondents were more likely to seek personal advice (more than two-thirds) than career advice (less than half) from siblings, even as they relied on their parents more frequently for both. In all instances, whether seeking professional or personal advice from parents or siblings, women were more likely than men to report that they frequently did so. A female respondent described her reliance on family for advice:

> *I find it difficult to make big life decisions without the support of either my sister or mother, such as renting a new apartment or taking a new job.*

Not All Advice is Equal

When respondents reported that they did not seek family advice, they often provided specific and thoughtful reasons why, demonstrating an astute ability to differentiate among family members who are best positioned to provide advice on various topics. They observed that, a parent's desire to help solve their children's problems notwithstanding, not every parent brings the relevant knowledge and experience to provide applicable advice. For example, one young lawyer distinguished between his parents' professional and personal advice:

> *There are some issues that my parents' advice is helpful on, but often, they don't understand the legal community or the [state's] job market. When I was still looking for work, it was difficult to talk to them about these things because they wanted to fix all of my problems, but didn't have the base of knowledge to do so. I've found it is important to keep some emotional distance in those cases from their advice. Obviously, as a close family, personal advice is more frequently sought and followed.*

Some Millennials described their strategy of seeking advice from the family member who has the appropriate expertise, seeking parental or sibling assistance accordingly. A respondent described this process:

Each member of my family provides advice to me, but often in different realms—for instance my father more often helps me with financial decisions, my mother with personal ones. My siblings offer a scattering of different kinds of advice depending—my sister may give advice re life experience, my brother may suggest ways of dealing with stress, etc.

Another respondent similarly differentiated among family members:

I am always talking to my dad and my husband about career advice and how to handle work situations. They are both entrepreneurs who lead companies, so they are excellent resources. My mom spent her career as a teacher in a union environment, so she is not as accustomed to being able to ask for what you want or to the idea of advancing to a new position every couple of years.

In several instances, Millennials did not ask their parents for advice because they were seeking to avoid the mistakes that they saw their own parents make, as this respondent described:

While I love my parents very much, I do not seek advice from them regarding career issues, personal issues, or financial issues because my parents have never made good choices in those areas. Even though I'm only 30, I am more financially secure than my parents. I have a rewarding career (unlike my parents), and I have a very happy, healthy marriage (unlike my parents).

In other instances, respondents declined to seek parental guidance when they knew their career aspirations clashed with their parents' expectations that they choose a career based on earning potential, as this respondent reported:

My parents have not been entirely supportive of my career choices because they put a higher importance on financial compensation than I do.

One young marketing professional similarly noted:

> *My parents encouraged me to major in science and take jobs with the highest pay regardless of the work environment. I have different thoughts about a career, so I am careful not to involve them too much in those decisions.*

This clash of career priorities emerged as the primary area where respondents felt unable to seek their parents' advice, for example:

> *My parents are hard-working, blue collar immigrants who worked hard to make sure we had opportunities that they didn't. As a result, my siblings and my dreams are very different from theirs. My parents have more of a "job" mindset where work was just a means to an end, whereas my siblings and I have been learning to have more of a "career" mindset, where our work means more than just a place to make money. It's been complicated.*

Respondents also reported occasional family strain as a result of opportunities available to them that were not as accessible to their families. One respondent described the tension she experienced with her mom, who did not work outside the home.

> *It's difficult to discuss careers with my mother, because she is a homemaker. I am a feminist and though I respect her choice to stay at home and be a caretaker, I often wish that she had pursued a professional career to do her part to advance women. Since this is important to me in my life, we have a disconnect when I try to discuss my career choices. When I try to discuss graduate or professional school, she dismisses it as too expensive. I am torn because I understand her concern in this economy and with her poor upbringing, but I also don't think she would do so if she viewed education as a valuable investment, as my father does. I wonder if she would have the same concerns if it were my brother who wanted to pursue a higher education. When I try to talk to her about my chosen field, public policy, she occasionally*

changes the conversation topic to my relationship with my boyfriend. I think this is because she doesn't really understand what public policy is, and also that she doesn't relate to that interest of mine.

These older Millennials also showed signs of a transition taking place in which advice is sought from a significant other, rather than family, as noted by this respondent:

I'm the oldest of 5, so only one of my siblings is even in a career, and 2 are still in High School (the same age as my students), so I have a very mentor-based relationship with them. Growing up very working-class, both of my parents have less job-security or work/life balance than me, and while I consider them friends, I don't consult with them often. I definitely talk with them regularly, but more often than not it is a discussion more than a consultation. That probably changed when I shifted into my later '20s. Before that, I did consult with my parents more about "grown up" things like insurance, loans, and job benefits. However, now that I am married and have a partner to discuss and decide these things with it seems less important. I still enjoy discussing and debating things with my parents, and even my brother close in age to me. My husband is an invaluable partner in advice, deliberations and decisionmaking.

These responses suggest that, for all their reliance on family, Millennials exhibit solid instincts for discerning when family members may not be in the best position to be helpful in certain circumstances. They also show that, as in generations past, Millennials eventually transition to spouses and similar significant relationships in their lives as sources of advice.

Elusive Adulthood, Transitioning Relationships

Boomers and Gen Xers—who are accustomed to aggressively making things happen in their own lives—have exhibited that same impatience as they try to help their children move forward in life. This extensive parental engagement has impacted the development of Millennials as they have grown into young adulthood. The workplace implications of this will be discussed in a later chapter.

Parental guidance reaches a particular intensity—some might prefer the word frenzy—during the college admissions process. Here, as one writer describes, parents have become "co-shoppers", in the search for the right college, and their deeply engaged role has been chronicled in numerous articles.[47] If the hoped-for acceptance is deferred by a wait-list notification, parents may continue their engagement as co-participants by trying to influence admittance, either directly communicating with or coaching their child through interactions with their college of choice.[48] A Millennial employee at a university career center described some of her experiences with parents:

> *During my time at the university career center, parents would occasionally call on behalf of their adult children. Often, they would ask to schedule an appointment with a career counselor for their son or daughter, but some would ask for more information on internship opportunities or the contact information for a potential employer. One parent even asked if she could speak with a career counselor about updating her son's resume. It happened enough times for us to adopt an unofficial policy of kindly telling parents that we only schedule appointments and communicate directly with the students. The worst part was, when I told parents that we would need to speak directly with their son or daughter, some of them didn't seem to understand why!*
>
> *As a Millennial myself (lucky enough to not have helicopter parents), I felt embarrassed for my peers. And I began to wonder about whether or not they thought this was normal. Do they realize that their parents are holding them back from career opportunities? Do they have what it takes to succeed in the professional world without Mom or Dad by their side? I mean, what's next? Mom negotiating a starting salary? The thought that some of them might even prefer for their parents to play a role in their professional lives was unconscionable. One time, a parent called asking for the number of an employer that her child was applying to for an internship. When I asked her why*

she needed the information, she said that she wanted to call and dis-
cuss her child's outstanding work ethic and interest in the internship.
When I told her that employers are not fond of receiving phone calls
from parents and suggested that her son or daughter call the employer
themselves, she said something like 'Well, it's just easier for them if I
take care of this.' I think I may have ended up giving her the number
but emphasized that her phone call may do more harm than good. I
can only be certain that the student did not get the internship—and I
wonder how successful they are in their career today.

As this response suggests, these behaviors can become so embedded that
they continue past college. A Michigan State University study found that
31% of the employers surveyed reported that parents of Millennials had
submitted a resume on their son or daughter's behalf, sometimes without
the child's knowledge. In addition, 26% reported that parents had called
to promote their son or daughter's positive traits to demonstrate that they
deserve to be hired or receive a raise, and 4% reported parents of Millennials
accompanying their son or daughter to a job interview.[49] Some workplaces
are responding to the bonds between Millennials and their parents by spon-
soring "Bring Your Parents to Work Day".[50]

Respondents continued the pattern of revealing an intra-generational
divide on the question of whether their parents are too involved in their
lives. Some of the older Millennial respondents disassociated themselves
from the popular narrative that they were raised by hovering parents,
even as they acknowledged examples of it in their younger counterparts.
A respondent working as an administrator offered a glimpse into these
intra-generational differences:

I do think there is a difference between people my age (26) and
those who are in college right now. The 'helicopter' generation grew
up with their parents literally doing everything for them. My mom
is a high school teacher, and I hear stories like this all the time, of
parents doing their kids homework for them, or calling to yell at the
teacher because their child failed the class. I obviously can't speak for
everyone of my generation, but I was not raised that way.

The intra-generational divide revealed in this quote emerges frequently in the survey responses. The quote also reveals another theme: Millennials criticizing behaviors attributed to others in their generation, but rarely identified as a self-criticism. More will be said about this in subsequent chapters.

Whether assisted by protective parents or not, Millennials worry about their ability to manage economic independence as they seek to make their way in the world during a financially precarious time. It is a concern, as well, for their parents who wonder whether the ties that bind them to their children will be reinforced indefinitely through their need to provide economic support.

Chapter 5

Parents Can You Spare a Condo? Perspectives on Parental Financial Support

From Stranger Danger to a Dangerous Economy

The global economic crisis has proven to be the ultimate early test for a generation raised to exude self-confidence. Like generations of parents before them, the parents of Millennials have sought to give their children a strong foundation in order to achieve greater economic success. It is, after all, in the collective DNA of parents to hope and expect that their children will prosper beyond their own level of achievement. But the combination of the significant economic success achieved by the Baby Boomer generation, their deeply engaged parenting style, and the lingering financial crisis may make this generational legacy harder to accomplish than at any prior time in history.

The data is daunting. The Urban Institute reported that: "Younger cohorts' average wealth is simply no longer outpacing older cohorts. . . . 65 to 73 year-olds today have far more wealth than 65–73 year-olds did in 1983. More generally, the net worth of those 47 and older is roughly double that of someone the same age 27 years earlier. Today's adults in the mid 30s or younger—the prime time for career and family formation—benefitted little from the doubling of the economy since the early 1980s and have accumulated no more wealth than their counterparts 25 years ago."[51]

The Millennials' reputation as entitled and sheltered by overprotective parents becomes more entrenched when the issue of financial support is added to the mix. The general perception is that this is a generation supported by parents who have never made them seek an entry-level job and who continue to help them maintain the lifestyle they had as children into their adulthood. Here, too, the reality is far more complicated than the popular stereotype.

Providing Shelter in a Storm

Data supports the anecdotal perception that Millennials are financially tied to their parents longer into their adulthood than the economic dependence experienced by prior generations. One author reported that: "Today 85% of college graduates have either come home or have stayed home"[52]

According to the Pew Research Center: "Millennials are more likely to be living with other family members (47%) such as their parents, than were the immediate two previous generations at the same age (Gen Xers, 43%; Boomers, 39%)."[53] More than a third of the Pew respondents (36%) stated that they depend on financial assistance from their families. Even those who are employed reported that they receive assistance: of those Millennials working full-time, 14% reported needing family financial support.[54]

The reality behind all the data is more complex than the simple image of young adults on the parental dole. It is impossible to separate issues of parental financial support from the economy. Even where parents and their children are committed to a path of economic independence, education costs, diminished job prospects and other financial impacts of the economic crisis have served as game-changers.

Today's young adults face an employment outlook that is challenging at best and can be particularly discouraging depending on one's chosen field of study and geographical location. According to the Economic Policy Institute, "Entry-level wages fell among both women and men college graduates from 2000 to 2007, declining by 2.5 percent among men and 1.6 percent among women, and tumbled further in the recessionary years after 2007. This means that young college graduates who finished their education in the last five years or so are earning significantly less than their older brothers and sisters who graduated in the late 1990s."[55]

Moreover, those Millennials who entered the job market at the peak of the recession in 2009 faced a nearly 18% unemployment rate. As a result, Millennials were forced to look at ways to reduce expenses. In their 2009 survey, for example, Pew reported that 13% of those between 22 and 29 moved back home due to the economy.[56]

The data demonstrates improvement since then, but two variables add to the continued challenge. The first is that the employment rate for recent college graduates has not rebounded to pre-recession levels. By February 2013, only 62.9% of Millennials were reported as working, of which 31.2% worked on a part-time basis; 9.7% of Millennials were reported as unemployed, while 27.4% were considered out of the workforce entirely.[57] In a comprehensive article analyzing global employment data among young people, *The Economist* magazine calculated that " . . . all told, almost 290m are neither working nor studying: almost a quarter of the planet's youth."[58]

Second, far more than ever before, "not all degrees are created equal". According to the Northeastern University's Center for Labor Market Studies, "more than 40% of recent humanities graduates are working as bartenders, retail sales associates, and at other jobs that don't require college degrees—double the share of those with technical majors."[59]

Millennials are left to work through this maze of high unemployment and student loan repayments, relying on the help of their families and their own skills to get them through. Of particular interest, one study reported that in the US, 35% of employed Millennials have supplemental income from their own business.[60]

Don't Judge Me By Your Crisis

Survey respondents frequently expressed concern about the stability of their employment prospects and the precariousness of their economic future, as this health care worker noted:

The next generation has to work harder to get the same things as older generations because of the economy and the recession.

Some respondents resented the unfairness of being judged by how they cope with diminished opportunities and limited financial flexibility, particularly by the generations they perceive as having created the economic difficulties. One respondent stated:

I think Generation Y is viewed as having a low work ethic, but I think that is both inaccurate and very unfair. I read articles about how my generation is following different paths like traveling, volunteering, and living with their parents after college instead of immediately entering the work force. That is really unfair and disconnected, because I have many friends who did all those things after college, and it was because they couldn't find a good job. The economy makes it hard enough to find a good job if you already have professional experience, but recent graduates are at the bottom of the pool it seems.

I got my job because I knew my employer personally, and when I was applying for jobs it was frustrating to see a requirement of 5 or 6 years experience for what were categorized as 'entry-level jobs.' Less young people are following traditional professional paths, but I argue that it is due to lack of opportunity, especially when compared to the opportunities older generations had straight out of college. And whose fault is that? I would say that it's the older generations who have created this economic environment and then judge the young and unemployed as unmotivated or lazy.

The economic crisis deeply impacts how Millennials perceive their opportunities for financial stability. It also affects how Millennials view those senior generations who criticize young workers while seeming to be disconnected from their own contribution to the troubled economy.

The Long Chain of Student Debt

Like so many other issues involving Millennials, the timing as to when economic independence will be achieved is far more nuanced than a mathematical analysis of how long parents will subsidize rent payments as their Millennial children search for jobs in a troubled employment market. The financial reality that Millennials face is that, unlike any generation before them, many are graduating mired in staggering amounts of student loans: even as this generation represents 200 billion dollars in spending power, it owes more than a trillion dollars in college debt.[61]

Even if Millennials find employment, they may not initially earn enough to allow them to relieve their loan burdens: "And the student market will continue to borrow while balancing major risks accompanying the accumulation of debt. Recent data shows that the salaries earned by graduates aren't enough to pay off their debt. And this is limiting economic recovery and the ability to keep students above the poverty level."[62]

It is important, however, to ensure that discussions about the burden of student loans do not overshadow the impact of education on long-term earnings. Over time, the benefits are clear: " . . . college debt represents just over 1 percent of lifetime earnings for the typical college graduate. It also offers a return on investment of between 6 and 8 percent . . . "[63] But for Millennials mired in debt today, the future seems far away.

In the short-term, at least, for many who incurred significant debt on the path to their career, parental assistance is more a necessity than a luxury. Many respondents saw financial assistance as a logical obligation of parents if they can afford to help their children avoid or minimize student loans, particularly when they are graduating during a time of high unemployment. They were generally comfortable with the notion that if parents themselves enjoy economic stability, then some level of prolonged financial support for their children seemed appropriate in a perilous economy, as this respondent noted:

[P]arents of Gen Y seem to be more financially stable and can give more to their kids . . .

One respondent compared the debt burden many Millennials carry following completion of their higher education with the student loan debt borne by predecessor generations:

> *I think the older generation sees our income and compares to where they started off. However, with higher income usually come school loans to pay. There is a trade off. They didn't come to the work force with debt close to $100,000.*

A Millennial who worked in a demanding job spoke about the way managers at work complain about her generation as being too fixated on how much money they will be earning. She then listed her monthly basic expenses and detailed the payment obligations she faces on her substantial student loans. Although her income would have been sufficient to cover her basic expenses, the added student loan repayment obligations left her with no discretionary income. She noted:

> *We are aggressive about asking for more money because of our crushing student loan debt.*

When employers fail to understand the extent to which student debt load drives the Millennial generation, they may incorrectly judge their workplace behaviors and misconstrue their concerns about compensation.

Motivated Beyond Dependency

Several respondents defended the reliance on the parental safety net and did not believe such support diminished any motivation to achieve. For example:

> *. . . I know a lot of people who are just as motivated and work just as hard even though their parents have the money to send them anywhere for school, anywhere to travel, and they will be set up well when their family passes.*

But not all respondents concurred that the economic security some in their generation enjoy is without impact on their work ethic or drive to succeed. Moreover, some respondents were blunt in their negative assessment of those who did not need to work to afford the benefits they enjoyed. One even offered a test for determining whether the financial support their peers receive is too high:

> There is a whole subset of my generation who came from families that allowed them everything under the sun and told them everything they did was just great. Not my family. I'm not going to say I worked three jobs through HS and college, because I didn't, but that's a product of my parents working hard to see that their children could focus on education. I think you can tell a Gen Yer who has that sense of entitlement from another Gen Yer very easily—ask them if they pay their own car insurance or cell phone bill.

Some saw a connection between Millennials' expectations for the future and the safety net of their economic dependency, for example:

> I've personally seen several people from my generation turn down job positions or give up hope looking for jobs, because what is offered is less than their 'dream position.' Having to start 'from the bottom' seems looked down upon. Of course, this can differ depending on necessity. Most of those whom I have seen turn down positions were able to move back home with their parents.

A government employee stated that her peers seemed to view supplemental family support as a way to achieve their earnings expectations:

> I think many members of my generation expect their parents to make up the shortfall of their incomes or tuition in grad school and that they seem to feel they deserve promotions faster than they can be earned.

At the heart of these comments lies a fundamental observation regarding behaviors that frustrate Boomers and Xers in the workplace. To these senior generations, Millennials have baseline expectations that are far higher than what seems reasonable. But to Millennials, that baseline is established by their own life experiences. If they have grown up in a relatively comfortable environment with expectations about the quality of life they should expect to achieve, the early financial assistance that parents provide may simply be keeping Millennials from starting in reverse.

Notwithstanding troubled financial circumstances, the optimism that is often ascribed to Millennials emerged as respondents expressed how they will respond to the economy. A student juggling classes and part-time work in education saw the economic crisis as a clarion call to his generation:

> *Given the events of the last year and the increasing effects of the financial crisis, my generation has woken up. More than ever before there are discussions of what should be sacrificed and what needs to be done to achieve success. We are not a lazy generation and we have been called to action. Every generation in American history has defined itself relative to the crises it faced and how they responded. Our crisis has arrived and I believe that we will (and are prepared to) rise to meet it.*

Competitive Pressures

As Millennials emerge into the workplace, they face a particularly competitive environment. This need to compete for diminished job opportunities is similar to the competition-teamwork frame that marked much of their secondary school years. A remarkable aspect of the way Millennials grew up has been their ability to hold two simultaneously conflicting views together. They were raised in an era of open circles and team bonding. But they have also faced intense competition due to their large population and an increased focus on competition for college admissions.[64]

For many Millennials, higher education has been the goal that spurred a childhood and adolescence filled with activities that would demonstrate achievement. The competition to impress college admissions officers has been fierce. One author noted: "While in 1975, only 50% of high school graduates nationwide went to college, 86% attend today."[65] Other data shows that enrollment in higher education increased by 26% between 2007 and 2012, which equates to approximately 193 million people.[66]

Competition follows Millennials into the workplace as well. One respondent noted that competitive pressures are both pervasive and highly motivating:

> *Competition is very high in our generation (more so than each decade that predates it), and as such, we have to work harder to have the same professional success. I am always available to do more.*

These competitive pressures impact how Millennials perceive their ability to move past the economic challenges they are facing. Job security is no longer a reliable concept. Moreover, as Millennial branding expert and author Dan Schawbel noted, "The competition for your job isn't just American engineers, marketers, and financial analysts; it's everyone around the world now. . . . The Internet is now the glue that binds everyone together, without boundaries."[67] Millennials are not simply competing with their talented classmates; for many positions they are competing with talented individuals around the world.

Not Me

When respondents described a negative aspect of Millennial behaviors, they often distanced themselves from those same qualities they ascribed to others. For example, some respondents worried that the Millennials' childhood experiences may make it more difficult to adjust to difficult economic circumstances that differ from the more robust economy that existed during their early years. Generally, however, these concerns were stated as observations about others, and not personal reflections. A student in the science field expressed concern that others in her generation were not handling financial independence responsibly:

> *While some of us were not brought up that way, I think there is an additional component to this that we as Generation Y cannot avoid,*

and that is that most of us grew up during continued financial prosperity and had parents considerably more prosperous then their own. As a result, a good portion of Generation Y does not know what it is like to 'work your way up' or struggle financially. Hence so many young people are graduating from college and immediately going into credit card debt buying expensive electronics, furniture, and clothing they think they 'need' because it was provided for them by their parents previously.

A lawyer in her early 20s blamed parents for not having demanded more:

I think many people haven't had to work for what they got as children and young adults. I think parents of Gen Y'ers failed to teach discipline to their kids and just gave in to their demands.

Another respondent distinguished between the career advice her parents provided and the actual financial support that is given to her peers:

My mom played a large part in my early career development. She helped me create my resume and did mock interviews with me. In addition, throughout my life, she's discussed her own career issues with me, and has advised me about what is or is not a good work environment. I also credit her with encouraging me to pursue a line of work I feel passionate about. I have friends whose parents are a bit too supportive, however. My mom clearly stated that we were not allowed to move back home absent serious emergency or illness. While she wanted her children to be happy, she has also given the frank advice of "take the job you need to pay the bills." Some of my friends, however, moved back home after college so that they can spend a year searching for a job or 'finding themselves'. That's a bit much.

Once again, an intra-generational divide emerged as some respondents distanced themselves from their younger cohorts who they saw as receiving too much financial support from their parents. For example, a respondent in the retail sector criticized younger Millennials as less reliable because of their parental safety net:

> *I am on the cusp of Generation Y. I'm married with children, and I've been financially independent since I graduated high school at age 16. I paid for college myself and wasn't handed anything. I see with a lot of recent college grads that work for me that they DO feel entitled, they want respect the second they walk in the door (without feeling the need to earn it) and don't take work seriously (because they don't need to—a lot of them have their parents paying for their apartments and other expenses).*

Perhaps these respondents' unwillingness to ascribe negative generational behaviors to themselves is rooted in the fundamental confidence Millennials seem to exude, notwithstanding a troubled economy and lingering economic dependency. Millennials bring into the workplace a self-respect that is fundamental to their world view and a self-confidence that was carefully nurtured by their parents. Once at work, however, that inner confidence and self-respect often drives everyone else crazy for one simple reason: other generations interpret these qualities as conveying a sense of entitlement.

Chapter 6

What Does the Mirror See— Entitlement or Self-Respect?

We were told by our helicopter parents we could be whatever we wanted to be and have anything we wanted to have as long as we worked hard. Now [we are being told] we shouldn't want so much.

This respondent captured the tension between the way many Millennials were raised and the way they are currently perceived. The generation raised to be self-confident is viewed as entitled when in the workplace. This popular stereotype emerges in much of what is written about Millennials.

One effect of this hyper-focus on building confidence in young Millennials was noted by author Ron Alsop in *The Trophy Kids Grow Up*. To many observers, he stated: "Their self-esteem seems to know no bounds."[68] In 2012, a high school graduation speech by English teacher David McCullough Jr. captured the impact of the protected upbringing and high expectations that Millennials and their parents share by stating that, if everyone is raised to be special, than in fact, no one is. The speech immediately went viral as the "You're Not Special Speech".[69]

It has become the reputation that endures: Millennials are seen as having been indulged by parents, coddled by teachers, and treated too sensitively by coaches. But these same parents, teachers and coaches frequently ignore their own complicity in shaping the Millennials' behaviors by lamenting that the young generation is too "entitled" and is unwilling to work hard.

The perpetuation of this stereotype is at the root of much of the generational discord in the workplace. Describing an entire generation as "entitled" misses much of the underlying complexity and related cultural context, and masks far more defining characteristics of the Millennials.

A closer look reveals that Millennials may simply possess a higher degree of self-confidence and self-respect than did previous generations at a similar age. The irony, of course, is that the qualities which senior colleagues in the workplace find disconcerting are the same ones they encouraged through their parenting roles.

The problem may lie, however, in what was not sufficiently taught during the Millennials' childhood years. It may be that as parents imbued their children with confidence, they missed an important ingredient: humility. Millennials may be facing a more difficult path at work because their supervisors do not see their self-confidence as tempered with sufficient modesty.

Defining Entitlement

The word "entitled" may be the most defining—and damning—term used by others to describe Millennials. Several questions were included on the survey to gauge their perspective on the meaning of the term as applied to their generation. The responses revealed a wide variation in the way Millennials view what it means to be seen as entitled. For example one male respondent stated:

> *Entitled refers to a person who is focused more on what he or she is due, rather than what he or she owes.*

Similarly, a teacher noted:

> *Generally, I think that the word "entitled" is used to describe us as a generation that feels that certain things like financial success and personal happiness are rights rather than privileges or rewards. They see us as unwilling to sacrifice or endure hardship.*

Another zeroed in on the way the term is used in the workplace context:

> . . . I guess when I hear people say entitled, I think they mean that we think of ourselves as more valuable to the workplace than we actually are, especially recent grads with limited marketable skills.

Some challenged the underlying concept of characterizing an entire generation by one word. For example, a respondent in a post-graduate program stated:

> . . . I believe that for every GenYer who is most certainly going through life feeling entitled, there are also many GenYers who are struggling to get through and achieve what they desire, and are putting in lots of hard work and effort and have no sense of entitlement whatsoever. I'm not sure what the division is of how many fall into the former and how many fall into the latter, but in both my upbringing in suburban Long Island, my undergraduate education at a private university that attracted many affluent students, and now my post-graduate school . . . where a diverse range of students are my classmates, I have experienced as many entitled students as I have hardworking ones. It is difficult for me to say with any precision as to why the older generations tend to focus only on the 'entitlement' aspect of our generation.

Other respondents saw the term as a short-hand critique of the Millennials' ability to handle negative experiences. One offered this perspective:

> I think [people view] members of Gen Y [as feeling] that they should not have to experience pain or hardship. And if they work hard, they are 'entitled' to the rewards of 'playing by the rules' (i.e. admission to an Ivy League School, good salary, robust 401(k), good looking spouse, nice car, smart kids, etc.). If these things don't come to them, despite their hard work, then they are frustrated because they haven't gotten that which they were entitled to receive.

For many respondents, entitlement was not a negative attribute as long as it was tempered with well-placed appreciation for the source of their confidence and optimism. Several expressed gratitude to their families as they described their expectations for future success that they felt others call "entitled":

> I think a lot of my generation feels they are entitled, but I also feel that many know how good they have it and are thankful for it. I am grateful to know that my parents could step in and help me out if I was in trouble financially, and I am so grateful that I had all the luxuries growing up that I did. Sometimes this may come across as me acting as though I feel entitled, but if one were to ask me, or look closer, I think they would realize how appreciative I am for all the advantages I have had.

Some respondents attributed the attention that was showered on them while growing up as typical behaviors of loving parents, and emphasized that what they do with these opportunities matters most, as this respondent in the marketing field highlighted:

> I think 'entitled' can often be misconstrued. The parents of our generation worked extremely hard to give us the opportunities that we have today. My parents worked multiple jobs in order to provide us with the best lives possible—sports, music lessons, choice of college, etc.—and give us the opportunities that they didn't have growing up. While this characterization is accurate for those who believe they don't have to work hard to go far and everything should be handed to them, I think for those of us who have had values passed on to us, we work hard and understand we have been given these opportunities because of our parents. It's not entitlement but more of a sense of the possibilities that exist because of the groundwork our parents have laid to get us here.

Underlying Gratitude for Great Expectations

Not all respondents saw the label of "entitled" as incorrect, but did challenge the derisive context in which other generations use the term. Generally, respondents understood the connection between the label and their upbringing. Some even noted a clear progression from their parents' life-long messages that they are special to an expectation that they will be amply rewarded—and soon. For example, a respondent observed:

> We have helicopter parents. But they taught us well. If you are a hard worker, what is wrong with expecting a lot? I work extremely hard and expect my employer to realize that and compensate me accordingly (thus, I feel entitled).

The notion that many Millennials feel both special and "owed" appeared as a consistent theme:

> I do think Gen Y tends to think that the world owes us, that employers should be happy to have us—not the other way around.

A college student observed:

> We feel like we can do anything and that we deserve to do anything we can put our minds to. I think it comes from people telling us all of our lives that we can achieve anything. It could just be the people I'm surrounded by at school, but everyone thinks they deserve the best job or the best opportunities and that, just because they have [high ranking college] on their resume or transcript, that they are going to get that.

Many respondents agreed that greater educational opportunities lead to higher expectations for success that is both internally and externally driven. A respondent in the marketing field noted:

> I think there is a certain expectation that comes from being

a well-educated, hard-working individual, and we want to be rewarded for it.

A college student similarly observed:

> *I think we are an entitled generation, as frustrating as it is to say. We have been given everything, and we've been constantly praised our whole lives. Therefore, we expect that sort of thing to continue. But at the same time, we have high expectations and will work hard to get them.*

This sentiment was repeated by a number of respondents. They did not accept the notion that the opportunities and advantages they had when young negated their own desires to work hard to succeed, as this post-graduate student observed:

> *I think that many of my peers have been given advantages that our parents may not have had, be it educational, or in a networking aspect. I think that once given these opportunities my generation is very hard-working.*

Another respondent both defended the work ethic of Millennials and linked feelings of entitlement to their expectations for engagement at work:

> *My peers from my undergrad years . . . have a strong work ethic and are not as concerned about how much they will be paid. But they do harbor a sense of entitlement. They feel that they deserve work that is interesting, engaging and challenging. Many of these peers were sorely disappointed with their entry level positions after graduation.*

These expectations for opportunities and engagement have deep roots in the culture in which Millennials were raised. One writer noted: "Millennials started to come of age . . . at a time when they were able to place more demands on the workplace in terms of comp expectations, work-life balance, and so forth, having been raised in an era of consumer control and a world in which they were free to create their own . . . From 'Build-a-Bear' to 'choose your own ending' stories, from choosing the next color of M&Ms to 'voting people off the island'—so they felt comfortable trying to call their shots as much as they could in other aspects of life."[70] The expectation that they could also write their own workplace story can be seen as a logical outgrowth of this upbringing.

Some respondents who saw their reputation as rooted in a legacy of encouragement noted that the realities of the workplace have tempered behaviors. A part-time professional stated:

> *I think my generation was pushed so hard as youths. We were told that as long as we worked hard at school, we could do/be anything. When we entered the workforce, it was a huge reality check—opportunities for more responsibility and advancement come much more slowly. I am much further behind in the job world than I thought I would be at this age, and it's eroding my self-esteem.*

Another stated:

> *We were raised to think that you could have it all—successful career, happy family, and rich personal life. I think that those expectations may come across as entitled, and the reality that you cannot have it all may result in a negative attitude until expectations adjust.*

The Celebrity Factor

Since their early adolescence, Millennials have been bombarded with messages that encourage attention-seeking behaviors and the idea that fame is easily achieved. Beginning with MySpace, and later Facebook and YouTube, social media has encouraged Millennials to develop an online presence. By constantly broadcasting their lives to each other, it became reasonable to assume everyone else is interested. Photographing and posting experiences can become more important than the experiences themselves. These publically lived lives have contributed to the perception of Millennials as over-indulged and entitled, and fueled the stereotype that they have grown up with an unrealistic expectation of early success and perhaps even celebrity.

This view that fame is easily attainable also stems from lifelong exposure to people who turned into overnight celebrities on a vast array of television channels. Where their parents grew up with television stations dominated by three networks, Millennials were raised with an entire cable TV industry devoted to attracting their loyal viewership. The quantity of offerings directed to a young audience grew along with the generation, and the explosion of "Reality TV" programming coincided with their developing entertainment tastes.

Throughout the formative years of Millennials, the lines grew increasingly blurred between reality and Reality TV. Child stars like Lindsay Lohan and Britney Spears morphed from personas of fresh-faced innocence to dark public meltdowns. For stars like Paris Hilton and Nicole Richie, and the many others over the years whose lives have played out on camera, Reality TV has become reality. All of these images generally contribute to the stereotype of Millennials as self-indulgent.[71]

A respondent who recognized that popular culture contributes to the negative perception of Millennials challenged the fairness of the stereotype:

> *Certainly, the people they show on Reality TV shows these days portray my generation as entitled, but I don't honestly believe that typical people like myself carry around an entitled attitude.*

Even as Reality TV images contribute to a stereotype of self-indulgence, it is more likely that the sheer quantity of media available has an even greater impact. For a generation raised in front of television and computer screens, the expectation of instantaneous responses and instant gratification impacts how they view the world and how others view them.

With so many shows creating new celebrities, fame can feel deceptively achievable, particularly to ambitious parents and their energetic children. It is difficult to avoid a celebrity culture which fosters the image of a younger generation influenced by a glamorized link between fame and fortune, and where both seem to come without effort. In a story about the expensive—and often fruitless—search for young stardom that parents engage in with their children, a reporter wrote: "In a technical sense, [fame] is more attainable. With the growth of Disney, Nickelodeon, and other kid-focused networks, there is greater demand for child actors. And when international pop star Justin Bieber can get discovered by uploading a few grainy clips of himself to YouTube, kids from every corner of the country feel they, too, can catch their big break without much effort."[72]

This perspective is similarly captured by a respondent who noted that when popular culture suggests that wealth and celebrity can be attained simply through family pedigree, rich friends, or a Reality TV show, it reinforces a disassociation between success and hard work:

> *Previous generations have had to work hard for their success and happiness, and now this generation would love nothing more than to ride on the coattails of those efforts. After all, one of our biggest celebrities is Paris Hilton, who has done nothing more to earn her fame than being born into a rich family. I think that just about says it all.*
>
> *Even as respondents had differing views about the source of their reputation as entitled, they did not see other generations as immune from the same criticism.*

Sorry, Wrong Generation

Many respondents turned the tables on the use of the word "entitled" challenging its application only to Millennials. For example, several respondents expressed frustration that prior generations neither seek, nor otherwise seem to respect, the opinions and ideas of younger employees. They saw the reluctance of older generations to engage their ideas as examples of far more "entitled" behavior than the same label applied to Millennials. One respondent stated:

> *I think anyone who grew up with a silver spoon feels entitled regardless of their age. I also think anyone who has never had to work hard feels entitled regardless of their age. In the workplace though, I have come across more entitlement from the older generations. I think*

they feel more entitled then younger generations. They think that they are more knowledgeable and should be listened to without question from anyone of a younger generation.

Just because you are older doesn't mean you are always right. And if you dare question them, well, watch out. They are less willing to consider other possibilities, to explore new options, or to listen to what you have to say. And offering criticism is just not even an option with most.

Another respondent dismissed the entitled label as an example of the Boomers' failure to take ownership of their own negative contributions to the world:

[Referring to our generation as entitled] seems like cynical Baby Boom-speak. If anything, the time for Millennials is urgent given the state of the world the Boomers have left it in.

The Label Does not Fit

Some respondents rejected the portrayal of Millennials as entitled as an unjustified judgment:

I don't think older generations realize that even if we act entitled, we actually do work for a living and work for our perks.

These respondents observed that the label needed to be understood in a broader cultural context that links the hopes and dreams of each new generation with the accomplishments of their predecessors, and the expectation that the next generation should achieve more. They also dismissed the application of the word as unique to Millennials, correlating the approbation as historically attributed to youth. They saw entitlement as a description that could be used to describe any member of a generation, with no greater applicability to Millennials. These observations were consistent with one commentator's response to a *Time Magazine* cover story about Millennials entitled "The ME ME ME Generation." The author provided images of prior young generations covered by major magazines through the years, including a 1976 Tom Wolfe *New York Magazine* cover story entitled "The Me Decade".[73]

A respondent observed this desire to stereotype generations in their youth:

> *Every generation can be characterized as 'entitled.' The whole point is to make the next generation more fortunate than the one that came before it. Entitlement is more about attitude and how you treat people. Any person who looks down on another can be considered having an 'entitled' attitude. For every Harvard graduate with a lofty pay-check, there are several dozen steel mill workers in the Midwest in the same age range trying to get by. Long story short, generalizations are almost always stupid, and the only reason they are almost always stupid is because removing the word 'always' would make the statement a generalization.*

Another stated simply:

> *The people saying such things do not remember what it was like to be young.*

Similarly, a Millennial in the public relations field observed:

> *I don't [see our generation as entitled] because setting higher expectations is what every generation has done. That's how society progresses over time.*

Another saw a broader application of the term:

> *I believe the concept of Entitlement applies to America in its entirety—not just Gen Y. It's part of the culture, but has become more recognized in recent years which may create an erroneous relationship to Gen Y.*

Respondents also generally did not agree that the stronger economy they experienced in their childhood diminished their goals or their drive to achieve them:

> *It seems that, in general, the US has enjoyed growing wealth as a nation for at least the last 60 years. Therefore, each successive generation since World War II has been raised in a more wealthy country than its predecessor generation. I think this is the underlying motivation for using the word 'entitled.'*
>
> *Each new generation should be entitled to inherit the metaphorical house that the previous generation has enjoyed and hopefully improved during its tenure. However, if 'entitled' is referring to a generation that is less driven, I vigorously disagree.*

Intra-Generational Differences

As with other responses to survey topics, respondents again revealed a generational division between older Millennials who have been in the workforce and younger members of their generation. Although the survey results overall showed an even split between those who thought the characterization of their generation as "entitled" was accurate and those who did not, there were two interesting differences. The first is that more than half of the younger Millennials (56.5% of those in the 18–22 year-old age range) saw the term as an accurate description, compared to those Millennials in the 26–31 year-old age range (less than 46% agreed). The second difference was that, behind the numbers, older Millennials offered stronger comments, describing their younger cohorts as the appropriate recipient of criticism. So even though a higher percentage of younger Millennial respondents agreed that their generation's reputation as entitled was accurate, their anecdotal comments were far more measured than comments from the older cohort of the same generation. For example, a lawyer expressed his view of the entitlement label in intra-generational terms:

I see younger generations than me expressing their concern for how much is expected of them over and over again. It actually frustrates me and I wouldn't characterize myself in the 'older generation' yet.

Another respondent in the older Millennial age range also spoke of an intra-generational divide:

I have noticed with folks a few years younger than me (maybe 5–6 years younger) that they seem to have a disconnect between what they want and what they have to do to get it. They also seem less concerned with keeping commitments and the value of their word . . .

A respondent in the marketing field stated:

I would say the younger half of my generation DEFINITELY is [entitled]. For people my age [28+], we earned money for a car. For people my brother's age—he is 22—they expect a NEW car ON their 16th birthday.

Another respondent attributed the attitude of entitlement among younger Millennials to the financial success observed in prior generations:

[W]e as a generation feel as if we have the right, right now, to the monetary success that our parents worked hard for and that took time to build. I am on the cusp of Generation Y and Generation X and have seen younger individuals that I have worked with act in this manner.

This intra-generational split sometimes had respondents sounding like they could be multiple generations apart. For example, a respondent who was a teacher offered this tough assessment of younger Millennials with whom she had worked in the past:

I remember being 26 and interviewing interns, I can't tell you how appalled I was! They all wanted HUGE salaries, Fridays off, their own office etc and for doing nothing . . . these kids are in big trouble. I have always been successful in my work and have always had bosses tell me that I was amazingly motivated and had the strongest work ethic of all the young people they knew. I stood out because I wasn't afraid of hard work or working hard . . . I grew up wealthy and spoiled but certainly worked for what I have, appreciated what I got, volunteered, was expected to work and knew the meaning of the words "thank you." Nothing is free. These kids want to be CEOs overnight with no work put in . . . Kids are entitled, they are given cell phones, money and sexualized clothing at a young age. No one works, people are hired to write college essays, there is no community service or sense of obligation to society.

Some younger Millennials, however, had a far more measured perspective. One respondent who both worked full-time and attended college stated:

Some in my age group are [entitled] but people need to stop lumping us all together. I worked for everything I've been given (or earned) in my life.

Not Me Redux

Once again, Millennials were more likely to attribute characteristics to others in their cohort that they did not necessarily see in themselves. Respondents who viewed their generation as exhibiting "entitled" behaviors distanced *themselves* from the label, denying the applicability of that term to the way they lived their own lives. Instead, they referred to "others" who seem that way, while stating clearly that they themselves were not. For example, a lawyer noted:

I think the older generations feel like Gen Y has a sense of entitlement in that they don't need to work as hard to make it to the 'next level' or next career move. I personally see it in colleagues but I don't feel the same way about me, as I think I was raised differently. In my mind, hard work is necessary to move up the corporate or career ladder.

A respondent in the information services field was pointed in his criticism of others, as he deflected any from himself:

Gen-Y often gets stereotyped as the 'entitled' generation. While I have to agree that the vast majority of Gen-Y carries this entitled attitude, I do my best to break away from that image. I hope others my age despise that stereotype as well and do what they can to not come off as 'entitled' to others in the workplace.

A public relations specialist succinctly disavowed any notion of acting entitled:

I do not carry myself in an entitled way. I am much too straightforward and honest about myself and my background for people to think that.

Another stated:

I do think there are a lot of people who feel [they are entitled] . . . thus all the credit card debt people have now a days! People feel like they (need) a new car, furniture, huge house, etc., right after getting their first job, like they deserve it, even if they don't have the money. This is definitely a 'Gen-Y' phenomenon . . . but I try very hard not to fall into this!

Similarly, a respondent in the administrative field stated:

I think that the . . . characterization is not applicable to me. I have never felt entitled to anything, and I'm anything but spoiled. But I have met peers who are definitely afflicted with a sense of entitlement and a need for instant gratification. People have little respect and patience anymore.

One respondent saw the criticism as accurate for some, and expressed worry that the label reflected poorly on Millennials overall:

I think my generation has been told that we are entitled to certain things if we graduate from college. We are entitled to a high paying job that we like, a good work/life balance, etc. A college degree meant something very different to generations before us, and now, everyone has one. I think the big shock for a lot of people comes when they graduate and realize that nothing is actually going to be handed to them, or that they may not get their dream job. Some people, unfortunately, continue to believe that they are entitled and I feel like it reflects badly on our generation as a whole, even though a lot of us are willing to put in the time and hard work.

Another credited her upbringing as responsible for the differences she observed between her own behaviors and that of her fellow Millennials:

I think when people call members of Generation Y 'entitled', they basically mean 'spoiled'. I think that a lot of young people from my generation believe that they can and should have anything they want, simply because they want it. Personally, I was raised by a mother who taught me lovingly but firmly that I am no better than the next person. Therefore, I deserve no special treatment. I thank her for that every day.

One respondent criticized members of his generation for being unwilling to match their efforts to their desired results:

I believe our generation is characterized as 'entitled' because many members of our generation are perceived as people who expect maximum return on minimal effort. Many in our generation, from my own experience anyway, want immediate reward for whatever they think they have done, which is usually the bare minimum. Many of them are critical of others and complain about much around them, yet they do not seem to take any accountability for themselves and their own contribution to whatever they are unhappy about. I fear our generation is exchanging accountability and responsibility for entitlement, impatience, and distrust.

Economic Circumstances as a Determining Factor

Yet another intra-generation gap may exist within the Millennials. Among the many comments expressed by respondents about their views of the entitlement label, particularly strong feelings emerged about the role of childhood economic circumstances and upbringing. The responses suggest that many Millennials judge each other by the economic circumstances in which they were raised. Those who perceived that their fellow Millennials had greater economic opportunities are more likely to be critical of their reputation as entitled.

Without naming the behavior as entitled, a graduate student spoke of the influence of early affluence on many in her generation, and the related impatience that can cause in efforts to achieve the same degree of comfort when on one's own:

> . . . [M]any of the people in my generation don't want to have to wait to have nice things. We don't want to have to wait to go on the vacations that we want. It seems like we see our elders have these things and we want them, but we don't want to wait until we are middle-aged and have saved for them to get what we want.

One respondent who grew up with limited financial means expressed concern about the entitled behavior of others in her generation:

> I worked with high school juniors for ten years . . . and there was a definite sense of 'you owe me this grade/experience/whatever' . . . that seemed to grow more acute with the passing years. Many of my peers and those younger than I am seem to have an 'I want it so I'm owed it' mentality. As someone who has worked since she was 16 and paid to put herself through college and law school, I find this attitude both annoying and sad. The outlook that you'll value most that which you have to earn seems to have been lost.

A law student working part-time observed:

Most of the Gen Y students at my law school, for example, do not have jobs outside of school. Many have not ever had a job. Many of them have parents who pay for their education and expenses. I think this leads to a sense of entitlement, even if that sense happens to be subconscious. It is most striking to the few of us who go to law school full-time, work, and have other outside obligations. . . .

Noted a Millennial in the advertising field:

I . . . think that certain groups of our generation can be 'entitled'". Personally, the people I have encountered that were raised in upper-class or upper-middle class homes and attended private schools, seem to have more of these characteristics than folks I know who grew up middle-class and lower-middle class.

A public relations professional in her mid-20's also emphasized the link between entitlement and economic circumstances:

I have been supporting myself for the past few years and do not expect handouts from anyone, parents included. I do not accept money from them or anyone else . . . I don't sit around and feel 'entitled' to having a great paying job, nice work hours, enough spending money to go on a nice vacation, get promoted every year, etc. I understand the idea of 'paying one's dues' but sometimes I also have to pay an arm and a leg.

A graduate student disavowed the label by simply pointing to her own immigrant background:

I immigrated to the US. In many ways, 'entitled' is the last word that comes to mind.

These perspectives are similar to the comments of respondents who distanced themselves from behaviors they recognized in their fellow Millennials. The views are also critical of the notion that all Millennials experienced a privileged upbringing. This distinction is particularly important because it provides the perspective of Millennials whose economic background does not comport with the image of this entire generation as being born into privileged circumstances.

Losing Entitlement to the Global Crisis

Although the Millennials' reputation as entitled dates back many years, it would be a mistake to assume that the behaviors that may have given rise to that reputation are unaffected by the extraordinary economic circumstances this generation has faced since 2008. Respondents recognized that, notwithstanding the opportunities they may have experienced while growing up, the global economic crisis deeply affects how they now perceive their current and future career success. The experiences of their childhood stand in sharp contrast to the near economic collapse that coincided with their entry into the job market. For some, that means a significant change in personal circumstances; for others, it may mean that the American Dream they were raised to seek feels more elusive than ever.

Two years after the economic crisis began, a poll of 18–29 year-olds by the Harvard Institute of Politics found that: " . . . six in ten (60%) are concerned about meeting their current bills and obligations and almost half (45%) report that their personal financial situation is bad. Among America's undergraduate population, 45% are concerned about their ability to stay in college given the state of the economy."[74] Another survey approximately a year later reported that 72% of the Millennials polled felt they made compromises in order to enter the job market, for example, accepting a lower-than-expected salary, fewer benefits, or less preferred geographical location.[75] This data stands in contrast to the perception of this generation behaving consistent with their reputation as "entitled".

Survey respondents expressed significant concern about how they will fare as a result of the economic climate. One part-time administrative worker spoke of the stark distinction between his generation's reputation as compared with the economic reality of the times:

The boomers did a good job by us. We've gone to good schools and all of that, without facing things like a draft or massive economic failure. Until now. I certainly have heard that I'm entitled, but given that I'm entering the work force with a [high] unemployment rate, I think everybody can go ahead and shut the hell up about that.

Similarly, a public relations specialist noted:

We were brought up VERY different from the previous generation. Our generation has always been pushed to the next level and told to never settle. Our parents busted their butts to get us into great schools and gave us incredible opportunities. So we bring this into the workplace and are judged for it. But what do they expect? Our attitude may be a bit aggressive but anyone who has been in the workforce over a year has learned to tone down their attitude and swallow their pride.

This comment highlights another aspect of the economy that has stymied Millennials. Even if they are able to find a job, their growth and development opportunities seem more limited than ever by a workplace that is spending less on training young employees. This leaves young workers still feeling adrift even after they are employed. And workplace data supports their concern. One study found that "55% of workers in the U.S. reported they are under pressure to develop additional skills to be successful in their current and future jobs, but only 21% said they have acquired new skills through company-provided training during the past five years."[76]

A respondent in the financial services field similarly highlighted this dilemma:

Some may think that [we are entitled], but I disagree. We have to work just as hard and it seems that there are less opportunities and less companies willing to train and promote than in the past.

The slow pace of the economic recovery has resulted in many Millennials feeling adrift in a workplace unwilling to invest in their success. Accordingly, they feel forced to recalibrate their goals and determine how they can succeed without the safety net of support they may have had as adolescents.

The Beat Goes On

Respondents frequently articulated a philosophical perspective that demonstrated wisdom beyond their young years. They shared a resigned recognition that workplace realities will necessitate the adjustment of youthful attitudes. Even with these adjustments however, essential questions remain. Are Millennials, like other generations before them, making adaptive changes in their expectations as they grow into their early adult years? And even if this is so, do their adjustments remain consistent with the early successes they were primed to expect, but are simply tempered to fit the economic circumstances they are facing? For example, a young woman in the sciences noted:

I don't consider myself to be entitled, but I do sometimes struggle with the concept that I can't have the luxuries I used to have when I lived with my parents (even though I've been an independent adult for about 4 years). Sometimes I think the label 'entitled' is over-used and intended as an insult, which I don't agree with. But there are definite differences between what my peers think they are deserving of and what I understand my parents thought they were deserving of when they were my age.

A woman in her early 20's noted:

I think a lot of people in my generation have this idea that if they want something they deserve it. That said, I also think that as we grow older the line between desire and deserve is clarified a bit.

Some respondents wisely saw a connection between their generation's characterization as "entitled" and the idea that a sense of entitlement may be the foundation for all important achievements in every generation. For example, a government employee observed:

Entitlement is not an entirely bad thing, but in the past decade it has acquired a negative connotation. Entitlement has allowed us, as a country, to come far with regards to civil rights, gender and human rights issues. These are some things for which people should feel entitled. I think that each person has a different perspective on what they are or are not entitled to. I have met many people from older generations who have similar 'entitlement' complexes as Generation Y'ers.

Where Confidence and Entitlement Merge

The survey responses and other data about the Millennials suggest that the frequently portrayed stereotype of this generation is misperceived. Perhaps when youthful enthusiasm is mixed with a child-centered upbringing, the word "entitled" becomes a euphemism for what happens when a sizable portion of a large demographic is raised to be self-confident achievers. Where others see entitlement, today's young adults see self-esteem—the same self-esteem that their parents encouraged them to develop from the time they were babies.

As one respondent stated:

They misunderstand our self-respect.

A law student emphasized this point:

I tend to think of this sense of entitlement as being part of my generation's self-confidence. Misplaced or not, I think that confidence helps people take risks and succeed when they otherwise might not.

Similarly, a Millennial in the engineering profession stated:

I think the only way I can really relate to this question is on a personal level, and I know that I have worked hard to accomplish all that I have accomplished, and so I don't feel entitled. I feel that what I have done I have done through hard work (and some luck!) and trying not to take things for granted. If I in any way feel entitled, it is only because I think that I can do pretty much anything I put my mind to.

Millennials are members of a large generation raised during a unique time in history. They have been able to experience relative economic prosperity and increased technological innovations. As they age and have children of their own, Millennials can only benefit from the vast array of resources and choices that will be available to them. Such choices will likely exist in even greater abundance than they experienced in their youth due, in large measure, to continued technological advances. One can imagine a future generation of young people entering the workforce as their beleaguered Millennial bosses express frustration with their entitled ways and dismay about the ways they communicate.

Chapter 7

He Talks, She Texts— Is Anybody Listening?

Conversations with Boomers and Gen Xers became particularly animated on the topic of Millennials and their communication styles. In particular, senior generations express concern about Millennials' reliance on technology, their discomfort with face-to-face communication, and how they express themselves. One issue not generally addressed, however, is the set of unique challenges Millennials encounter as they bring their exceptional technology skills into the workplace.

No prior generation has had to face the odd assortment of communication and technology transitions that Millennials confront daily. At home, Millennials rely on social networking and text messages for their preferred forms of communication. Actually speaking on a cell phone provides a secondary back-up. And emails are, well, so yesterday.

But work is a different story. When Millennials walk into work, it is not unusual to feel like they are stepping back in time. Their primary means of communication may be face-to-face, by telephone, or by email, and they may even be prohibited from using social media. And, contrary to the experiences of nearly all Millennials in their personal lives, their workplace phone is likely connected to wires, which requires staying in one place for the duration of the call.

This means that Millennials are continually adapting to the communication styles of those with whom they work, even though they more efficiently and effectively communicate differently on a personal level. This is not an adaption that prior generations had to make. Back in the day—any day—people communicated at home in the same way they did at work. The choices were limited: letters; telephones; face-to-face. As technology advanced, other forms of communication entered the mix, but there was not a dramatic difference between how people communicated in their personal lives and how they communicated at work.

Not so anymore. Millennials live in a constantly evolving world of communication options that allow them easy access to each other. But once they enter the workplace, the options differ wildly from job to job, and, frequently, even within a single workplace.

As a result of this significant variance, Millennials must demonstrate a quiet sophistication and ability to adapt that is both admirable and unnoticed. With each new job or assignment, they need to immediately assess the communication capabilities of their colleagues and determine whether there will be an easy technology fit, whether they must adapt to a less efficient style of communicating, whether they will be expected to assume the role of teacher to help their colleagues communicate better, or whether they will face co-workers whose unwillingness to learn to use technology or maximize its efficiency impedes workplace effectiveness.

Growing Up Digital

At the core of any debate that exists about whether Millennials are truly a different generation or whether they are simply exhibiting behaviors of youth that have existed in all generations, there is one distinction that is irrefutable. Millennials have been exposed to technology of various sorts since birth and have grown up within the digital world.[77] We do not yet know the full impacts from a technology-immersed life on the developing brain. We do, however, see the immediate behaviors that have emerged from being "conditioned by technology to become bored and frustrated during the momentary gap [waiting] for a response to an e-mail or [a] web browser to open."[78]

Millennials expect to adapt to the fast pace of each new change. They do not view advances in technology as something they would choose *not* to learn, as some of their more senior colleagues sometimes do. In fact, as John Palfry and Urs Gasser wrote in *Born Digital: Understanding the First Generation of Digital Natives*, the use of technology among young people is "changing the way the world works." Palfry and Urs further stated that, even as the full impacts of the changes cannot be known, " . . . they are profound and will alter all manner of dynamics over the coming decades, if not centuries and beyond."[79]

According to Pew Research Center data, Millennials see their use of technology as a distinguishing marker when comparing themselves to other generations: "They are more likely to have their own social networking profiles, to connect to the internet wirelessly when away from home or work, and to post video of themselves online." And the Millennials' use of cell phones for texting far exceeds that of Gen X and Baby Boomers.[80]

Technology guides how Millennials communicate with one another, shaping their social patterns. Texting has replaced telephone calls and contributes to a generation always able to be on the move, always able to communicate where one is or soon will be. With such ease and fluidity of communicating while on the go, social planning becomes a relic of the past.

Technology is also affecting economic patterns, significantly influencing other generations as well. As consumers, Millennials make purchasing decisions in ways that were unfathomable a decade ago. As one study of the Millennial consumer noted: "For this generation, the definition of 'expert'—a person with the credibility to recommend brands, products, and services—has shifted from someone with professional or academic credentials to potentially anyone with firsthand experience, ideally a peer or close friend. U.S. Millennials also tend to seek multiple sources of information, especially from noncorporate channels, and they're likely to consult their friends before making purchase decisions. For example, more Millennials than non-Millennials reported using a mobile device to read user reviews and to research products while shopping . . . 'Crowd sourcing'—tapping into the collective intelligence of the public of one's peer group—has become particularly popular."[81]

The internet has also provided the forum for lives to be lived publicly. Privacy boundaries, compared to previous generations, have crumbled. In her book of essays written by teen-aged girls, Amy Goldwasser stated that this generation may be the first to have such chronicled and exposed lives: "It's how you conduct your friendships, get to know people, break a heart, manage your family, flirt, lie, make plans, cancel them, announce big news, and, most important, present yourself to the rest of the world. You're fluent in texting, e-mailing, and IM'ing. You're blogging and constantly amending your profile . . . Regularly . . . you're generating a body of intimate written work."[82] In discussing the confessional nature of many web sites and discussion boards, Psychology professor Jean Twenge noted the tendency to tell "everyone about your experiences and feelings, no matter how distasteful."[83]

Another commentator compared the technology used today to record life events with the scrapbooks of the past: "If a scrapbook was something you kept for yourself to archive your memories, Instagram is that scrapbook, except shared with everyone."[84] In other words, prior generations chronicled their lives, but aspects of those experiences that could be tangibly captured were shared selectively within the close geographical circle of friends and family. The internet provides for every experience to be recorded and distributed widely.

Technology has also resulted in Millennials serving as unwilling participants in a massive experiment. What will it mean for a generation to grow up digital and distracted? What is the impact on a developing brain from a lifetime of multi-tasking between online distractions and whatever may be happening in real time? Will future generations be unable to focus in depth on specific tasks? If not, what will be the potential complications?

Answers to these questions are emerging in some early studies, for example: "Research on the brain's response to electronic media . . . suggests that digital natives have higher baseline activity in the part of the brain governing short-term memory, the sorting of complex information, and the integration of sensations and thoughts—so, in certain respects, computers make you smarter. . . . But other research suggests that excessive, long term exposure to electronic environments is reconfiguring young people's neural networks and possibly diminishing their ability to develop empathy, interpersonal relations, and nonverbal communication skills. . . . With more time devoted to computers and less to in-person interactions, young people may be understimulating and underdeveloping the neural pathways necessary for honing social skills. Another study shows that after long periods of time on the internet, digital natives display poor eye contact and a reluctance to interact socially."[85]

And what will be the impacts on family cohesion when parents raised on iPhones have children themselves distracted by the technology of the future? Millennials are bringing their exceptional expertise and comfort with technology into this uncharted territory of the future.

Adjusting to Differences at Work

Technology is not only changing the way the world works, it is changing the world of work. Even in the midst of the economic crisis, Millennials emphasize the importance of access to state-of-the-art technology when they are considering a job.[86]

The Millennials' comfort with and recognition of the power of technology was evident in many of the responses in the survey. An overwhelming majority of the respondents identified themselves as technology proficient, with more than 97% stating they were somewhat or very tech savvy. Interestingly, male respondents considered themselves more tech savvy than female respondents: 55% of the men described themselves as very tech savvy, compared to only 37% of the women.

Survey responses also demonstrated the differences between how Millennials communicate personally and how they communicate professionally. Respondents communicated most frequently via text (more than 86%) and social networks (more than 75%) with their friends. Yet in the workplace, respondents often faced limitations in their use of text messaging and access to social networking sites.

In assessing the technological capabilities of more senior generations in the workplace, only 7% of the respondents thought of their older co-workers as very tech savvy, and nearly a third described them as not savvy.

These responses may have significance beyond whether those supervising Millennials understand how to use a computer. For example, one study reported that 45% of executives at smaller organizations and 29% of executives at larger organizations stated that their CEOs rarely or never factor their company's social media reputation into decision-making, and that they are not monitoring, analyzing, or responding to comments made about the company by users on social media outlets.[87]

Moreover, for many older workers, social media can be threatening. Generally, if a business run by Boomers embraces social media as part of its marketing strategy, the implementation will likely fall to a younger, tech savvy employee. But some senior managers may not be ready to cede that aspect of their business, worrying about the loss of control that they may feel as a result. As noted in an article analyzing the tensions that can arise in a multigenerational workplace: "Because older workers tend to view knowledge as power, they sometimes hoard it to stay in control."[88]

To young employees adept at social media, the unwillingness to use it strategically is viewed as a missed opportunity for the company to maximize the reach of its message and to cement its brand identity. It is also a disappointment to the younger workers because they are not being encouraged to use their skills to their best advantage. It is even more disheartening when refusal to engage is more a control mechanism than a decision made in the best interests of the organization.

In their survey responses, Millennials frequently highlighted the communication gap they experienced. Nearly 30% of the respondents stated that they communicate differently with managers in the workplace then they do with their peers at work, and more than 24% said that they are less effective when unable to use their preferred communication methods at work.

Respondents regularly expressed frustration with having limitations imposed on their ability to use technology to its optimum benefits. They described having to adapt to the inefficient expectations of others, even where the failure to take advantage of simple technologies could result in a lower quality work product, for example:

> *I work with a group of people who don't use the automatic spell check. Since I was in middle school, I have had my misspelled words highlighted for me.*

This respondent then identified her own insecurity with how others may view her written communications if her spelling errors were not auto-corrected. She worried that, without the spell-check feature upon which she always depended, there would be errors in her work. To older generations raised with a strict focus on grammar, spelling, and punctuation, the notion that a machine would be needed to check their work is anathema. This particular example may be unusual but in other contexts has wide implications for how the generations communicate. Her point, and similar points made by others, demonstrates that when producing a work product, Millennials frequently rely upon efficiencies and tools of technology that had not been available to other generations when they were young. Accordingly, tools that senior generations feel they do not need may be options on which Millennials have grown dependent.

Global data reinforces these concerns and demonstrates that all workplaces would benefit by reviewing the impact of their own technology practices and requirements on workplace effectiveness and Millennial retention. A survey of more than 5,500 Millennials around the world—including both students and employees—found that nearly half of those between the ages of 18–22 "expect not only to use the computer of their choice once they are on the job, but also to access their preferred mobile and technology applications."[89] The study further found that, once in the workplace, Millennials were disappointed with the quality of emerging technologies provided, as compared to the traditional technologies available.[90] Another study exploring the effect of the generational differences in technology use found that: "More than two in five of those questioned said they felt that their use of technology was not always understood, and some felt held back by outdated and rigid work styles."[91]

Communicating Across Generational Barriers

When survey respondents were asked whether they felt that older generations were clear in their communications at work, more than 50% reported that they were only somewhat clear and more than 6% stated they were not clear. The responses further showed a distinct age variation: 51% of younger Millennials (age 18–22) expressed that older generations were clear, but only 40% of respondents between the ages of 26–31 felt similarly. One possible reason for this difference is that younger workers are likely to be given less sophisticated assignments and, therefore, require less detailed instruction, where older Millennials are more likely to be assigned more complex tasks for which they may be seeking greater clarity in the explanation.

Several respondents described how their interactions with other generations impeded their efficiency or effectiveness. In some instances, the respondents felt the inefficiencies arose from their supervisor's failure to trust their judgments regarding the use of social media on behalf of their employer:

> *I work for a PR firm, so we are trying to adopt social networking to keep current. It is my responsibility to maintain/update, but I am required to get my boss's approval on all content [which] slows the process down.*

Similarly, another respondent stated:

> *I do all the online communications, marketing & PR. I often find I have to explain my reasons for doing something in a particular way to my Boss (she's 39). I end up wasting a lot of time having to back track to make things crystal clear for her, which leads to quite a bit of frustration on my part.*

Many respondents expressed frustration that managers did not understand the immediacy—and in some respects, simplicity—of social media:

> *My supervisors are concerned with what we post on our Facebook account, and I currently need to have any article, link, event, etc. approved before posting. I see this as a generational difference: for me, posting something on Facebook is not binding the agency to the event in any way, but is a way of generating "buzz" around an idea tied to our mission.*

Some respondents saw the changing patterns of the workplace, including the ways in which offices are configured, as an indication that the customary devices of the past are obsolete. For example:

We were talking about how managers use the phones to call us at work. I'm an auditor and I don't have a permanent desk, so I never go to a place with a phone and I never check my phone's voicemail. However, if you were to e-mail me, I'd get right back to you. The person who calls me won't be getting a response.

Employees and their supervisors are likely to have significant differences in their communication styles. By failing to understand and bridge these differences, however, the workplace suffers from unnecessary inefficiencies and the impacts of conflicting messages.

Restricting Communications and Other Acts of Futility

Research indicates a significant shift in the use of technology among younger Millennials, which will not be news to any parent of a Millennial still in high school. Research supports the growing use of real-time alternatives to email, such as social media sites: "young Millennials (14–17 years old) are more focused on real-time, collaborative communication."[92]

Moreover, the Millennials' comfort with sharing information about themselves and each other on-line has profound implications for how privacy will be managed in the workplace. As one survey noted: "Millennials' attitudes about security, loyalty, privacy, and work style are colliding with the policies and norms" of employers.[93] Globally, 30% reported that they are open about themselves and their friends online and in some countries, such as China, Germany, Japan, and Brazil, that number is higher.[94]

A 2013 study of Millennials' use of technology in the workplace found: "The majority of Millennials say they carry out personal tasks during work hours. Though keen to perform well at work, it is virtually impossible for them to leave their personal lives behind, as they typically check Facebook, conduct IM chats and send and receive text messages on their devices throughout the day. This is seen as a right rather than a benefit."[95] While some might read this statement as fueling the "entitlement" reputation, it could also be seen as an expectation of flexibility to communicate with friends consistent with the way they have been doing so for much of their lives.

Of particular significance to employers, the study identified how vast the divide can be with respect to the effort to maintain workplace norms and policies in a vastly changing technology climate. A stunning 66% of Millennials reported they do not abide by IT policies generally, and that: "45% of employed Millennials globally use social networking sites at work, whether prohibited or not." Nearly 30% said they do not even know if their company has a corporate IT policy.[96]

This expectation of around-the-clock accessibility to social media becomes particularly understandable in the context of how Millennials experienced social media throughout much of their lives. As true natives in the digital world, Millennials were generally unsupervised in their on-line lives. As one author noted: "A paradox about Millennials is that this is a generation whose parents would not send them outside to play without the watchful eye of an adult. Yet, they could venture into a virtual world that held as much, if not more, potential danger as being outside without a parent. This generation has had relatively little censorship of the complexity of their virtual world."[97]

Consistent with these studies and observations, many survey respondents brought with them to work an expectation that they can interact freely with others during the day. The question that is unanswered, however, is whether these interactions hinder their ability to do the job, or serve as momentary distractions. This response, for example, sets up the concern without answering it:

> I gchat (on Gmail) a good part of the day with friends who are also at (their own) work.

The Millennial reliance on technology begins even before entering the workplace. These habits have raised concerns in the classroom and, when translated to the workplace, create the impression of being disengaged from work. For their teachers and their supervisors, the adjustment to what Millennials see as simply a way of life is challenging. In an article in the Chronicle of Higher Education reporting on studies of classroom behaviors, professors described students as constantly using technology for communication, academics, and browsing of social media sites during class.[98]

One Millennial expressed concern about the implications of lives lived at the center of constant distractions:

> *We love multitasking and have such short attention spans—we are easily distracted and more often than not, treated the problem with Ritalin instead of learning how to focus and control impulses. Our generation is seen as living on phones, always being connected to friends and personal lives through texting or Facebook etc. We value our personal time, but we have a hard time separating personal time from work time (aka, putting our personal lives aside while we're at work).*

Both Millennials and senior generations have a role to play in addressing the challenges posed when technology allows for continuing intrusions in the workplace. The opportunities for distraction will only increase. Determining where and how to erect boundaries will be a challenge for all generations.

Adept at Adapting

Respondents described the negative impact on workplace effectiveness arising from the frequent adaptations they needed to make because their workplace lacked updated technology. For example, they often must move between their updated software at home to outdated technology at work. That adaption takes time and causes inefficiencies. A survey respondent in the science sector spoke of this transition between the software version available at home but not at the office:

> *It can be hard. You go home and use the most current software and then have to come to work and remember the software from 3 years ago.*

Even more significantly, respondents repeatedly described how they were diverted from their assigned tasks to troubleshoot their own technology problems or to help others solve theirs. For example, a respondent compared the way in which Millennials address their own tech challenges compared to the way older generations rely on younger workers for technical fixes:

> *In my experience, my previous boss, who is a generation older than myself, refused to learn any new technology, even though it would make both of our jobs much easier and more efficient if she were to learn certain programs. Another issue was with her blackberry—she refused to learn how to use it. Anytime anything went wrong she would wait until I was in the office to call the company to fix it, or fix it myself. This wasn't a problem, just a difference between my generation who can't function if something goes wrong with their cell phone and will drop everything to figure out how to fix it, or immediately run out and buy a new one.*

Other respondents similarly expressed frustration with the compounded inefficiencies that evolve from the technology divide, for example:

> *I think that the older generation is . . . at a disadvantage from an efficiency-standpoint because they do not know how to use the technology available to them. I cannot tell you how many times I hear an older partner instructing his assistant to enter his time into the time program or transcribe his voicemail (very archaic). On more than one occasion, older partners have "advised" me to dictate my documents rather than typing the documents myself. They have no clue that "Generation Y" can type faster than most assistants and that they master computer technology in such a way as to promote efficiency.*

Some respondents were similarly puzzled by missed opportunities to use technology to make tasks easier. For example, while acknowledging the importance of interpersonal communications, a respondent expressed a concern that technology is not used to facilitate these interactions more efficiently:

> *. . . [P]hone communication over all other forms is heavily pushed in my office. I agree it's important, but . . . I often find myself making calls I don't need to—i.e. to set up an appointment when I could just*

send an Outlook Invite . . . I certainly hold that there is an important time and place for phone and f2f meetings, but there is often a lot of computer/electronic steps that can be taken prior to those more personal touch points.

A marketing professional expressed frustration with a manager who was unwilling to learn to communicate in the same way that her employees did:

I use messaging software to speak to coworkers. It would be fabulous if my boss would use it, too, so we could all communicate simultaneously through a chat program, as we all telecommute. Unfortunately, there's some technology she's not quite ready to adopt.

Respondents recognized that it is harder for older generations to learn technology, but they resented the missed opportunities for greater efficiency that resulted. For example:

I think (and I've heard others express) my generation uses technology to work more efficiently so we don't have to spend as much time at work. It can be frustrating to older generations to have to learn the technology so we can whip through something quicker, but it's frustrating for us to have to sit and plod through something using a certain system or method when there are better ways out there.

Millennials saw a particular inequity in the reluctance of older generations to learn a new technology that could significantly improve workplace functions, knowing that they themselves lacked the luxury of ever refusing to do a task they thought would be difficult. As one respondent stated:

The older generation is almost scared to learn the new tech ways and just expect gen Y to handle. It's hypocritical. If we ever did that, they say we're not pushing ourselves hard enough. But if they don't take initiative, why should we?

One young professional observed the opportunity that can be found in the frustration:

> *I just had another 'more experienced' person tell me that they couldn't use a very easy to follow project management software because they are 'tech-challenged.' I have noticed more and more that this is an excuse for people who simply don't want to try to use a technology that, once learned (and it's really not very hard, I promise) is actually very useful. This is something that Gen Y doesn't really get. We've grown up with tech and have learned by trying it. So when you tell me you're tech-challenged and won't get it before you've even logged in to try it, I'm annoyed. For people who want to work with Gen Y leaders, it's ok if you don't get it and need our help—in fact that's great. It's not ok if you don't even try. The sooner you can get over your fears the better off you will be. So, on the flip side—great opportunity for reverse mentoring.*

Power Plays and the Need for Control

It is one thing for Millennials to feel they must adapt to inefficiencies that exist from working with different styles. It is quite another, however, to feel purposefully undermined by senior managers whose discomfort with technology resulted in significant inefficiencies that severely hampered productivity. Many respondents spoke of such situations, for example:

> *For one of the partners that I work for, I submit all of my work in paper form. He will not read it if I send it to him electronically. He also gets very upset if he asks me for something and I respond by looking for it on my computer. He wants me to constantly have paper copies of everything at my fingertips.*

In some instances as the above, the anecdotes were so confounding that one had to wonder whether an unwillingness to allow technological efficiencies was simply a way for a senior leader in the workplace to exert power. One particularly egregious example was noted by this young professional:

A partner forced me to sit in her office and read through a 100+ page document, looking for every use of a certain term, when I could have gone back to my desk and searched the document electronically in less than 5 minutes.

A respondent in the engineering field described a similar experience with an older colleague:

I have one older supervisor who would continually call me and ask me to print something for him and bring it to his office because he didn't know how to properly send the document to the printer. While I didn't mind helping him, I found that to be a complete waste of my time and skills.

Such comments lead to the question of whether more is going on in some workplaces than a simple fear or discomfort with technology among older generations. Boomers and Gen Xers, used to feeling in control, may find it disquieting to see themselves in a rapidly changing work environment where younger workers seem better equipped to manage change. Perhaps they cope with their fear of change, at least on a subconscious level, by taking steps that serve to delay the inevitable.

Ignored Suggestions

Several survey respondents reported that when they offered suggestions to improve efficiencies, their recommendations were ignored. A respondent in the engineering field said:

I mentioned that if IM was available it would cut down on all of the walking and waiting that we do to communicate with other groups. It was voiced during a committee meeting to improve our working environment, and the people that were running it were in their 50's-60's and didn't take it very seriously. I was written off for being younger.

Another respondent noted:

> *I suggested that we use instant messaging in the office to bridge the gap between those that are regularly in the office, those that work from home, and those that travel and primarily are on PDA devices . . . I suggested it to my immediate managers who thought it was a great idea but then did nothing.*

Occasionally, Millennials offered examples of their ignored ideas that proved to be missed opportunities for their employers to gain a competitive advantage. A public relations employee recounted one such experience:

> *While working as a Media Coordinator . . . I tried to implement a social media initiative. One aspect was to include a Twitter account where I would post daily either events or deals or even simple stuff like the weather. But, when I tried to do it, I was told by my 52-year old supervisor that it was a waste of time—that Twitter is useless and a pain and no one would be using it after a few months. . . . Twitter has only gotten bigger and . . . reporters use that to post stories and find sources. And we missed out on it.*

Professions Stuck in Reverse

Technological inefficiency in the workplace is not only frustrating to employees; it may negatively impact the bottom line or quality of outcome. Many respondents reported similar views of professions that seemed unduly reluctant to change their outdated practices. The legal profession was a prime target of frustration. Said one young lawyer:

> *I have suggested working remotely and communicating through email and other electronic messaging, but law firms are still stuck in a face-time rut.*

Another young lawyer stated:

I prefer to communicate by email, with co-workers and with clients. I generally scan and email court documents to my clients, because I think they appreciate receiving information quickly . . . I am on a committee at our office to develop a "paperless office." The reaction of older attorneys has been mixed, as some of them are not comfortable using computers and some of them do not even use computers and still prefer to work by dictating to their assistants.

Respondents identified similar issues in other occupations. For example, a professional in the marketing and PR field noted that, despite being in a profession whose clients are best served by updated tools of communication, co-workers do not necessarily take advantage of the opportunities technology can provide:

Sometimes my bosses think I'm wasting time on FB and Twitter when in all reality I am getting in touch with and "friending" reporters and potential clients for new business. They don't get it. They prefer to send out "marketing blasts via email." No one has the time to read those. Blogging and re-tweeting is far more powerful.

Even non-office work environments were criticized for ignoring opportunities that technology offers, as one young employee noted:

We do not have desk jobs—we are full time fitness, yoga, pilates instructors. All of our interactions are face-to-face, but a number of us believe that our company would be much more successful if it did more online—blogs, podcasts, etc.

Respondents also identified academia as an area of concern. Several respondents in the teaching field reported a lack of available technology in secondary and higher education, where insufficient resources significantly impact student learning. The unavailability of updated technology in schools can seriously hamper a young person's future opportunities in the job market. A university employee expressed concern that the educational experience of the students is diminished when technology is lagging:

I work at a college, and students expect quick, easy, and paperless communication. The college does not have the technological infrastructure to make this happen in all cases. Therefore, I spend too much time doing projects that should be automated, and students are less satisfied educational consumers.

One respondent who worked in higher education noted the safety implications when access to technology is limited:

I'm on-call for crisis management purposes, and we use an antiquated beeper system to communicate with campus police and our co-workers. Several of us have discussed the potential usefulness of cell phones or text-enabled phones in place of the pagers, but supervisors have not been receptive.

In some instances, understanding the power and usefulness of critical technologies can have far-reaching ramifications. One respondent reported on the way technology can make a difference in the justice system:

I work in a family court, and one of the newest ways to harass people is on Facebook and My Space. Another Gen Y-er and I spent about 30 minutes explaining how they work to the judges, explaining how they can be harassing, and explaining how to go about checking them if necessary.

This constant need to assess and adapt to limitations in technology demonstrates a talent that Millennials must regularly demonstrate in a context where others may not even notice that they are being accommodated.

Unrecognized Tutors

Respondents were asked how they most frequently interacted when working with colleagues who were not tech savvy. Here, too, the responses revealed an interesting age disparity. Although the majority of the respondents reported that they helped other colleagues, the younger respondents were more likely to be helpful: 65% of those 18–22 years-old and 64% of those in the 23–25 age range stated that they helped their co-workers learn new technology, as compared to 56% of respondents in the 26–31 age category. Conversely, 15% of the younger age range and 19% of respondents 23–25 years old said they would, instead, adopt the preferred style of their colleagues, even if it would be less effective, as would 23% of those 26–31.

Even with these age variations, it is clear that Millennials spend a lot of time assisting more senior colleagues. This results in a recurring challenge: the expectation that Millennials will serve as unpaid technology tutors to their colleagues. Many of the respondents reported that they felt like they had two jobs: the one for which they were hired, and that of technology teacher.

Young workers serving as the substitute IT Department emerged as a common theme throughout the responses. Stated an administrator:

> *Frequently, in my office, I have been the 'go-to' person when it comes to technology. From simple things such as making sure the computers have all necessitated updates to converting files . . . I seem to be the building's private tech support.*

One respondent pointed out how much of the day can be filled with helping others perform mundane tasks:

> *It seems myself and the younger members of our team often are asked to play IT department to diagnose tech problems and do day-to-day tech-related tasks such as set up email away messages and program voicemail prompts.*

Another young professional described various tasks which took her away from her regular responsibilities at her former job:

> *When I previously worked at a firm, I often had to teach the secretaries how to create forms . . . Often they knew how to use the program, but not all of its functionalities, so they were unable to get*

the most out of the technology. I had a similar experience with regard to older workers and keyboard shortcuts or ten-figure typing. If often ends up that younger, well-educated workers were doing menial tasks, just because they were able to do them quicker because of their ability to better use the technology.

This overreliance on Millennial tech support can have the effect of enabling older workers to ignore even the easiest paths to self-sufficiency, as noted by this accounting professional:

In general, they're slower when utilizing the latest in technology . . . They appear to be more timid, which causes me to spend time showing them how to do things (like in excel, or outlook email). It can be frustrating when they don't use the help features of computer programs. Most of the time, that's where I get my answers from.

A public sector worker gave up trying to teach in the face of a "pupil" who was unwilling to be taught self-sufficiency, and instead relied upon the work being done for him:

My former boss knew nothing beyond basic Internet and typing skills and used to call me into his office multiple times daily to perform simple tasks . . . or fix minor problems on his computer. This took up hours and hours of my time and was extremely frustrating. I tried to teach him how to do things for himself for about the first year, then gave up because he had no interest in learning when he could call me to do everything for him.

When Millennials are viewed as institutional tech support, their own job responsibilities can suffer. Respondents described how they resorted to protective measures in order to do their own job. One young man learned to manage the drain on his time through judicious sharing of his knowledge:

I've found that you have to be selective as to whom you reveal your tech-savvyness, otherwise people will treat you like a personal IT department and impede your own work with their constant questions.

Other self-help measures included direct communications with supervisors about the limitations on one's ability to undertake the responsibilities of others. Noted one marketing professional:

> *For a while, I joked that I was the IT department at our company (and I have no background in IT!). Whenever there was a question about how to do something in Word, Excel, Outlook, etc., I was the one the team would ask. I finally discussed this with my boss and we clarified with the group that although I'm happy to help here and there, my overall work is not to solve technical difficulties! It has since been much better.*

Overbroad Assumptions

Some respondents expressed concern that older workers mistakenly assume that every younger employee is a tech guru. A similar observation was made in a series of comments in response to the *Chronicle of Higher Education* article describing students distracted by their internet use during class. These comments identified an area in which Millennials seemed to lack sophistication, and that is with non-social media applications of technology, particularly practical software applications.[99]

Respondents also noted that the costs of keeping up in a rapidly changing market or learning industry-specific technologies pose limitations, particularly for many young people entering a new profession. One college student explained:

> *I have had experiences where, as a member of Generation Y, I was more behind on technology than a member of Generation X. Not that there is anything wrong with that but I felt like I was not doing enough homework or knew anything about it to understand the procedures or programs in a way that I could effectively do my job. But one reason for this could be because the programs are so industry specific, we are unfamiliar with it, or the prices make the programs inaccessible to become familiar with other than at work.*

Another young worker worried that he was unreasonably expected to be capable of solving all technical issues:

Older people constantly assume that I am more tech-savvy than I am.

Good Humor and Back-up Plans

Several respondents wisely noted that technology is not infallible, so it is important to develop procedures to work around the occasional glitches. The more ubiquitous certain practices become, the greater the possibility an error may occur, as one respondent observed:

I am a part-time law clerk for an attorney that is in his late 30's to early 40's. As I work from home or school, 99% of our communication is by texting and email. On numerous occasions, I have not received emails or texts from him and he has also mentioned that he has not received some emails from me in the past. The fact that we rely so heavily on technology worries me. I try to remind him to call me rather than text or email if time is of the essence, so I can be sure to respond immediately rather than worrying about not receiving a text or email.

Some respondents maintained a philosophical approach to the wide disparity of communication and technology capabilities in the workplace. A young man in the marketing field stated:

Among all age groups of employees, there are trendsetters, early adopters and laggards. Though there are much more early adopters among the younger generation and more laggards in the older.

For a few respondents, self-employment offered the best way to solve the communication divide:

I am the boss. I allow others to communicate with me via face to face, email, text message, phone . . . depending on the situation.

A particularly cheerful-sounding response was similarly offered by a self-employed marketing consultant:

. . . I work for myself . . . I can do whatever I want!

Some Millennials found comfort in a good sense of humor and the opportunity to share anecdotes. Consider the experiences of two respondents. The first reported on a search request:

True Story: My boss has on several occasions asked that I "look into the Google" to find information for him. Not "Google." "The Google."

The second told of a conversation he overheard:

I overheard a new VP on the phone, "Control A? Control Z? No . . . I don't use that functionality!"

Tech savvy Millennials need to develop a reservoir of good will for helping older workers, and then call on that stored good will as they work through other challenges and pitfalls they face at work.

Chapter 8

"You Cannot Wear That to Work!"

Research demonstrates that people develop initial judgments of others based on superficial first impressions that occur within 1/10 of a second of meeting someone.[100] Such a blink-of-an-eye judgment does not allow time for thoughtful reflection about an individual's strengths and weaknesses. Rather, it means that people are making judgments on the most rudimentary input of all: physical appearance.

In the workplace, these snap judgments can have a tremendous impact on career success—either positive or negative. For Millennials beginning their careers, such initial judgments can impede advancement, as Boomers and Gen Xers frequently complain about the overly casual wardrobe choices and communication styles of younger workers. Too often, these generations incorrectly interpret the Millennials' informality as a lack of respect, not recognizing that the roots of this behavior are far deeper and have little to do with a lack of generational deference.

Appropriate attire can be an important tool to help any employee steer through the political minefield of work. It is an area where judgments can be swift and harsh, and where a reputation can be affected without a word spoken. For young employees, understanding these dynamics can be critical to ultimate career success.

Beyond the Outfit

It is a generational rite of passage for an older generation to complain about how the younger generation dresses. And when those complaints are voiced, it becomes the right of the younger generation to sneer at the superficiality of adults who would judge a person by how they look. In this respect, the Millennials are no different.

The respondents seemed to dislike hearing other peoples' judgments about their appearance almost as much as people dislike discussing it directly with them. Unfortunately, however, the judgments are always present, impacting careers in ways Millennials may not ever see or hear.

When survey respondents were asked about clothing in the workplace, the more common response was that clothing is—or should be—irrelevant, especially compared to one's work product and related accomplishments. When respondents were asked, by occupation, whether wardrobe choices impacted their career success, less than half responded that the impact would be significant, even in professions not known for their liberal dress policies. For example, slightly over 20% of those in banking, slightly over 30% of those in retail and in marketing and public relations, and approximately 40% of those in the legal field responded that how they dressed would have a significant career impact. Surprisingly, approximately 35% of those in financial services, generally considered a profession in which conservative dress is expected, said that how they dressed would have no impact.

Many viewed attention to clothing as an artifact of a by-gone day. They saw today's workplace as more open and seemed to have a broad definition of "business casual". For example, one Millennial stated:

> Whenever anyone starts a new job, there is always the inevitable question of "what do I wear?", but I think as long as it's not jeans and a t-shirt, people are OK with business casual now.

But is this assessment accurate? Supervisors who view a young worker's appearance as unprofessional may make harsher judgments about that person's competency and capability. This may result in a lowering of expectations based on nothing more than first impressions—and clothing is what everyone sees first. The downward spiral starts before there is any idea that a problem exists.

Clearly, however, Millennials pay attention to how they look, and that interest emerges early. One survey stated that teenagers spend approximately 40% of their budgets on fashion, and further reported that their purchasing shows an "emergence of refined classic or preppy aesthetic, and preference for fashion athletic wear."[101] According to a website which provides data on teenage consumer spending, products bought by and for teens reached $208.7 billion in 2012.[102]

Notwithstanding Millennial attention to the latest fashion trends, however, many of the people for and with whom they work simply do not think much of their fashion selections. But the complaints are not about whether someone likes a red suit and hates the blue one. To Boomers and Gen Xers, it is about taste and appropriateness. These criticisms are, at their very core, an extension of the flip-flop admonishment, which seemed to seal the Millennials' fate as a generation that does not know how to dress.

The Flip-Flop Firestorm

For those who may have missed the Great American Flip-Flop Scandal, the story is instructive. In 2005, Northwestern University's women's lacrosse team won the national championship and was subsequently honored with an invitation to the White House. Their visit resulted in international attention when photos revealed that members of the team wore flip-flops to meet the president. Dubbed by an Associated Press writer as the "flip-flop flap", the incident sparked a media firestorm critiquing how this younger generation dresses and questioning whether the choice of footwear demonstrated a lack of respect for the office of the presidency.[103]

For the Millennial lacrosse champions—and their peer observers—the response was simply another affirmation of the "they just don't get it" culture of the adult world. After all, flip-flops had long ago passed from mere beach attire into the world of high fashion and are available in a large variety of colors, designs, designers, and prices. The team members themselves defended the choice by noting that their footwear selections were a dressier version than the common beach flip-flops.

The intense debate crystallized all aspects of the "Millennials don't know how to dress" comments that are frequently expressed in the workplace. The issue was framed in the language of respect: the team should have reflected proper respect for the office of the President by choosing appropriate attire from head to toe—literally. To older generations, flip-flops are the ultimate footwear sin in the workplace and the White House. Even some of the team members' parents expressed embarrassment when they learned of their daughters' footwear choices.

The fact that the incident captured national attention demonstrates the strong emotions people bring to a topic which reaches well beyond one's choice of footwear.

Appearances and Impressions

The responses to the survey questions on the topic of attire revealed that Millennials have varied and strong opinions about their own clothing selections, with little consensus on how to reconcile the judgments of others about what they wear. More than two-thirds of the respondents believed that how they dressed in the workplace did not at all impact or only somewhat impacted their career success. Men were more likely to state that their wardrobe choices did not impact their career success (28% of the men compared to 17% of the women) whereas 34% of the women compared to 26% of the men stated that how they dressed at work significantly impacted their career success.

A number of respondents spoke about the relationship between how they dressed and how they were perceived and evaluated at work. One young professional observed:

> I think it makes a lasting impression. I think that if people perceive you as a sloppy dresser, they will think you are sloppy in other ways as well. The way you dress is a form of nonverbal communication, it's meant to have an effect on the people you come in contact with.

Since we are a professional organization we are asked to dress in a professional manner.

Similarly, another respondent stated:

I think appearance is extremely important in the workplace. It shows how seriously (or not) you take yourself and your appearance. You can tell a lot about a person by the way he/she dresses.

Several respondents expressed their belief that looking good at work leads to feeling good about one's self, which then translates into positive interactions with others. A marketing specialist noted:

I think how you dress impacts how you carry yourself and how people perceive you.

A female administrator bluntly advised:

What you wear is the first thing that people see and judge you on. You should dress accordingly.

But acceptance of this aspect of human behavior does not imply that respondents were devoid of cynicism, as this college student revealed:

Appearance is everything. People are shallow.

Several respondents reported that their choice of attire provided an opportunity to look more professional and compensate for their youthful appearance, as this teacher noted:

I'd be afraid to dress in clothing too casual because I work in a high school and have been mistaken for a student in the past!

Dressing for the Job You Want

Many respondents recognized that their desire to wear more comfortable clothing is trumped by the reality that they are initially judged by their attire. They see that clothing matters, even though they may not agree with the fairness of a world where superficial assessments of one's attire can impact judgments about their performance in the workplace. Some respondents saw a direct link between their choice of attire and the quality of their work assignments and opportunities for advancement. For example, a professional in the engineering field noted:

> *The higher you are—in terms of hierarchy and closeness to the heads of the group . . . , or the more important your role—the better you dress. All young and ambitious workers dress professionally and act seriously. In return, they receive more important responsibilities in their work.*

Another respondent described the moment she realized that her attire could translate into future employment opportunities:

> *At my old job we worked in a small office in a small town and in the first few months no one cared what I wore. As I grew less and less satisfied with that job, I realized that if I happened to meet a potential employer dressed as I was I would be embarrassed to ask for a job. While it isn't necessary to wear a suit every day, I did start dressing more professionally (dressing for the job I wanted, not the one I had).*

Several respondents agreed with the perspective that it is best to dress in a state of preparedness for future opportunities. For example, a social services employee stated:

> *I believe you should be ready to meet anyone at any level at any time. I believe your boss will not want to promote you or your work if you do not represent the ideals of the company.*

The Ripple Effect

In offices where senior generations dress more formally, some respondents observed a ripple effect in the office. For several respondents, bosses who dressed well served as role models in their clothing selection. One young professional stated:

> I work for a man who has a lot of fashion know how, so I have to be sure that I dress well—though it's still casual.

Several respondents reported that they choose their outfits with their supervisors in mind, as noted by this student who worked part-time:

> I take pride in my appearance, and I think it is important to dress for success. I would rather be over-dressed than underdressed. I take my cues from my boss, and she dresses pretty professionally at work.

Another observed:

> Number one rule of thumb that a lot of people my age don't or won't get—look at how your boss dresses, and act accordingly. The partner from whom I receive most of my job assignments wears suits and abhors open-toe shoes, so guess what? I wear a suit and don't show my toes at work!

These comments make clear that other generations are always serving as role models, whether they realize it or not. Young employees often take their cue from those senior to them in the workplace.

Gendered Judgments

Judgments about clothing particularly impact women (of all ages). There is a seemingly endless array of articles, blogs, and related media commentary to support the perspective that women are often initially judged on what they wear, rather than what they say or do. An article describing how quickly first impressions are formed reported that looking polished is critical. For women, the challenge can be more burdensome: "Women are judged more harshly here. While 83% of senior executives said 'unkempt attire' (including wrinkled or too-tight clothing and visible lingerie) detracts from a woman's executive presence, a slightly smaller percentage (76%) said it undermines a man's. Moreover, women's professional polish includes tasteful accessories, manicured nails and a hair*style* versus a hair*cut*. Whereas, a man's polished look is based on clean nails, shiny shoes, a clean shave and manicured facial hair . . . ."[104]

Gender disparities in wardrobe choices emerged as a significant issue in the survey responses. Many female respondents expressed concern that judgments about how Millennials dress have a disparate impact on women. A teacher observed:

> . . . [T]he standards for women's and men's business attire are radically different, and I think that women's attire places an undue emphasis on physical appearance.

Female respondents observed both a double standard and a double bind. They described a workplace where women face greater obstacles in the choice of appropriate office attire compared to their male colleagues, and where they are under harsher criticism for their selections. This dilemma was summarized by a new lawyer:

> I still think women are expected to dress differently than men. And women who try to incorporate fashion into work attire, like me, are sometimes looked down upon in professional settings. I think it is very hard for younger women to walk the line of being fashionable but taken seriously.

Female respondents reinforced the difficulty of dressing to avoid harsh judgments, for example:

> If you are a woman you have to deal with the balance of not looking too sexy while not dressing like your mother.

Some female respondents who worked in male-dominated offices lacked senior female role models from whom they could learn clothing tips. For example, a lawyer stated:

I dress more formally than many of my peers and my male bosses. There are no female partners in my practice area, and several of the young associates (both male and female) follow the male partners' lead and 'dress down'. I make a specific effort to wear suits and 'dress up' more than the partners.

But others who worked in offices with senior women noted that such exposure did not necessarily result in wardrobe choices that Millennials would choose to emulate. Several respondents saw the attire of more senior generations as too constrained, for example:

Older women at work routinely dress in below the knee dress suits in grays, blues or blacks. They are often surprised by younger women who don't wear suit jackets, wear skirts slightly above the knee and wear nontraditional/non conservative colors.

Respondents also objected to the gendered judgments that came with their clothing choices. For example, one government worker noted:

Older women in my office often make comments about how women should wear dresses and skirts to work. I do not agree with this, as I believe it is a sexist expectation.

These gender distinctions in wardrobe selection were particularly evident with respect to the meaning of business casual attire. Women respondents generally felt that a double standard resulted in a more liberal definition of business casual for their male colleagues:

The older generations, specifically the men, dress in ways that I would never have thought of as work appropriate—beaten down khakis and faded polos. The women and the younger generations tend to dress in business or business casual attire. It's odd that the company professes to have a business casual dress code . . . I believe that if I were to dress in such a manner others would deem it to be inappropriate.

A working mother observed that her wardrobe of suits was easier to manage than business casual and helped her image at work:

I think as a young female lawyer I get a little more respect by dressing conservatively. Plus, it makes it easy to get dressed, and as a mom I'd rather go for speed than try to figure out an outfit of separate pieces.

Productivity Impacts of Casual Comfort

Respondents frequently described a connection between work attire and work output, with two elements to the analysis. The first related to comfort. For many, the desire to be comfortable in one's clothing equated to an ability to work more effectively and, in many instances, more creatively. For example, one Millennial stated:

I work for a creative department with a lot of graphic artists who feel as if 'business attire' stifles them. However, I feel as if our business attire is so casual that it really doesn't bother me at all. I would not like to work somewhere where I had to wear a suit every day. To me, being a little casual allows me to roll back my metaphorical sleeves when a particularly arduous task is called for.

These respondents reflected the belief that comfort should trump formality, but not good taste:

I think people should dress in what makes them most comfortable. I am more productive in jeans than I am in a suit I feel "stuffed" into. However, some people take advantage of not having a particular dress code, i.e. too short skirts, tank tops, etc.

Respondents generally saw a focus on attire at the expense of comfort as misplaced emphasis. A young professional in the marketing field noted:

> *I feel people are most productive in what makes them feel comfortable. My generation and my coworkers know when it's appropriate to wear jeans and flip-flops and when the situation calls for more formal business attire. When I worked at companies with business casual dress codes, it felt like my job was just a role I was playing and the dress code was my costume. When I can dress as myself, I feel like my work and job are mine, not just a role.*

A second element of the connection between attire and output that emerged from the responses related to clothing as a predicate to performance: if someone looks the part, it feels easier to assume that role. For example, one respondent noted:

> *I think dressing professionally at work is important. It makes me feel ready to take on whatever task I may have.*

Another in the public relations field similarly commented:

> *Our office dress code is very casual. This allows us to work in what makes us comfortable, which lends to overall better productivity. On days that I have a big goal to accomplish, I dress up. It makes me feel more professional.*

Through all aspects of the survey responses on this issue, there was a pervasive concern that older generations myopically leap to unfair conclusions about individuals based on appearance, instead of performance. A post-graduate student observed:

> *I think that there is a general belief that how you are dressed conveys something about your willingness to work hard or how seriously you take your work. Though I agree with this to a certain extent (and believe that it is not appropriate to wear extremely casual clothes*

to work), I think that employers often place too much emphasis on dress and discount great employees because they are not comfortable wearing a suit to work every day (especially, when there seems to be no compelling reason to do so).

Overall, respondents recognized that comfort and formality can conflict, but sought some middle ground that allowed talent to flourish in a less constrained environment.

Dressing for Different Audiences

Many respondents stressed that the selection of their work outfits varied, depending on the task, the setting, and the expected public or client interactions. Respondents who described a need to dress for external obligations, such as client meetings, resented being told what to wear on those days when they only see their office colleagues. They trusted their own judgment to determine when more formal attire is appropriate. For example, a young professional reported:

I work at a non-profit organization that serves low-income people. So, on regular work days, I do not bother to dress up, as too formal attire will intimidate clients. However, I am a lawyer, so when I go to court or meet with opposing counsel, I do have to dress up, either a suit or business casual.

Similarly, a marketing professional noted that although general workplace attire can be informal, direct client interaction changes that dynamic:

I think how you dress at work doesn't matter as long as you're clean and presentable. I think that dressing professionally when you have client meetings DOES affect first impressions and their trust of you.

But many respondents felt that if they would not encounter external clients or visitors during the workday, then casual dress should be the default.

For example, a respondent stated that the lack of opportunity to interact with outsiders should result in a more relaxed dress requirement:

> *Older partners tend to dress in suits, because in their day, there was a lot of face to face interaction with clients. Younger people at the firm dress more casually, recognizing that we NEVER see clients, ever, in this day and age.*

Some respondents even made clothing decisions based on which clients are being seen:

> *Older clients expect business dress. So that is how I dress.*

Dress Codes

70% of the respondents reported that they were subject to a dress code at work. It is interesting to note that nearly 75% of the women stated that their workplace had a dress code, as compared to 56% of the men. It is not clear whether this significant disparity meant there was, in fact, such a difference or whether it reflected the greater attention generally paid to what women wear at work.

Respondents also reported that they dressed more casually than senior generations at work. Of particular interest, although more than 46% of the respondents were in workplaces where older generations wore business attire, less than 34% of the respondents stated that they similarly wore business attire.

Many respondents felt that judgments about how one looks are too subjective to be fairly regulated by a dress code. Moreover, many felt that dress codes were unfairly imposed office-wide to address a problem caused by the few who consistently dressed inappropriately.

A marketing specialist noted:

> *Regulations are in place for the folks who don't have good common sense at the cost of those people who do. If you have client meetings,*

or interaction with external people, your appearance does matter. If you are in a cube all day and never see the light of day, why bother wearing uncomfortable heels, skirts, ties, etc.? Also, appearance is a definite judgment call and is never easily regulated because it can differ from person to person.

Respondents reported that, too often, dress codes were not fairly enforced. They questioned why workplaces insisted upon paper policies that were arbitrarily enforced, if at all. They similarly expressed annoyance with the way supervisors often avoided addressing the issues directly, resulting in an ad hoc approach to enforcing the policy, as this teacher noted:

> *. . . I think that it is important that if a certain office requires a certain dress, then it must be enforced by someone in power.*

Several respondents also described a double-standard. A part-time office administrator spoke about the hierarchy of dress she observed in her office:

> *The office assistants (which I am) are required to dress in business casual. The brokers often come to work in jeans . . .*

Many respondents expressed annoyance with arbitrary decisions about what may or may not be acceptable attire. One part-time worker revealed her own need for role models as she commented on the arbitrary enforcement of clothing choices in her office:

> *There are women at my office who show their cleavage off all the time. I wore a mid-thigh skirt to work once, and was told by HR that my skirt was inappropriate.*

Some who spoke of dress codes as arbitrarily instituted and enforced were additionally concerned that the requirements were not flexible enough to adjust to the circumstances of the workday. A young professional observed:

> *Personally, I feel like I'm always teetering on just being in*

compliance with the dress code, particularly when there are no hearings or meetings. It's very frustrating to be in an office where I see no one but have to wear a blouse and high heels (though to be fair, I've given up the heels in favor of some black Pumas). I think sometimes people perceive me as lazy because of the way I dress. . . . I just don't care that much about the way I look unless there's real reason to—like a presentation to a client. I definitely think people judge whether or not you are a competent professional based on how you dress.

Footwear remained a focus of attention and criticism—and flip-flops retained their pre-eminence as an object of generational divide. A postgraduate student who works part-time described a particularly arbitrary dress code:

I personally think some of the rules here are a little weird. For example, we can wear hoodies, t-shirts, and tennis shoes on Fridays with jeans, but never flip-flop-like sandals, and they are very strict about what kind of sandals we can wear. It's not a job where we're up moving a lot and it's not a safety issue either.

One respondent saw the written dress code at work as primarily a vehicle for governing the ways in which a woman's toes may be exposed:

The 'dress code,' such as it is, is not extremely strict anyways, just mostly reinforcing that business casual is expected and that, for example, flip flops are not acceptable footwear. But open toe sandals are fine.

Several respondents identified rules relating to jeans as a particularly frustrating example of arbitrary and unproductive line-drawing. For example, a lawyer observed:

We have a no jeans policy, but during the summer, they changed that policy to every 3rd Friday. Come on, that's almost impossible to remember and makes absolutely no sense. Why can't we do every Friday during the summer? The dress code simply makes no sense.

Another respondent who works in administration noted:

My office is business casual, which is pretty equalizing. If I had to characterize a generation gap, younger people feel more disenfranchised that we do not have jeans day on Fridays.

Body Piercings

Millennials are not the first generation to face the arbitrary decisions reflected in dress codes. They may, however, be the first to face the reactions at work to body piercings and tattoos, both of which Millennials have more of than other generations. The Pew Research Center reports that 38% of Millennials have at least one tattoo, compared to 32% of Gen Xers and 15% of Baby Boomers. The differences become greater with respect to multiple tattoos: half of the tattooed Millennials have 2 to 5 and 18% have 6 or more tattoos. Approximately 25% of Millennials have a piercing in a location other than their ear lobe, compared to 9% for GenXers.[105]

One young woman in the public relations field detailed her experience with others at work who disapproved of her tattoo:

In PR it is extremely important to give off the right tone with your clothes. . . . I have a tattoo, which is also a huge setback for me in the workplace. Although it is a simple design that could not be found offensive in any way, it has always been a problem. I am always asked to cover it up by older bosses and have actually been told on more than one occasion that I will never succeed because of it. These reactions have only come from older bosses, never from anyone under the age of 50. When I try to tell them that the stigma of tattooed people really doesn't apply anymore, that so many people my age have them that it really shouldn't be an issue, I get the same response I get when I say that women my age don't wear nylons and that there is a real shift away from wearing them: 'Well, when I was growing up that is the way it was, so that is the way it is going to be'.

At least this respondent was specifically told that there was concern about her tattoo. For many Millennials, however, an aspect of the generational divide on this topic is that the disapproval may not be directly addressed. This failure to communicate directly can lead to a false sense of confidence. One respondent expressed an optimistic view that her choice of piercings was acceptable to others at work:

I have a nose stud and no one has given me any trouble over it.

And perhaps no one will. Yet older generations in the workplace may have formed strong judgments based on stereotypes about people who arrive at work with tattoos and unusual piercings. Even more likely, and as will be discussed further, they may not directly express their negative reactions, but it will nonetheless impact their opinions. This presents a difficult challenge for the pierced or tattooed Millennial who assumes acceptance based on the silence.

Peer Disapproval

As with so many other survey questions, many respondents differentiated themselves from their peers. These respondents noted the less professional image they felt that others in their generation conveyed, while maintaining that they themselves dress appropriately. For example, a marketing specialist noted:

Our company has a very laid back style. I've always been told by my mother to 'dress for your next job', so I make an effort to be business casual on most days and pay particular attention to my attire when it comes to client meetings. My colleague, who is in the same age range as me, doesn't appear to have this same belief. She wears jeans and flip flops most days and even wears jeans to client meetings!

Sometimes, the observations reflected harsh criticism, such as this statement from an administrative professional:

I have had to send multiple young women home for inappropriate dress. Excessive cleavage is the most frequent offense. Even though I am a peer or only slightly older, I am regularly shocked by how clueless young women—and young men—are about the image they project and how it can hold them back.

An employee in the social services field also expressed surprise at the wardrobe selections of her colleagues:

I am routinely amazed at the casual dress of so many people at my company. Jeans are considered acceptable when paired with a collared shirt or a nicer blouse. I do not share this opinion and therefore choose to dress more professionally despite not being required to do so.

Another bluntly observed:

People dress like slobs at my work. Because my last job was at a company with a dress code and I still wear these clothes at my new job, I generally look nicer than everyone I currently work with. I think that I get more respect and am treated more professionally because I dress respectably.

An interesting twist on wardrobe frustrations in the workplace related to office athletes. Some respondents criticize those who engaged in athletic endeavors during the work day and failed to transition back into work attire, as this respondent indicated:

At the firm I worked for previously, a few of the attorneys were heavily into biking. One of the attorneys would return from his lunchtime . . . rides and would remain in his sweaty bike clothes for the rest of the day—even if he was meeting a client. This is something I never really understood.

The Economic Burden

For Millennials just embarking on their careers, the expense of a business wardrobe can be daunting. Although every young generation faces the cost of their first work-appropriate wardrobe, many Millennials are facing theirs in an economy that leaves them little room for discretionary spending. When one adds the economic burden of student loan repayment to the other costs of living, wardrobe expenses can stretch a young employee's budget too thin.

A number of respondents expressed their concern about clothing costs. For example, a new lawyer stated:

> I wear suits to work every day except Friday. It's an expensive dress code for someone who is just embarking on a new career path.

A recent college graduate stated:

> I will soon be working . . . and am going to have to wear business clothing. I am not looking forward to the expenses of that.

Some Millennials noted that they have changed their choice of shopping venues to meet their limited budget. One respondent stated:

> I am on the lower end of the pay scale here, but am required to dress just as professionally as those who make more than twice my salary. As such, I tend to frequent thrift stores and attempt to rise to the challenge, but it is a significant financial burden.

Wardrobe costs can be particularly challenging in professions where employees are expected to have a creative flair, such as in public relations. One such respondent stated:

> Working in PR can be tough. You are expected to be glamorous 24/7, yet we make no money. Our bosses are very well dressed and each has a unique style. The better dressed you are, the more respect you receive, no doubt!

Another respondent in the PR field noted:

> *Those who are managers or well-respected wear suits. Suits are too expensive for what I get paid, so it's hard to dress for the position I want.*

And as some respondents noted, the problem is not necessarily solved by having a job that requires a uniform:

> *Working in a hospital, business attire is required under a white coat (the tradition of wearing a white coat is another issue) for work in the clinic and in most specialties within the hospital, whereas scrubs are considered appropriate attire for surgical specialties. For a student, buying business clothes to wear in the hospital/clinic is just another expense added to that of the education itself—which perhaps pales in comparison, but is real nonetheless.*

Nor do the white coats of a medical job serve as a sufficient cover up to a boss with an eye for a wardrobe:

> *In my last job at a hospital, the physician we worked for required that the young men in our group wear ties and nice pants/suit pants and be cleanly shaved every day. He himself took a lot of pride in wearing a suit and tie every day under his white coat. He would make comments to the young men often about worn-out looking pants or sports jackets, if they had a 5-o'clock shadow, etc. And the young men would get very frustrated, because whereas the doctor could afford nice suits, they could not!*

In addition to the initial expense of purchasing an appropriate wardrobe, respondents saw their ability to dress well impacted by the related costs of dry-cleaning. This ongoing expense can be worrisome to Millennials whose salary barely covers living expenses, as this respondent in the marketing field noted:

Too often, younger coworkers are too casual, but it is expensive to buy and dry-clean business clothes and they certainly don't pay close to enough for much more than ramen! :)

Unasked Questions, Unspoken Answers

The implications of the nonchalant selection of casual clothing can be profound in a workplace if the supervisors and leaders disapprove of the choices. The effects of unconscious bias may perniciously come into play here. Boomers and Gen Xers may quickly judge someone's attire and, if they determine the choices are inappropriate for the workplace, pronounce the wearer clueless—and then extrapolate their judgment to additional aspects of that individual's job performance.

Millennials often describe work as an environment where it is difficult to discern how they are doing or what those senior to them think about their work, let alone how they look. Without specific feedback on their wardrobe selections, Millennials reasonably assume that they are making the right choice unless informed otherwise. This survey response is illustrative:

I will dress business casual, unless I know that I am meeting with opposing counsel or having depositions, hearings, etc. The older attorneys in the office wear suits on a daily basis. I am not comfortable doing that, and no one has told me that I have to do that.

And this is exactly the problem. Like the respondent with the nose stud, it is quite probable that no one will offer feedback suggesting alternative clothing choices. More likely, if the supervisors are annoyed by a young employee's attire, they will complain to each other about it or maybe even complain to another Millennial who is a better dresser. They are less likely to say a word to the person who most needs to hear the message, leaving the young professional with no reason to think there is even a problem.

One article describing a panel discussion of lawyers and judges illustrated this dilemma. To an audience consisting largely of Baby Boomers, a judge expressed concern about how women were dressing in the courtroom, with strong agreement—and explicit examples—echoed among fellow panelists. They all deflected, however, any responsibility for raising the concern with those whom they judged as inappropriately dressed younger lawyers: "As [the] moderator . . . turned the conversation to what could be done about the dress debacle, some of the attorneys and judges blamed law firms for not giving lawyers enough guidance, while others said law schools needed to do a better job of educating young lawyers on appropriate dress."[106] This discomfort with mentoring young workers on their clothing selections plays out in workplaces everywhere. It is someone else's problem to solve. In the meantime, the young workers who are the subject of disapproving looks may remain unaware of the judgment rendered against them and the impact of that judgment on other aspects of their job performance.

Where Clothes Are A Euphemism

Work environments can pose challenges that include unreasonable rules, mixed messages, or simply silent disapproval. Unfortunately, the lesson to be learned from the silence can be harsh: no one should assume that those in a supervisory position will look past superficial judgments about appearance and focus solely on the quality of their work. The issue can have a particularly negative impact if "office casual" is interpreted as a statement that clothing is irrelevant, especially compared to what one can accomplish. Most people would likely prefer to work in that place where only work quality matters. But most job environments are not that place.

However correct it may be to believe that it is superficial to judge someone on appearance, the reality of life in the workplace is that the senior person holding the opinion likely has the power in the relationship. As Jenny Blake, a Millennial author and micro-business coach who has chronicled her post-college experiences in a book and a blog, stated: "You will develop a reputation at work whether you like it or not. Remember that everything you do, wear, and say WILL be judged. Do everything you can to act with integrity and make a good impression on your co-workers."[107]

In most workplaces, there is a direct connection between clothes and culture. Respondents who understood this seemed best able to use this to their advantage. The importance of finding a workplace that is a cultural—as well as a wardrobe—fit permeated the Millennials' responses. They felt at their best when they saw that fit between their job functions and the workplace culture, especially one without seemingly artificial dress requirements. As a respondent stated:

> *In the job I just quit, the dress code was severely strict, and rather inappropriate for the job, and definitely posed a financial burden. My new job is quite similar to the one I just quit, and the dress code is much more appropriate to the setting. The atmosphere in my previous job was very uptight, and at the new job is much more relaxed, and I think part of that is because of the different dress codes.*

Not all wardrobe pressure is exerted by people more senior in the workplace. One Millennial noted the impact that her choice of attire had on others, with interesting potential career consequences. As a result of the office dynamics she observed, she made a decision to dress for the unexpected demographic who could most influence her work outcomes:

> *I just left a job where my supervisor expected (though not required) me to dress significantly more "professionally" than all my colleagues. I did initially, but soon realized everyone else my age did not dress that way. And my peers were much more stand-offish when I dressed up than when I just dressed in business casual. I realized they were much more important and helpful in my day-to-day activities, so I ditched the idea of dressing up.*

This respondent seemed to feel that she had to choose between pleasing co-workers who were important to her ongoing job functions, or dressing in accordance with her supervisor's expectations. The question left open is whether both objectives could be met. The politics of the work environment can significantly impact these choices and responding to these dynamics is an important aspect of succeeding in the work environment.

Respondents were clear that the lack of uniform enforcement of dress code requirements only made their decisions about what to wear more confusing. What they may miss, however, is that behind the arbitrary enforcement and double standards are Baby Boomer and Gen X supervisors loathing the thought of directly addressing a perceived breach in office wardrobe expectations. These workplace leaders may nonetheless be making quick and unspoken judgments. With respect to attire in the workplace, you either "get it" or you don't, even though younger colleagues might find it easier to "get" something if they would simply be told. Instead, these criticisms fall into the category of "How could they *not* know?", which also provides the cover of no longer having the responsibility to directly explain the concern.

Even more worrisome, that unarticulated judgment may also haunt other aspects of the respondent's career. After all, supervisors may assume, if this person does not know how to dress like the rest of us, maybe he or she also is not doing the job properly. This quiet judgment generally comes unencumbered by conversation, leaving Millennials to sort out whether there is a problem and, if so, how to resolve it.

The harsh reality that Millennials face is that, just because they are not told of a concern, the conclusion cannot be reached that a problem does not exist. The ability to understand this dynamic, however, is at odds with a childhood frequently enveloped by feedback, much of it positive or gently corrective. It is easy, therefore, to be lulled into a false sense of comfort that everything is ok because no one has said that anything is wrong. In the workplace, however, where problems are often rooted in poor communications, such false security can be damaging to one's future.

PART TWO

Chapter 9

Navigating Ambiguity and Other Lessons that Helicopter Parents Should Have Taught

As described in Part 1, throughout their early years, Millennials have shared a powerful bond with their parents and have often not been more than a text or cell phone call away from instant help, advice, or even a ride. This parent-child bond deeply influences how Millennials are traveling through adolescence and emerging as adults. Part Two of this book explores how that upbringing affects their integration into the workplace and is impacting Baby Boomers and Gen Xers. It also proposes adaptive behaviors that all generations can implement.

Emerging Adulthood

The hyper-focus on the Millennials during their developmental years has had some unexpected ramifications, which is now at the heart of how they are integrating into the workplace. Some researchers have identified an extension of adolescence and dependency that has slowed the Millennials' immersion into full adult status.

Clark University Professor Jeffrey Jensen Arnett describes an "historically unprecedented period" in the lives of the younger generation, using the term "emerging adulthood" to describe a new life stage between adolescence and adulthood. "The rise in the ages of entering marriage and parenthood, the lengthening of higher education, and prolonged job instability during the twenties reflect the development of a new period of life for young people in the United States and other industrialized societies, lasting from the late teens through the mid- to late twenties." [108]

In describing the cultural context of this period of development, Arnett notes that two key markers of emerging adulthood—the postponement of marriage and the postponement of parenthood—allow "the late teens and most of the twenties to be a time of exploration and instability, a self-focused age, and an age of possibilities." [109] Consistent with this concept of emerging adulthood, a 2010 Pew Research Center survey of Millennials also reported that Millennials are far less likely to be married or have children as compared with prior generations at similar ages. [110]

Author Bruce Tulgan observed the dichotomy between two concepts: "On one hand, kids grow up so fast today . . . ; on the other, they seem to stay tightly moored to their parents throughout their twenties". [111] In his own take on this period of emerging adulthood, Tulgan refers to thirty as the new twenty.

But this should not be interpreted as an opportunity to view the twenties as a time for unfocused exploration. In discussing the importance of building identity capital early in life, author Meg Ray states: "Twentysomethings who take the time to explore and *also* have the nerve to make commitments along the way construct stronger identities. They have higher self esteem and are more persevering and realistic." [112]

It is important to emphasize that the notion of emerging adulthood as a period of delayed adult markers is not one likely to apply to all social classes. As Arnett noted, young people who are middle class and above have "more opportunities for the explorations of emerging adulthood than young people who are working class or below." [113] Moreover, some Millennials do not necessarily appreciate the narrative that their transition into full adult status is any more delayed than in prior generations. One commentator wrote: "The millennials I know—and as a 27-year-old, I know many—don't often resemble the ones I see in journalists' nervous portraits. We do face many challenges, most notably the economics of being young during a recession we aren't responsible for. But my peers are working hard on careers, graduate school, creative projects, and relationships."[114]

Many survey respondents saw their generation as slower to achieve full independence, for example:

> *Things are changing—we are not married at 24 anymore and pursuing a career we will stay in for the next 30 years. Instead we are exploring many options and trying to find one that sticks while balancing our private lives that at times are complicated. Additionally, perhaps not for the better, more of us are earning higher degrees and spending more time in school.*

Some expressed concern that the significant involvement of parents in all aspects of their lives negatively affected their ability to adjust to the demands of work. A young lawyer spoke as a detached observer of his generation's reliance on others:

> *[B]ecause they grew up in a world where everything was "figured out", they thought that things should be "figured out" for them.*

As Millennials move towards full independence, they are still frequently confronted by behaviors at work that are anathema to the more transparent experiences of their youth. Possibly for the first time, Millennials will need to develop the skills required to assess and negotiate the politics of the workplace. Whether starting out in government, business, or the non-profit sector, Millennials are entering workplaces where they are meeting people with a mix of personalities and expectations that warrant quick assessments and adaptive responses. No matter how accomplished the Millennials have proven to be in their academic pursuits, workplace savvy calls for an entirely different set of skills that are critical to career success.

Discomfort with Ambiguity

The workday can be full of treacherous moments where a hesitant response to a question or assignment can send a career reeling backwards, or where a mistake can linger in a supervisor's memory for what seems like eternity.

Ironically, even with—and perhaps because of—all the parental hovering, Millennials may lack the navigational guidance needed to help them maneuver around the many landmines dispersed throughout the workplace. Millennials have both benefitted from and paid a price for the significant parental involvement in their lives. An unintended consequence of this close relationship may be that many are entering adulthood less skilled at independent problem-solving.

With parents engaged in so many aspects of their lives, Millennials became used to significant adult input into their decisions. Problem-solving was frequently part of a collective process that generally included the advice—and even the active involvement of—their parents. Teachers and coaches were also trusted sources of guidance.

This comfort with a joint approach to addressing issues in their lives, and the long-held expectation that older adults will encourage and engage them, has affected how Millennials are adapting to the workplace. Having experienced a highly structured childhood where activities were planned and free time was a rarity, Millennials tend to be uncomfortable with ambiguity. Moreover, they anticipate that those senior to them in the workplace will provide detailed information and specific guidance with each assignment, just as their teachers did in the past.

The Millennials' expectation of clarity and support plays out with great irony at work. Even as Boomers and Gen Xers engage in solving their own children's problems, they demonstrate little patience when other people's Millennial offspring seek support and guidance in their own workplaces. Instead, senior generations are frustrated by young workers who seem less skilled at problem-solving and less savvy about negotiating their way through the day-to-day struggles of the workplace than they were at similar ages. Significantly, they often miss the connection between their own parenting styles and the behaviors they see in front of them each day at the office.

As a result of these dynamics, the Millennials' entrée into the work force has been marred by the negative assessments of senior leaders who do not recognize the roots of the Millennials' discomfort with assignments that lack clarity and detailed instruction, and their expectation for frequent feedback. These senior generations miss the underlying incongruity that, once understood, can make an essential difference in the integration of Millennials into the workplace. As noted in a book on managing Millennials: " . . . Millennials are perceived as autonomous, but that does not mean that they do not welcome direction. After being acknowledged for their ability and potential, they are open to a high level of direction as to how they can go about using their skills."[115]

All of this ambiguity and uncertainty can lead, for some, to what is termed the "Quarterlife Crisis"—a response to the changes, choices and instability felt by Millennials after a clearly defined path through childhood and adolescence. As the authors of a book on this life stage stated: "The extreme uncertainty that twentysomethings experience after graduation occurs because what was once a solid line that they could follow throughout their series of educational institutions has now disintegrated into millions of different options. The sheer number of possibilities can certainly inspire hope—that is why people say that twentysomethings have their whole lives ahead of them. But the endless array of decisions can also make a recent graduate feel utterly lost."[116]

As Millennials seek to work through these choices, they do so in an economy emerging from crisis and growing at what feels like a glacially slow pace. As a result, their former aspirations feel more like a luxury as they struggle to simply find work.

Internships That Once Were Jobs

Internships have long been viewed as a way to meet and impress potential future employers while gaining valuable work experiences. The essence of an internship was rooted in the expectation that eager young graduates work without pay for a practical learning opportunity that may lead to employment. Particularly in a competitive job environment, young graduates have scrambled to be competitively positioned for their future careers by seeking experience-based learning.

This arrangement has been significantly transformed in the last several years. The economic crisis and related job losses have led to an explosion in the number of positions that are called internships, but do not resemble the carefully developed programs of the past.

Many Millennials now enter the job market having completed a number of experiences that may have been internships in name only. As internships bear more of a resemblance to an entry-level job without pay than the antici-pated educational opportunity, the question is whether these positions are bringing this generation any closer to full-time employment.

The data suggests that employers may no longer be maintaining their side of the expected bargain. For example, a 2012 survey found that 91% of the employers surveyed said students should have one to two internships before they graduate, even though half of those employers had not hired any interns in the previous six months. Moreover, 79% of the employers surveyed offered full-time work to 30% or fewer interns.[117]

Another article reported how college graduates are trapped in an "internship vortex" described as "permaterns": " . . . those perpetual interns, mostly in their twenties—who have been battered by the winds of the recession and are holding out hope that the conventional career wisdom that an internship leads to a job isn't folklore from a bygone era—like the 1990s."[118]

Once considered an opportunity for structured learning in a work environment, internships are now under legal scrutiny.[119] A recent wave of high-profile lawsuits has shed light on internship practices and, as of this writing, has resulted in some victories for the plaintiffs. For example, a New York court held that unpaid interns who worked on the movie Black Swan lacked any educational benefits and performed low-level tasks that did not require specialized training. Accordingly, the court found they were improperly classified as interns and were, there-fore, entitled to pay for the hours they worked.[120] Other lawsuits have resulted in significant financial settlements.[121] Combined, these efforts may change the way post-education internships are structured and result in a re-evaluation of whether intern roles are more appropriately clas-sified as paid employment.

Once they are finally in the workplace, Millennials face additional challenges arising from their generation's reputation. Senior generations frequently complain about young employees who do not want to work as hard as they did, and who are disloyal as exemplified by the frequency with which they change jobs.

Chapter 10

Definitions at Variance: Hard Work, Loyalty, and Self-Perceptions

Primed to Work

The perspective that Millennials are impatient in their desire to maintain or exceed the economic comfort of their childhood is often conflated with an image of Millennials as not being willing to "work their way up". The data demonstrates the inaccuracy of this notion; rather, the research shows that Millennials are prepared to work, and work hard.

The survey responses show that Millennials see themselves as a generation primed to excel, having spent years focused on achievements that could propel them to the best possible colleges, graduate programs, and fulfilling jobs. They see this work ethic applied to their jobs, contrary to the harsher judgments they face from others in the workplace. Not only did nearly two-thirds of the respondents disagree with the notion that Millennials have less of a work ethic than older generations, virtually all (94.5%) believe that they are willing to go beyond what is asked of them at work, with nearly 70% stating that they are always available to do more, and 25% willing to occasionally perform extra work on projects.

A respondent who works in higher education observed:

> *The friends I know who have achieved success in their careers*
> *have worked very hard for it. No one has been rewarded for laziness.*

Some respondents felt undermined, however, by the belief that other generations see them as lacking a strong work ethic simply because Millennials may have grown up with greater physical comforts. Data suggests they are correct in this impression. For example, one survey reported that only 20% of employers rated Millennials "above average" with regards to their willingness to work long hours relative to non-Millennials in similar roles and 47% of the employers rated Millennials as having a "below average" willingness to work long hours compared to members of other generations. The results from the Millennials showed stark disagreement: 55% of Millennials reported themselves above average in their willingness to work long hours and only 15% of Millennial respondents stated their generation was below average.[122] Millennials view these assumptions by senior generations as unfair and worry that they could negatively impact their opportunities to advance professionally.

A workplace survey of 44,000 people from across the world concluded that "Millennials and non-Millennials are virtually equally committed to the workplace."[123] Despite the questions raised about whether Millennials are less committed to work, the data tends to diminish generational distinctions on this issue.

The data does, however, suggest differing perspectives on what matters in the workplace. Unless Baby Boomers and Gen Xers better understand what motivates their Millennial employees, retention will continue to be a source of frustration for employers.

A graduate student further emphasized the point:

> *The manner in which we go about getting what we want is different from past generations—we have access & skill in technology so it may not seem as though we are 'trying' as hard, but it is just a different era.*

The Continued Pattern of Differentiation

As with nearly every question in the survey, many respondents drew boundaries between their own behavior and the behavior of others in their generation:

I think certain members of generation Y have a terrible work ethic, although I do not consider myself to be one of them.

A teacher drew a similar boundary:

I know that I have an exceptionally high work ethic thanks to my parents. I don't think all of gen Y have a low work ethic, especially those I went to grad school with, but many of my students exhibit low work ethic.

This continued pattern of differentiation could have significant workforce ramifications. Is there truly a split between how Millennials perceive others in their generation behave, as distinct from their own actions? Or do these responses reflect a clouded mirror, through which Millennials do not clearly see their own qualities?

This matters if Millennials are not honestly assessing their own behaviors in a clear light. Particularly because they are being judged by the stereotyped impressions of others, it is important for Millennials to be sure they understand how their own individual behaviors are perceived.

There can be no doubt that Millennials see their work ethic as integrally tied to a holistic view of their lives. Work is important, but it does not necessarily take precedence over family obligations, personal relationships, and health and wellness. One respondent summarized this recurring theme:

I have a very strong work ethic . . . I put 110% into my work and always make the most of my time. I am available to do more, but not if it will interfere with my family time.

If you define work ethic as being a work-aholic then yes, I do think that Gen Y has less of a "work ethic." I believe that I have a VERY strong work ethic, and this is evidenced by being in the top 15% of my law school class, working 3 part-time jobs, and participating in school organizations. I will not, however, let my life become all about work . . . Just because I will not compromise my values to work does not mean that my work product will be any less. I take pride in my work and will always produce quality work and have a strong work ethic. The older generation confuses quantity with quality. You do not have to be a work-aholic to have a good work ethic.

Echoed another:

We have realized that work doesn't have to be your life and we have found ways around being forced into this lifestyle. It's not that we work less and feel that we deserve the same benefits.

The overall theme from the respondents is consistent with other research on this generation: working hard is fine, but work as the sole or even primary purpose of one's life is seen as folly. Rather, Millennials see work as a place in grave need of an efficiency make-over. A young worker in the public relations field stated:

[It's not that] my generation doesn't work hard, we just work differently.

A Different Definitional View

Respondents expressed frustration with workplaces that seemed to care more about adherence to inflexible rules and requirements than the quality of the work product. They saw hypocrisy in written policies about lunch hours or breaks that were verbally overwritten by superiors telling employees that it is best not to take such breaks in order to impress others. A respondent described such a situation:

I have never been a real fan of "time cards." I hate having the value of my day and work regarded only in terms of arriving at 9 am on the dot. Can't be early because I don't have permission for overtime, can't even be one minute late because gasp . . . you're late. And no matter what, you have to stand there and wait the extra minute to make sure the clock says 5 pm before you can leave. Even if that means you just stand there with your coat and wait. For some reason that is acceptable, even though no one is doing any work that way either. . . . I have been told to eat at my desk because it shows good work ethic. I have been told that even though I get breaks, it is better not to take them because it doesn't look good to my boss to leave my desk—he actually told me that! . . . With those types of statements, it is just so obvious that they are not interested in quality work, but just putting in the time.

Other respondents similarly reported that their commitment to their job was negatively impacted by inflexibility at work, a supervisor's poor management skills, and a failure on his or her part to ensure fairness by properly addressing difficult employees. For example:

Older generations aren't as flexible about time. As in, if one is expected to work a certain number of hours a day, I think it's ok to come in a little later (30 min) or leave earlier (30 min) so long as one is working at least the minimum time required and one isn't behind on work. I do this and often work through lunch to leave 30 minutes earlier (although I'm supposed to have a 45 min lunch) but get dinged for this so will just need to have the more structured schedule, which is annoying and not the most conducive to my working style.

We had a few bad experiences with employees the company would not get rid of despite demonstrated and well-documented incompetencies and HR violations for fear of lawsuit. It made me lose faith in the company.

Another respondent similarly highlighted the mixed messages and perceived hypocrisy that diminishes effective job performance. The comment also highlights a central distinction between how Millennials view work, compared to how they perceive other generations do. Specifically, Millennials see their work as tasks to be completed, not hours to be spent:

Many older generations view work ethic in terms of hours worked, while many younger people view it as work completed. And I am no exception. If I can get 10 times more work done by taking regular breaks or something, why wouldn't I? . . . And there are many times I work 10–12 hours a day in order to complete a project on time. When that has happened, I have actually been told that I should not claim those hours and a good worker would "gift" those hours to the company to show a strong work ethic. Something I think is ridiculous and know it is illegal. . . . I work my butt off to get everything done in my day a few minutes early so that I can clean my work area and prepare for the next day, that way I can get right to work the next day. But I have been told that this is viewed as a sign that I don't work hard since I have time to clean my desk. While at the same time, my boss has an area that he can't even work at and has pulled me away from my own work to clean it for him. Who's really lacking the ethic there?

This tension between measuring productivity by hours worked seems anathema to a generation raised on devices that promote efficiency and multi-tasking. It is a tension that emerges throughout the responses on workplace practices. Resolving these irreconcilable views of the workplace will be an important step in developing an engaged younger workforce.

The Heart of the Intergenerational Disconnect

The easy and frequently expressed criticism of Millennials at work is that they lack self-awareness and do not understand the patterns of behaviors that frustrate older workers. This misses the essence of the generational disconnect. It is more likely that the behaviors other generations are witnessing reflect an unwillingness to conflate unrelated concepts. Millennials see antiquated practices in the workplace that hinder their ability to optimize how they manage their work-life responsibilities. That they do not expect to acquiesce to the status quo does not mean that they lack a work ethic or are disloyal. One young lawyer saw in her generation's approach to work an unfairly drawn connection to that fallback concept of "entitlement":

I think the older generation confuses 'entitled' with forward-thinking. I think we see through the bullshit better and force the older generations to rationalize ideas or concepts that no longer work. We don't think it is necessary to do the 'tried and true' method when that method clearly does not work.

Respondents also expressed confidence that their track record of success will naturally flow into opportunities at work for early promotions and career development. This perspective sometimes conflicts, however, with that of older generations who may see young employees as having overly-aggressive expectations, being less willing to work as hard and long for their rewards as did Boomers and Gen Xers, and more likely to move on whenever expedient.

Millennials get the disconnect. While almost all of the respondents viewed themselves as having a strong work ethic, less than two-thirds believed that older generations perceive them to be highly motivated. Millennials' respond to the negative image that other generations have by drawing on their internal strengths and believing that their energy and goal-driven behaviors will propel them forward.

This expectation that things will work out helps buoy self-confidence and deflects disappointment, but is misread by many Boomers and Gen Xers, who see younger workers as not sufficiently compliant and as demanding too much from the workplace. Millennials understand that Boomers and Gen Xers pride themselves on their ability to withstand long hours at the office, but balk at the notion that the endurance these senior generations demonstrated throughout their careers must be a prerequisite to a young person's future success.

Respondents generally felt their generation has significant drive which is not inconsistent with a simultaneous focus on effectively managing their workday to maximize time for other aspects of their lives. As one respondent noted:

I think Gen Y understands how to do less in order to get more— meaning we don't waste our time on things that don't matter and still get the same results as the older generations. We are more efficient and therefore don't have the need to work 9+ hours every day.

Some respondents suggested that just because each generation may have a different world view, it does not mean that one is better. As this health care worker stated:

> I don't think the work ethic of younger generations is less than, I think that it is different. Older generations seem to be very focused on providing for their family, while in my experience the younger generation is more focused on fulfillment.

Your Bad Management is not my Lack of Loyalty and Work Ethic

In addition to the criticism that Millennials are not hard-working, they are plagued by the perception that they are a generation without loyalty. For example, in a study of more than 6,300 job seekers and Human Resources professionals, only 1% of those in HR saw Millennials as loyal to their employers, and only 11% stated that they were hard-working. In that same study, 82% of the Millennials described themselves as loyal and 86% saw themselves as hard-working.[124] Other research confirmed that the majority of Millennials are interested in developing a long-term relationship with one employer, contrary to the view of this generation as unwilling to stay loyal: "54% of Millennials want to stay in the same job and don't want to job-hop . . . "[125]

Senior generations err when they judge the loyalty of Millennials to their workplaces by equating loyalty with a commitment to stay in the job. Millennials see loyalty as expressed through their dedication to *perform* the job, but not necessarily to forego better opportunities.[126] A survey of Millennials and employers asked whether Millennials are more likely than other generations to leave an organization for another opportunity. Approximately half of the employers and 90% of the Millennials said yes. Of those, 66% of the employers believed Millennials would leave their organization because of a perceived lack of advancement opportunities, while only 48% of Millennial respondents agreed; 62% of employers cited "no loyalty" as a reason for leaving, compared to 35% of Millennials; and only 45% of employers believed high ambition constituted a reason for Millennials to leave one organization for another, as compared to 75% of Millennials.[127] This survey reveals a mismatch in perceptions that is regularly confirmed in other data. But retention becomes an elusive goal if employers do not understand what would drive their employees to leave.

A worldwide cross-generational survey discovered that "Millennials are more likely to leave if their needs for support, appreciation and flexibility are not met, while non-Millennials are more likely to leave if they feel they are not being paid competitively, or due to a perceived lack of development opportunities."[128] Additionally, the survey found that, "the economic downturn had a significant impact on Millennials' loyalty to their employers. In 2008, 75% of respondents from around the world expected to have between two and five employers in their lifetime, but in 2011 that proportion fell to 54%. Now, more than 25% of Millennials expect to have six or more employers, compared with just 10% in 2008."[129]

Survey responses demonstrated a close connection between flexible work environments, feeling valued at work, and the reciprocity of loyalty. The vast majority of respondents reported feeling somewhat or very loyal to their current employer (92%). The results also revealed an interesting gender distinction: male respondents reported lower levels of loyalty to their employers, with 12% of men stating that they considered themselves not at all loyal compared to only 7% of the women. While the percentage of respondents feeling somewhat loyal towards their employers were similar (48% for the men and 46% for the women), more women reported feeling very loyal to their employers (47%) than men (40%).

Significantly, the respondents rated themselves as more loyal to their employer than they rated their employer's loyalty to them. When asked how loyal they considered their employer, respondents (83%) felt that their employers were somewhat or very loyal to them in return, compared to the 92% that described themselves as somewhat or very loyal to their own employer. The degree of loyalty differed in that only 32% of the respondents described their employer as very loyal to them, even though nearly 46% saw themselves as very loyal to their employer.

One respondent described her early disillusion with bosses who made no effort to foster loyalty:

I have felt loyalty to my jobs in the past, but more because of a personal need to please and not let people down than a desire to stay at the company. It has also been made clear to me, from previous bosses, that I shouldn't be naive about a company's loyalty to me—that we are all replaceable! Talk about unmotivating.

I just recently changed jobs for better pay, better learning opportunities, and job location. At my previous job, my kids were at a daycare provided by the employer, which was located at the office location where I worked. When another office location was short on staff, I was expected to go to this other office (an extra 30 minutes away), but still had to drop my kids off at daycare where I usually worked . . . my employer said, oh well, too bad for you. I also was then almost an hour later picking the kids up, costing me overtime at the daycare. This was why I left—they didn't seem to care about my loyalty to my children and my family time, so I didn't feel much loyalty to them either and started looking elsewhere.

Respondents spoke of experiences where they felt their loyalty was ignored in the face of corporate downsizing. Several described experiences in which such corporate decisions were made unnecessarily painful. For example:

I learned first-hand that companies have no loyalty to employees . . . [W]hile on vacation I received a voicemail saying I was laid-off. He actually laid me off in the message . . . Another example, our company needed to find $50,000 in the budget. So, instead of my boss putting his new office furniture order on hold or taking a pay cut himself . . . they rid my position. I was told 5 minutes before the end of the day and the day after I put a deposit down on a new apartment and on wedding reception reservations. The paperwork for my laid-off notices and checks were all dated 3 days earlier, meaning, they knew they were getting rid of me but . . . There was no regard at all for me, just that they knew it was better to fire people on Fridays at the end of the day.

Another respondent spoke of a company's passive-aggressive approach to terminating employees:

> *The company I work for technically is employing too many people right now, so has cut all of our hours, but has an order from on high not to fire anyone (they'd have to pay unemployment). So, essentially, they have been making life difficult for us hoping that a few will quit. That is far from loyal to employees who have been working for them for over 5 years.*

Anecdotes revealed how direct communication, even in the face of difficult decisions, could have made a difference. For example:

> *I worked at a PR agency for nearly three years after graduating college, starting when they were very small and eventually reaching almost 40 employees. When the company faltered due to bad financial decisions by the owner, he immediately started hacking people—ending when I got fired on my birthday (via phone). It was something that really affected me because I felt absolute loyalty to that company— like I think many of my generation do to their first jobs. I think that relationship of "you matter" means a lot to my generation because of the way we were raised.*

The responses show that Millennials see the concept of loyalty as a highly individualized response to how people treat each other and how leaders manage. They see institutional loyalty as a fiction, focusing instead on the individual relationships that people develop with one another that result in behaviors of trust and loyalty. For many respondents, what mattered was whether their employers treated them as if they mattered as individuals:

> *I have found that if the employees feel the company cares about them it increases . . . loyalty. At [former job] I didn't feel that anyone felt very secure and no one was very happy. As a result no one stayed at that company for long (unless they were nearing retirement). At [current job] most of the staff has been here for several years and*

have no plans for moving on. It's a very different environment and everyone has a strong feeling of purpose.

A clear theme emerged from the respondents: loyalty is earned, and the lack of reciprocal loyalty diminishes morale, impedes performance, and leads to attrition. A respondent in the marketing field described in detail how these issues intersected:

I entered the work force in 2002 in the design industry for new construction. At the time the industry was booming, people who entered the industry just two years before me were making 6 figures. My timing was terrible. I worked 70 hour weeks with a 6-figure income in mind, but as I started to work up to it the housing market crashed and instead of salary increases I took salary cuts. The owners of the company changed their mindset and told us our reward was a pay-check and we should be happy to have one even it is was 20% less than the year before. After this experience I realized the importance of work/life balance. I missed friends' weddings, birthday parties, etc because I was too busy working. I cannot get that time back. Now I am focusing on starting my own business. When times are good you feel needed, but when markets crash owners will protect themselves first and don't care about you or your family.

I have always been an incredibly loyal employee, rarely even looked for new jobs while at a current job, because I felt it was unfair. . . . But, in the end you are expendable. . . . If someone were to offer me more money and flexible hours today I would be happy to give my two weeks' notice.

I believe the times have changed and the idea of working for one company your entire life is gone. My father-in-law worked for the government. He started right out of high school and retired at 50 with a pension. Stories like this will be rare in our generation. So work ethic and motivation have changed. . . . I focus on learning new skills that I can continue to apply. I want to make sure I am improving myself. This will benefit the current company I work for, but more important it will protect me and help me get my next position.

Many respondents identified a connection between their own loyalty and whether they felt their efforts were appreciated. When hard work goes unnoticed, the result is diminished morale, as this respondent observed:

One weekend my co-workers and I came in and worked 13 hour days to meet a clearly arbitrary deadline. The department head was not at all appreciative. That kind of squashed my willingness to go beyond—for example volunteering for weekend conventions, etc. There is no comp time or overtime at my job, but if I at least felt appreciated I would be willing to do more. As it is, I will give 100% on my responsibilities but I am less willing to go beyond them for no appreciation and no compensation.

Another respondent similarly noted that when employees feel unappreciated, it is easier to trade salary for greater control over one's life.

My brother (who is one year older) is going through something similar to me right now with a boss that expects him to work all the time for less pay and no recognition. He is quitting [his manager-level position] in order to have a better balance in life, despite the pay cut.

Several respondents were fortunate enough to feel their hard work was noticed and met with appreciation. The results were far more conducive to a productive work environment. For example:

I work hard and pull long hours when needed without being asked. My boss recognizes this and appreciates my drive and therefore is flexible when I need to leave work a little early or take a long lunch to do personal things. This type of appreciation is very motivating to always strive to do my job well and I definitely do not take advantage of my boss's generosity.

Another described changing jobs for a better work environment:

I have noticed that for myself job loyalty is much more contingent on work environment than on pay. Friends of mine remain at jobs that pay less because of the environment they enjoy/benefits they receive, and I left a higher paying job for a lower paying job because of the environments that they had.

Some respondents felt that loyalty did not prevent looking for other opportunities. They believed that they could demonstrate loyalty while performing their job, even if continuing to seek a position that would be more fulfilling, as this respondent noted:

I find that my peers, and myself, are loyal to the company they work for in the sense that while they are there they give 100%, however that loyalty does not keep us from looking for other positions that might be more satisfying.

A few respondents found a way to stay loyal to their employer forever, as this respondent in the IT field stated:

Can I skip all these loyalty questions? Because when you are your own boss, it's hard to not be loyal to yourself.

Technology is More than a Tether

As a result of their lifelong comfort with and mastery of technology, Millennials demonstrate a healthy degree of skepticism about the rigid way senior generations view the relationship between work and time. Respondents repeatedly emphasized their view of technology as a game-changer, and were stymied by the challenge of getting other generations to understand its full reaches. They could envision a future where technology could be woven into the fabric of the workplace in a way that delivers meaningful flexibility and work options. That vision, however, seemed frequently thwarted by limitations that held back the full reach and potential of technology as a tool for rethinking work.

Clear themes emerged from many of the responses: technology should work for, not against us; and using technology to work smarter should be viewed positively. As one respondent noted:

My sense is that generation Y is less willing to put up with "bulls**t" if it's just there based on the idea of dues paying or the "this is how I did it when I started out" kind of corporate hazing. I think gen Y expects the ability to work smarter instead of harder, since we have grown up observing how technology makes things so much faster/easier.

Another respondent observed:

Again, it's all about efficiency. It's not that I don't want to work hard for long hours, I just don't want to waste my time working hard for long hours on something that can be done quicker another way.

Several respondents saw criticism of their generation's work ethic as related to the misnomer of entitlement and the failure of older generations to maximize the benefits of technology. For example, a college student noted:

I think we are generally misunderstood as being entitled when we really just want to use technology to increase efficiency and therefore have more time to do as we will.

Another respondent similarly observed that Millennials' facility with technology causes others to misunderstand their work ethic:

I feel that Gen Y has a work ethic that is equal to that of older generations, but we are able to get more accomplished due to the new technology that is available to us.

As noted in earlier responses, many respondents expressed frustration with workplace norms where people continue to be judged by the amount of time they are physically at the office—and appearing to look busy. The strict adherence to time makes little sense to a generation primed to see technology as an opportunity for new ways of communicating and performing tasks that should logically extend to the workplace, as this respondent noted:

I work at a place where even if you don't have any work to do, you are expected to sit there and wait for work to come in. I would rather spend time with my daughter or running errands while I wait for work to come in. It drives me crazy to sit at my desk. I don't feel like I can propose this solution (i.e. email me when the work comes in) because my boss is very inflexible. He once got angry at the staff because they all left at 5.15 instead of 5.30. They had nothing to do! It just seems inefficient to me. If my boss had a better handle on technology, I think he would realize that I can be available to him even when I am not in the next room.

Many respondents identified an interface between the benefits of flexibility for themselves, and the benefits to the workplace. For example:

My bosses are not flexible with things like 'leaving when your work is done' or flex hours . . . This gives me less time to rejuvenate once I'm home, then I stay up later, then I'm more tired and when I'm done with all my duties, I don't understand why I can't leave the office. I feel like we are wasting energy. If bosses allowed for more flexible hours to employees they trusted, I personally would be much more productive and save my company money on electricity etc.

Respondents particularly rejected the way in which senior generations viewed technology as an opportunity for around-the-clock accessibility rather than as a way for work to be done more effectively and efficiently. As the barriers between work and home have blurred, all generations should be concerned about the effect on people's health and stress levels. One article observed that technology has resulted in: "nothing less than the loss of barriers that insulate us from modern capitalism. Today, not only is home more like the office—since 1980 the number of Americans whose principal place of work is home has doubled—the office is more like the home."[130]

This theme emerged continuously: rather than serving as a vehicle to make lives easier, technology has become a tether which lengthens the work day and provides constant connectivity. The promise of efficiency and greater flexibility offered by these devices has become illusory. As one respondent noted:

> *Work is all consuming with the use of email and cell phones; it is nearly impossible to get away.*

Professions that demand extraordinary hours and favor a face-time culture were particularly frustrating to the respondents. Noted one lawyer:

> *[W]ith such advanced communication technology, it still surprises me that lawyers have to put in so much time at the office. I find myself more motivated to work at home without the continuous distractions of other attorneys, partners, etc., however, I feel that, if I worked at home (even one day a week), that could potentially hurt my opportunity for advancement.*

These responses reveal that Millennials understand that unchecked technology adds extraordinary stress to their work demands. They also recognize the impacts on health and wellness in a way that more senior generations seem less comfortable addressing as a workplace issue.

The Lure of Entrepreneurship

Notwithstanding the challenging economic climate, Millennials are bombarded with examples of young people who followed their dreams to significant—and early—success. There are the obvious and renowned global figures such as Facebook founder Mark Zuckerberg and Beyonce Knowles who turned her singing talent into a billion dollar brand. There are lesser-known billionaires and millionaires whose key roles in tech companies have reaped significant economic rewards. And there are those Millennials who have emerged as leaders in a variety of fields, and have been highlighted in books and blogs.[131]

These peer role models have had an impact. They are helping to spawn a generation that is searching for their own brand of success. Particularly in a troubled economy where a significant percentage of young workers are still having trouble finding traditional job opportunities, entrepreneurship beckons as a hopeful alternative. As noted in a New York Times article: " ... the tools to become an entrepreneur are more accessible than they've ever been. Thanks to the Internet, there are fewer upfront costs. A business owner can build a Web site, host conference calls, create slide presentations online through a browser, and host live meetings and Web seminars — all on a shoestring."[132]

Many respondents were supportive of those seeking an entrepreneurial approach. One post-graduate student observed:

> *I hang out with a lot of people who want to be independent and do their own thing—entrepreneurs, academics—really strong personalities. I can see how quitting a job to pursue something entrepreneurial can seem irresponsible. . . . But, I think a lot of Gen Y kids are looking for something they want to do.*

Another described finding that sense of commitment and meaning:

> *I am incredibly loyal to my position as Co-Director here, and to my colleagues because we've built this organization together. Since the Founder . . . hired my Co-Director and I two years ago, we have invested our time, money, energy and vision into the organization, and that investment makes me want the best for the organization, and to build my future in alignment with it.*

It is possible for workplaces to respond to this lure of entrepreneurship by providing opportunities that appeal to Millennials seeking new horizons. For example, travel may be a way to retain younger employees, particularly as centers of economic power broaden globally. As one study noted: "In an increasingly globalised world, international experience is seen by millennials as a vital element to a successful career. Millennials have a strong appetite for working abroad, with 71% keen to do so at some stage during their career."[133]

Creative employers would be wise to tap into this interest in entrepreneurial opportunities. The economic climate should serve as an incentive to rethink how, where, and when work is conducted. Millennials can play a key role in that process.

Work that has Meaning

Survey respondents confirmed other research demonstrating that the majority of Millennials seek meaning in their work and a shared commitment to core values. In a survey of Millennials, nearly 60% were willing to sacrifice 15% of their salary to work for an organization whose values they share. To have a job that endeavors to make a social or environmental difference in the world, 45% of the student respondents said they would give up 15% of their income.[134] In the Clark University Poll of Emerging Adults, 86% of the respondents agreed with the statement that: "It is important to me to have a career that does some good in the world."[135]

A report on workplace trends noted that in a 2009 survey of new college hires, 86% stated that they would consider leaving an employer whose social responsibility values did not meet their expectations; a 2012 survey of student values reported that 58% of the respondents would accept less pay to work for a company whose values they shared.[136] This data and others like it reinforces the importance of social responsibility as a recruitment and retention tool.

Author Courtney Martin, in rejecting the portrayal of Millennials as focused only on themselves, writes of the sophisticated understanding that many young people bring to the complexities of the world's problems. She writes: "We are not, on the whole, entitled, self-absorbed, and apathetic. We're overwhelmed, empathetic, and paralyzed. . . . This is not a quiet generation; it is a generation searching for its own way."[137] Other research on Millennials' connection to social causes reported: "The generation that was taught to recycle in kindergarten wants to be good to the planet and believes that collective action can make a difference. Millennials believe that working for causes is an integral part of life, and they are drawn to big issues."[138]

Millennials are also pushing workplaces to increase their community involvement.[139] They seek a level of engagement that is far removed, as a book about retaining Millennial employees describes, from "the old paradigm for corporate charity" such as a competitive effort to match employer contributions. Rather, there is a preference for "a more hands-on, personal, and direct approach to charity."[140]

It is, therefore, not surprising that even in the face of a sobering economic climate, Millennials are demonstrating a strong desire to be engaged in work that matters.[141] Many respondents tied their motivation and work ethic to their engagement in the job, for example:

> *I think the younger generation has to be interested in what they are doing in order to be motivated. My friends who have found jobs/ fields that they love are highly motivated. I have watched some friends struggle to find what they love and really flounder in different organizations—however, once they do, they really thrive and are willing to work VERY hard.*

One respondent briefly summarized the theme embedded in many of the responses:

> *I work for a family run business in the midst of several corporate conglomerates. It's really rewarding, to not only champion the underdog, but to even outperform our competition.*

The importance of meaning and engagement continued as a prominent theme throughout the responses. One described how friends have pursued a variety of opportunities in their search for meaning, and noted:

> *I would say all of us value having a career that energizes us over a high salary. We strive to live below our means.*

One respondent described her money/meaning trade-off in the context of a packed life:

> *I have a very busy schedule juggling a full-time career, a part-time job, two graduate programs, and my board responsibilities . . . I work for a nonprofit suffering the effects of the recession. I believe in its*

Mission; therefore, I sacrifice monetary compensation and better ben-efits, knowing that I could find it elsewhere.

Similarly, another respondent stated:

I think the older generations aren't used to the fact that we are looking for careers that we enjoy rather than careers that make money.

The conflict between higher compensation and opportunities for mean-ingful work can lead to family tensions. One respondent noted her family's differing perspectives regarding the trade-off between income and other values:

My family and 3 siblings are all productive and successful, but we have all chosen very different paths. My lawyer sister and invest-ment banker brother think me leaving corporate for teaching is insane purely because of the money. My entrepreneur brother thinks I made the right choice . . .

Survey respondents recognized that not all jobs can be personally fulfill-ing. Those are the instances where money emerged as an important factor. Where work demanded an inordinate amount of time, respondents were more likely to be focused on the monetary rewards.

This can result in another area of missed communication at work. Mil-lennials are often described as in a hurry to make a lot of money. But there are two compelling factors that may underlie those instances where Mil-lennials seem hyper-focused on income. The first is where a student's debt burden is high and loan repayment obligations must be the top priority.

The second factor may be more workplace specific. If a job offers little meaning and profit is the sole motivator within the company, a Millennial employee may be focused on compensation because that is the only advantage of the job. If young workers only see managers and other employers focused on profit, it is logical that they may respond similarly. One lawyer noted:

I think the younger generation is better able to assess the value of personal/family time, and therefore expect sufficient pay to justify time away from what they've assessed to 'really matter' (i.e. family time, personal time, etc.). Work, for the younger generation, is not necessarily in and of itself the part of one's life where personal satisfaction and fulfillment will be achieved.

Overall, the survey responses demonstrated a remarkable ability to starkly analyze one's current work environment and adapt behaviors accordingly. If careers are not proceeding as hoped, or if talents do not feel recognized, Millennials will reassess and respond accordingly. For example:

Work is integral to my life, and I actively pursued a career that was important to me, my values, and my personal goals. As such, I find that my job is a part of my personal time — and I don't regret that. However, like most Gen Yers, I am frustrated that despite putting so much effort and time into my work that I am not given greater leadership opportunities. I would easily give up more of my personal time if I could be granted more opportunities for professional growth. Until that happens, though, I have decided to hold back a bit and concentrate on personal activities, like my volunteer work.

These responses represent one of the most significant inter-generational disconnects. Where senior generations perceive disloyalty and a lack of work ethic in younger workers, Millennials see themselves responding to work-place rigidity by finding new positions or becoming engaged in other activities. Millennials also recognized the lost opportunities to use their talents in a way that is both beneficial to the workplace and efficient for the employers.

The retention of Millennials has a great deal to do with the level of engagement they find in their work. But whatever the motivation for staying in their jobs, Millennials can be significantly influenced by the way in which senior generations provide feedback and respond to questions.

Chapter 11

Moving Forward with Feedback

Ask Me No Questions, I'll Tell You No Lies

Another major source of inter-generational conflict in the workplace arises from the perceived frequency with which Millennials ask questions and raise concerns. The complex behaviors that have their roots in the childhood of Millennials are now causing consternation at work. Parents who encouraged their children to be assertive sent them out into the world with specific advice: to aggressively pursue their goals, to speak up, and to ask questions. By the time they enter the workplace, where (most) parents do not tread, Millennials may reasonably expect that those in roles of authority will be as eager to offer them advice and listen to their questions as other adults in their lives have been.

As a result, employers are complaining that younger employees want to talk through workplace issues, be sure they understand assignments, or otherwise have their questions answered. This sets up a dynamic where senior generations—who already see themselves as overworked and lacking sufficient time in the day to meet their obligations—are expected to respond to frequent inquiries from younger employees. These workplace leaders wonder why Millennials are not figuring things out for themselves. And in many cases, they may simply view the interruptions as a lack of respect for hierarchy.

This issue gets to the heart of the way in which all generations judge whether they are respected at work. The desire to feel respected crosses all generational boundaries. For senior generations, respect is often equated with deference to one's position of authority, which means attention to hierarchy and position. For Millennials, respect is equated with being heard. As a generation whose opinion and ideas were sought throughout their lives, they have grown up comfortable expressing their opinions and asking questions. In the workplace however, such questions and comments are easily misinterpreted as a lack of respect.

This disconnect arises most frequently when Millennials ask questions about assignments and then seek feedback when the work product is completed. This is an area where senior generations frequently miss the connection between how Millennials were raised and how they interact at work.

As analyzed in prior chapters, many Millennials grew up accustomed to trusted relationships with adults in their lives who answered questions, provided guidance, and otherwise helped them achieve their goals. Learning was incremental. At each bump along the way, assistance was generally available. And for each paper turned in, each race completed, or other milestone achieved, there was a parent, teacher, or coach to help analyze performance. This ongoing feedback stream served as the foundation for how Millennials learned and developed new skills.

With this background, Millennials are pouring into workplaces with every expectation that the adults there will treat them similarly. They trust that their supervisors will provide the same caring feedback to which they have grown accustomed. Instead, Millenials more frequently may find workplaces where they are offered little or no feedback outside of an annual review process that is, in many work environments, perfunctory at best. Moreover, their questions are often interpreted as a desire for praise only. Consequently, Millennials end up misunderstood by older colleagues and, in many cases, this can contribute to a negative assessment of their abilities.

There is irony in this disconnect. Boomers and Gen Xers who are frustrated by these behaviors when other peoples' Millennial children enter their workplaces are often the parents whose children are exhibiting similar behavioral patterns in the workplaces of others.

Tell Me You Love Me

Perhaps no title has been used more frequently to describe Millennials than "Trophy Kids". The term originates from a place of well-meaning intentions. As children, their effort and participation were encouraged and recognized. Instead of—or sometimes along with—awards for star performers, team members would each receive their own trophy.

This concept of team support made its way into classrooms and school activities, resulting in a generation accustomed to frequent compliments, positive reinforcement, and even grade inflation. It is only natural that Millennials would expect positive feedback to continue once they enter the workplace. One poll of over 1000 Millennials found that more than 60% of the respondents "wanted to hear from managers at least once a day".[142] Feedback has for Millennials become an essential learning tool. Accordingly, if senior leaders hope to maximize the potential talents that Millennials bring to the workplace, they will need to adapt to the generation's expectation of and desire for frequent feedback.

Survey respondents described a need for feedback that went far beyond the image attributed to them as a generation who wants positive reinforcement instead of constructive criticism. Millennials see ongoing feedback as a way to understand how they are progressing. Just as they learned how to improve in school and their other activities through regular feedback, Millennials similarly seek direction in the workplace. As one respondent stated:

> It's not just 'a job' to us, it's our life. We won't take positions in 'corporate America' just because our parents did. We saw how bored and stressed they were every day. We are not entitled, however, when we put our heart and soul into an organization. We want recognition and we want to know we're doing a good (or bad) job and how we can improve. A simple email of 'great job' goes a long way for us. We're not 'entitled' to being recognized but we see this as a natural thing to do.

For Millennials, feedback serves the role of helping them respond to the dynamic nature of the workplace. As an article describing ways to motivate Millennial employees noted, "The millennials have learned that in times of change one needs a constant source of feedback . . . to be on the mark and adjust performance accordingly. Since job requirements and expectations are constantly in flux, yesterday's feedback may no longer be relevant today. Constant feedback, thus, is not to pump up a frail ego as much as to help them stay on track to continue to do good work for the employer day after day. Feedback and praise serve as reinforcement as well as a corrective mechanism for this generation."[143]

Survey respondents recognized that the early encouragement they received helped them become confident. They also understood that they were raised to view insecurity as a quality that does not facilitate future success. Respondents often identified the link between an upbringing steeped in confidence-building measures and their desire for early career success. Many appreciated the efforts that went into helping them become confident young adults encouraged to pursue their dreams. The challenging aspects of that focus, however, did not go unnoticed. For example, a respondent in the engineering field spoke about the impact of the "everyone gets a trophy" thinking during their early years:

> If you are taught from a young age that everyone is equal at everything then you feel that you should have everything you want. Why not? You are just as good as the next person, right?

Others also spoke about the down side of always being primed for success. For example, one respondent noted:

> I happen to think that our desire for . . . money, status, satisfying, self-fulfilling careers is true. . . . If anything, we may have been taught unrealistic expectations for what it would be like to be in our 20's in the workplace and how quickly we would experience success.

Respondents also commented on the high price paid by some members of their generation who, shielded from disappointment since birth, may be inadequately equipped to handle disappointment in adulthood. They worried that being primed to expect success can limit one's resilience to persevere and rebound from disappointment. Ultimately this can pose numerous challenges to career advancement.

Experts have similarly raised concerns about the development of resilience and perseverance in the Millennial generation. For example, in an interview about her book concerning depression in affluent teenagers, author Madeline Levine commented, "we need to have, internally, an authentic, robust, resilient sense of who we are, and the self-esteem movement sort of neglected that [. . .] My husband showed me this great little cartoon of a kid who's in soccer clothes, and he's approaching his dad with this huge trophy, and he says, 'we lost.' And that's the self-esteem movement."[144]

Respondents recognized that a person who lacks resilience will be more inclined to blame others when something goes wrong, rather than introspectively evaluate how to learn from the experience and move forward. But blaming others for negative experiences impedes the opportunity to grow and mature, a concern addressed by this respondent:

> *Many people in my generation expect others to do our work for us. This does not mean that we are unwilling to work, but it means that we want, and expect, others to help us, to hold our hand, and to often give us guidance far longer than we probably need it. This was exceedingly evident in law school where people blamed career services because they could not find a job, or blamed the professor when they did not understand the work. While some of the complaints were justified, many people failed to take responsibility . . . .*

It is clear that none of the generations have a fully accurate view of each other. Millennials are seeking transparency and feedback from generations whose behaviors often demonstrate discomfort with direct and open communications in the workplace.

Passive-Aggressive Comments are not Feedback

Many respondents felt particularly thwarted by feedback that was not constructive, or that could even be characterized as passive-aggressive. A government sector worker provided an example of this behavior:

Our office is business attire (most wear suits every day), but we have a "Jeans Day" once a month, which people can earn the privilege of participating in by donating to charity. On jeans day a couple months ago, our boss (elected official) walked in wearing a suit and the first thing he said to me was, "Wow, wish I could wear jeans." I hadn't seen him in a couple weeks, so it was sort of a slap in the face . . . he could have said, "Hi, how are you? How is your work going?" without making me feel like I was doing something wrong. This actually annoyed me a lot.

To some, this anecdote may simply demonstrate the oversensitivity of a young worker. But the example shows the reaction of a Millennial employee hoping for a positive interaction with a boss, only to be disappointed by a flip comment. If the comment were simply an off-hand remark in a relationship in which there was frequent contact, it may have gone unnoticed. But when the norm is minimal interaction between supervisor and employee, the negative reaction to even mild sarcasm may be better understood.

Other respondents spoke of supervisors who managed through passive-aggressive behavior, rather than by addressing the underlying issues. For example:

I was planning on attending a birthday party for a friend out of town during a weekend. I had to cancel my plans last minute for an assignment that only had punitive value. It was essentially an assignment to teach me a lesson for being sloppy earlier in the week. I should not have been sloppy but I'm not sure if the response was merited.

Some respondents identified a passive approach to feedback, which generally consisted of hardly any at all. For several, the lack of interaction was a key factor in their decision to change jobs, as this respondent noted:

The place I work has a great reputation, but I have not been well supervised or trained. So I am going to switch jobs soon and use this is a springboard to something in which I can learn more.

The Millennials' desire for meaningful feedback can be seen in data demonstrating that this is an area where technology is seen as a poor substitute for direct conversation. Of note, a global generational study found that when it comes to communicating about their career plans and progress, 96% of Millennials still want to talk to their employers face-to-face, just as 95% of their non-Millennial counterparts do.[145] This suggests that Millennials seek direct interaction for advice and guidance, which is likely similar to patterns they experienced when they were younger and spoke with parents and other adults in their lives about their career goals.

To break down these barriers, each generation must communicate clearly their goals and expectations. The workplace functions more effectively when assignments are clear and transparent, and when feedback is used as an ongoing performance development tool.

Effective feedback can be a tool that develops the next generation of leaders. Attention to inquiries can yield new ideas. Opportunities abound for those workplaces willing to think creatively about the many ways to develop the full potential of Millennials.

Chapter 12

Rethinking the Workplace

If It No Longer Fits

For the most part, Boomers and Gen Xers adapted to the workplace they inherited. Doing so may have required some adjustment, but the fit was eased by a lack of dissonance between their upbringing and their expectations from work.

For Millennials, the circumstances upon their entry into the workplace are different in significant ways. The biggest game changer is technology. It is hard to imagine that, for most Boomers, the invention of the fax machine was a major breakthrough (that also became obsolete) in the span of their careers. Boomers began typing on a manual typewriter, which then became electric, and later morphed into the mag card typewriter—a major breakthrough in 1973 which was followed a year later by the IBM Memory Typewriter. The point, however, is evident in the consistent use of the word "typewriter" in describing these changes.

Compare this slow evolution to the high-stress, fast paced work environment Millennials face which is fueled by technology that changes at a dizzying pace. So far, the tools of technology at work have served primarily to increase the demands on their time and energy, and limit opportunities for constructive interaction. And to those with a vision for a more flexible workplace, technology has not yet been allowed to fulfill its promise.

The economic crisis has been exacerbated by a workplace that, to many newer entrants, feels like no one in charge is paying attention to the people who work there. Respondents described Boomer and Gen X leaders who are not sufficiently focused on managing in the workplace where they became so successful. They also spoke of inflexible rules that contribute to an atmosphere which appears nonsensical—sometimes even toxic—to newer employees.

This frustration with the workplace environment may be manifested in data showing that Millennials are more stressed than other generations. A study conducted for the American Psychological Association reported that 39% of Millennials surveyed stated that their level of stress increased in the past year and 52% said it kept them awake at night in the past month. More than any other age group, Millennials reported being diagnosed by a health care provider as having depression (19%) or an anxiety disorder (12%). On a scale of 1–10, with 1 being "little or no stress," and 10 being "a great deal of stress," Millennials scored 5.4 on average, above the national average of 4.9. In addition, 49% of Millennials reported that they did not believe or were not sure that they were doing enough to manage their stress.[146]

Survey responses identified several sources of stress in the workplace. In particular, respondents saw a work environment in which leaders clung to vestiges of an outdated economic model structured on the father as breadwinner and the mother as homemaker. This model, however, has bordered on extinction throughout most of the Millennials' lives.

As families grow increasingly reliant on two-earner households, significant burdens exist on the allocation of available time at home. New York University Professor Kathleen Gerson described the dramatic change that is taking place in family structures: "During the closing decades of the twentieth century, the 'family wage', which once made it possible for most men (though certainly not all) to support nonworking wives, became a quaint relic of an earlier time."[147]

Yet even as the single earner supported by a homemaker has ceased being demographically accurate, another component of the workplace economic model has persisted: the notion of time in the office as a marker of commitment to one's work. Tech-savvy Millennials wonder why flexibility remains a rarity in so many workplaces, when they have all the tools they need to integrate their work, family, and personal responsibilities. Instead they see themselves as too frequently expected to adapt to a rigid face-time culture whose unnecessary persistence is at the heart of extraordinary work-life tensions.

It is this workplace which represents the unfinished revolution of the Boomer generation that changed just about everything else, then stopped short of implementing needed cultural change in the workplace. Rather, they embedded their behaviors as competitive overachievers who, in striving to reach their own goals, ignored the lessons they were teaching their children. As noted previously, Boomers and Gen Xers promoted the concepts of team-work, sharing, trust, flexibility, and fair-play as parents. Yet they too often neglected to integrate these life lessons into their own leadership style at work. And now it is up to their Millennial children to redefine this workplace and create a new legacy for their own sons and daughters.

This is a tough challenge for Millennials who are entering the early stages of their working life at a particularly precarious time. The changes that Millennials are poised to make, however, may actually be helped, not hindered, by a difficult economy where keeping employees engaged and energized at work should be particularly mission-critical.

The data is clear and definitive. Based on simple math, Millennials are the future of every work environment, so keeping them engaged is of the utmost economic importance. Workplace cultures which seek to keep employees engaged are more profitable and suffer far less expensive attrition. The Sloan Center on Aging & Work at Boston College notes that "higher levels of engagement are associated with several positive business outcomes and when employees derive a sense of meaning and fulfillment from their work, they tend to experience positive personal outcomes . . . "[148]

One study estimates that employee disengagement costs the United States economy $370 billion each year in reduced productivity.[149] As author Tamara Erickson wrote: "Organizations that foster and sustain engagement realize major returns on those efforts: improved shareholder value; higher levels of productivity and profitability; and increased organizational stability."[150]

Family Matters

Research on the Millennial generation consistently documents commitment to a life in which family responsibilities are not overshadowed by work. According to data from the PEW Research Center, 52% of Millennials stated that "being a good parent is one of the most important things to them." This compares to 42% of Gen Xers who answered a similar question in 1997, when they were in the same age range.[151]

Another study of undergraduate and graduate students offered important insight into how Millennials view their own economic goals. The survey asked the respondents to rank a series of factors as "essential" or "very important" to their life goals. The results identified the following as ranked in the top four: (1) being financially secure; (2) having a partner/being married; (3) having a job with impact on causes that are important to them; and (4) having children. Critically, one of the choices, "being wealthy" ranked significantly lower, which demonstrates the impact of the economic crisis on this cohort: economic security is a priority, but wealth is not.[152] The concern for financial security becomes clearer when seen through the prism of the impact of student debt, as two-thirds of the undergraduates and three quarters of the graduate respondents stated that they expect to owe money when they graduate.[153]

For workplace leaders, it is also important to understand that the Millennials' work-life concerns start at an early age. A college student who works part-time emphasized this focus:

> Work/life balance is HUGE. I find myself having a hard time separating the two and finding balance so I am continually working at it. I find this in a lot of my other co-workers who are my age.

No Longer A Women's Issue

Women in the workplace have long been the primary advocates for the development of policies that support better work-life integration. But women are no longer alone on the front lines of the work-family flexibility debate. The Boston College Center for Work & Family, whose work includes cutting-edge research on the changing role of fathers, found that: " . . . fathers want to have more time to be with their children and they aspire to do more at home."[154]

Similarly, in the Clark University Poll of Emerging Adults, 60% of the respondents reported that they would sacrifice some career goals to achieve the family life they want. Importantly, the study further noted: "But there is a modern twist to this theme: although traditionally it is mainly women who have sacrificed their career goals for the sake of family life, in our sample young men were just as likely as young women to have this expectation."[155]

Shared Millennial values can be seen in numerous surveys conducted over the past several years including the emergence of flexibility as a gender neutral issue. One survey reported that, nearly three-quarters of those responding reported that they would give up 15% of their salary for greater balance between work and other areas in their lives.[156] A Bentley University survey of Millennials reported that 70% of the respondents said having the ability to set their own hours is somewhat or very important; 60% reported similarly on the ability to work from home.[157]

This focus on work-life may prove advantageous to their health. For example, the Families and Work Institute reported that dual-centric employees (those who give equal priority to work and family) and family-centric employees (those who place a higher priority on family than work) "exhibit significantly better mental health, greater satisfaction with their lives, and higher levels of job satisfaction than employees who are work-centric." They are also less likely to experience burnout and stress-related illnesses that take a toll on companies and society in terms of related costs of addressing these issues.[158]

An international employer's study of its global workers from 158 countries found that 71% of Millennial respondents (compared to 63% of non-Millennial respondents) believe that their work demands interfered with their personal lives. Furthermore, 64% of Millennial respondents claimed they would like to occasionally work from home.[159] The study also found that even as finding a better work-life balance is important to Millennials worldwide, "the issue is particularly important for Millennials in the more developed economies of North America and Europe and in the East region, where work/life balance has a stronger bearing on turnover, commitment and job satisfaction than in other parts of the world."[160]

Too often, however, even when a flexible work policy exists, supervisors may send mixed signals which discourages the use of an available option. In a survey of workers asking whether their team leader or supervisor supported the use of flexible work arrangements, Millennials were the least likely of all age groups to believe that their supervisors supported the use of such options "to a great extent".[161]

Significantly, both male and female respondents to the author's survey reported having concerns about work-family integration even *before* they have children. Nearly 99% of the respondents agreed that work-life balance is important or somewhat important to them. This was true of men (95%) and women (99%), as well as parents and non-parents alike (both at 99%). Nearly 75% of the respondents reported that they would definitely or probably change their job for more family time. A similar percentage indicated that they would not give up family time for more compensation or opportunities at work. When this data was analyzed by gender, a majority of both men (61%) and women (75%) agreed they would be unwilling to give up family time for increased compensation or opportunities at work. Here, too, this strong response came from both parents (90%) and non-parents (71%).

Male respondents demonstrated their strong interest in ensuring that their jobs do not negatively impact their parental role. For example, a male respondent in the public relations field anticipated how his current work schedule would change once he became a father:

> *My job necessitates long hours and often I work far longer than I would prefer, however I volunteer myself to do so. I've worked the same job for two years and if I had more of an issue with the work/ life balance, I would have left long ago. That said, as a 24-year-old single male I do not have much responsibility outside of work, and I could very much envision my desire for more free/family time shifting in later years.*

A few respondents were experiencing a life stage that older Boomers in particular are now experiencing en masse: parents who need care.

Work-family issues invariably will extend beyond the needs of a spouse and children.[162]

A respondent spoke of her caretaker role and the importance of a responsive workplace culture:

> *My workplace takes the work-life balance very seriously. There are many different programs aimed at keeping that balance and keeping employees happy. When it comes to family issues (personal experience—mother has a terminal condition), I have been told to spend time focusing on my family. Taking time off to take care of my mother has never been an issue.*

The Specter of Stigma

Notwithstanding what may be a mutual commitment to sharing family responsibilities, the workplace can still be unforgiving to people who venture out of their expected roles. As Professor Gerson wrote: "When it comes to their aspirations, women and men share many hopes and dreams. But fears that time-demanding workplaces, unreliable partners, and a dearth of caretaking supports will place these ideals out of reach propel them down different paths."[163]

As described earlier, Millennials' commitment to sufficient time for family and personal well-being impacts how other generations perceive—or, rather, misperceive—the Millennials' work ethic. Noted one respondent who worked part-time:

> *If I would make comments about how much I'm working, [older] people would say that younger people don't work as hard, and that when they were young they worked harder . . . I think it's more of a value shift towards work-life balance than that the younger generation isn't working as hard.*

Although respondents seemed confident that their generation is making better life choices, some expressed worry that their career path will be negatively impacted by rejecting the road traveled by senior generations. A respondent in the legal profession stated:

> *I think older generations don't realize the importance of having time outside of work for yourself or your family as much as younger generations do. So I think they would assume that I am less motivated than they are.*

These work-life decisions cause deep internal conflict among young people in the workforce. Each choice looms as a potential conflict between career success and career stigma. For men and women, the risks can feel daunting. For example, even where workplaces provide written policies with respect to caregiving leave and flexible hours, supervisors may undermine the written policy. Men who seek paternity leaves may be quietly told that using the benefit may result in less challenging assignments and slower advancement. The professional who is hailed as a great dad when he coaches his kid's soccer team somehow morphs into an uncommitted employee if he seeks reduced hours or a more flexible schedule to pick-up his children from day care.

For women, the challenges are pervasive and long-standing. Women have borne the brunt of the work-family conflict for decades, with negative impacts on their careers. Data abounds showing that women lag behind men in achieving leadership roles and are not paid equitably for comparable jobs.[164] And similar to the mixed messages of paternity leave policies, even where workplaces offer flexible work arrangements, utilization rates demonstrate that a stigma often attaches to the use of those policies.[165]

Young women also face an added burden when their commitment to family time is viewed by senior women as a rejection of the choices they made earlier in their own careers. Female respondents described feeling negatively judged by those who sacrificed to succeed. They acknowledged the price their predecessors paid, but also saw sacrifices they do not want to make for themselves:

> *I do feel like a lot of older people that I have worked with expect a large commitment to work, when in my life, my commitment lies*

with my family, and work is a (distant) second. This is especially evident when I've worked under women who don't have children. I tell my friends a lot that our generation got screwed by woman's lib! I'm glad I have the opportunity to "do anything", but then you are expected to do all of these things. A lot of the original feminists are now woman in their 50s and 60s, in positions of power over a lot of us "gen y-ers", looking down on us because we don't devote every second to our career, or want to have families before we're forty, or at all. I've had many 50-somethings think I was crazy for only working part time, including my mother-in-law who never worked when her kids were small. It's like they can't believe you would want to do what they feel like they didn't have a choice about.

Respondents also felt stymied by employers who failed to appreciate the retention benefits of a workplace that facilitated work-life integration. One respondent described her experience in an unsupportive government environment:

After my son was born, my employer at the time (DA's office) eliminated previously available part-time positions for working mothers of young children. After returning to work full-time for several months and learning that I would not be able to scale back my hours, I resigned. I spent a few months at home and then found a part-time federal clerkship which currently provides me with a wonderful balance between time at home and legal work (20 hours/week). Given the choice between full-time (really more than full-time given the stress/time demands of preparing for a full trial load) and staying home, I did/will stay home, but I much prefer to remain engaged in my profession and am glad to have found a way to make that happen.

Another described her decision to leave based on workplace inflexibility:

I left my previous employer solely because of the location of their offices. I would have worked for them for my entire life, but they couldn't accommodate professional growth while working remotely (as opposed to in their offices).

The responses clearly demonstrated that Millennials significantly value work-life flexibility and its availability leads to loyalty and engagement. A respondent highlighted the retention benefits and resulting job loyalty that ensues when flexibility is available:

The opportunity to work part-time or with a modified schedule has created enormous job loyalty for me and other young mothers I know.

Another respondent similarly stressed her own priorities:

I think our work ethic is different . . . again, it's about work-life balance. I'm not going to volunteer for overtime or special projects that take extra time away from my kids . . . but while I'm at work I am very motivated and feel like I "do more" than a lot of my older co- workers. So just because I don't want to work a ton extra or stay late doesn't mean I'm not a good worker . . . I just have a life outside of work that is more important than getting ahead in my career.

Some respondents identified the time before they start a family as an opportunity to focus on developing their career, but even these responses indicated that they viewed the intensity of this commitment as a temporary "all-in". One respondent saw this temporary period as a time to launch one's career, and seemed undaunted by possibly having to change jobs multiple times to find the correct fit in the future:

I'm currently unmarried with no children and willing to sacrifice quite a bit now to enhance my career—but once I'm out of my twenties and have put in the time to launch my career, I expect to have balance between work, personal, and family life. For my generation, balance like that isn't a hope, it's an expectation. I think we know that you don't have to stay at one job for 50+ years to be successful, and so are not as tied to obscene-time sacrifices to keep a position, and all-around society is more health/wellness focused with a lot of attention paid to finding balance in all areas of one's life.

The Public Discomfort with Personal Time

As difficult as it is to find workplaces with policies that help employees better manage their work and family responsibilities, finding a workplace sensitive to personal time is even more difficult. It is far less socially acceptable to take time away from work to address personal needs.

Yet for Millennials, staying healthy and maintaining friendships matters and they expect to have time in their life for both. And research demonstrates that they are right to do so. Studies show that when employees experience high levels of emotional exhaustion in their organizations, their job performance suffers. Worker well-being has positive consequences for the workplace as well as the worker.[166]

Consistent with this other data, respondents confirmed that maintaining friendships, exercising, and otherwise enjoying life are important and should not be sacrificed to work. The majority of the respondents were not at all, or only somewhat, satisfied with the time they spent at work compared to the time they had available for themselves; only approximately one-third of the respondents felt satisfied with the amount of personal time they had available. More than 40% reported that they would be unwilling to give up personal time for more compensation or opportunities at work.

For many, this desire for more personal time was enough to consider switching jobs, with 62% reporting that they would definitely or probably switch jobs to increase their personal time. This data reflected some gender variation which may itself reflect a concern about stigma: 31% of the men said they would not give up personal time for more compensation or opportunities, compared to 42% of the women.

A respondent who described herself as highly motivated stated:

I think that working 40 hours a week is too much and does not leave enough hours in the day for personal time, which is very important to me. I would be willing to take a pay cut and work only 32 hours/week.

Another similarly noted:

> *I would take less compensation for more personal and family time if that was an option to me.*

Respondents spoke unabashedly of the connection between their personal time and their mental well-being. For example, a college student linked time for friends and family with his emotional health:

> *There has to be a balance of time to spend on school, family, and friends. They are all crucial in my life. My family is more important than all, but I feel a balance of all is important for my sanity.*

When a Millennial is asked to work late, the request may be met with some resistance if the reason for staying late is viewed as unnecessary and interferes with other plans. A respondent offered insight into the tensions that arise when Millennials seek to keep a personal commitment:

> *[M]y generation expects to work hard, but be able to define our own workload and set limits on what type/volume of work we are and are not willing to do. I've heard [criticism] mostly in the context of being asked to work late by the older generation and having a response from the younger generation that, for example, it will inter-fere with a yoga class or dinner plans. It is not well received by the older generation. . . .*
>
> *I believe the simple explanation is that Gen Y grew up hearing that we can do anything we want to do and to stand up for ourselves, so when someone 'impedes' our ability to do what we want to do, we resist and speak up.*

The respondents so consistently spoke of living life fully across multiple dimensions that it is hard to imagine they will not be successful:

> *I believe work is important . . . However, it is not my life. I love spending time outside; surfing, swimming, enjoying the beach, my*

family and my friends. I want to laugh, smile and enjoy my day. Work can do that, but it isn't my entire world. As my dad told me, Everything in Moderation. For me, that goes not only for work, but for play. You can work hard and play hard, but do not have to give up one for the other.

The Currency of Time

Millennials are a generation born to workaholics whose pace can be exhausting not only to those who live it, but to those who are watching. Senior generations frequently hear from Millennials the statement: "I don't want your life." The statement is not meant to be insulting, but it is grounded in keen observation and personal experience. One respondent noted:

After working 14 hour days for a year, I finally left my upscale job for a more stable job that allowed me more personal time. It was one of the best decisions I've made. I regret all of the times I had to cancel with people and will never get those times back. The stress was also very unhealthy in that particular job, so leaving that has been a huge weight lifted. I have less money, but I've never been happier!

The bottom line is that Millennials see a different bottom line for themselves. Their currency is time. They seem acutely aware of life's trade-offs, and the one resource they can never have back is the one most precious—time.

One aspect of valuing time is being able to reasonably make plans and be able to participate in the lifecycle events of friend and family, as this respondent stated:

I have a GREAT paying job for a 25 year old. But I am away from home for a solid 6 months. When I'm at work, I don't get to go home at night, I don't get weekends off, and I don't even get to call home every night. I miss holidays and birthdays. I'm looking to take a $50k pay cut to work longer hours, but be able to be home most evenings and have holidays with my family.

Another respondent's comments regarding time concerns revealed how others might view the potentially inherent contradiction in her statement:

There is no amount of money that would take me away from proper work/life balance. That is not to say that I am unwilling to work long hours.

This simple statement sets up the core conflict regarding time in the workplace. Respondents frequently expressed that even though they guard their time, they are willing to do what is needed. To them, senior generations seem to focus more on the way in which Millennials appear to protect their time.

A respondent noted:

[Older generations] discourage vacations and working anything less than full-time, which usually includes 10 hour days. Additionally, they believe you should do anything and everything for your job, while sacrificing your personal life. If you don't have these same values, they label you as lazy, even when you are not.

Some respondents expressed a willingness to work hard before their life circumstances impose other commitments on their time, but even those comments placed boundaries to protect their personal time. For example:

I run a start-up company. So finding that balance between my personal and professional life is something I always strive for. I don't mind working long hours right now while I'm single and without a family. But I would like to make more time for traveling. Personally, I think making "Me Time" is essential to your overall happiness.

Millennials are bringing a new dimension to the issue of workplace flexibility. For decades, discussions about flexibility focused primarily on so-called "work-family balance". But if this rigid interpretation is tied to a presumption that users of flexibility have children, what does it mean for a generation who is marrying and having children later in life than predecessor generations? And what about those who may not choose to have children, but nonetheless value time for other interests and responsibilities?

Some childless respondents stated that they felt their personal needs were seen as secondary compared to co-workers with children. They expressed frustration that more is expected of them because they do not have children, as this respondent noted:

> *I think that people with children have no respect for the personal time of people without children. I was once told I should work the day after Thanksgiving because I 'have no family.' I have parents, grandparents, and a husband—but because I have no kids my personal/family time didn't matter.*

Clearly, Millennials are bringing an expansive perspective to the concept of work-life integration that offers an opportunity to create a healthier work environment for all.

Work-Life Integration in a Troubled Economy

The contrast between the messages Millennials received while growing up regarding their opportunities for success and the challenges caused by the economic crisis served as a recurring theme in the survey responses. Many saw the economy as having at least a temporary impact on the way Millennials approach their job prospects.

For Boomers and Gen Xers who may be hopeful that the economy will force Millennials to make permanent changes in their expectations, survey responses supported other data demonstrating that short-term compromises are unlikely to be part of a long-term strategy. As noted in one research paper: "During times of recession, Millennials lower their expectations regarding the work-life balance and social atmosphere. However, their expectations regarding job content, training, career development and financial rewards remain high, suggesting that these expectations are largely embedded within the generation."[167]

One study found that 58% of Millennials surveyed said they were willing to make compromises to secure a job during the economic downturn.[168]

As the study noted, however: "The risk for employers is that as economic conditions improve, the compromises many millennials were forced to make will no longer seem acceptable as opportunities arise elsewhere and many will move on as soon as they can."[169]

Many respondents were keenly aware that the economic crisis was significantly impacting their immediate hopes for sufficient time and flexibility to address their family's needs.

> *Work/life balance doesn't exist in this economy. Face time has taken on a new importance. In addition, it is clearly communicated that men and women who take time off for family will be greatly hampered in their advancement.*

Even in a difficult economic climate, however, respondents who worked in demanding (some might say unforgiving) professions emphasized that their family and friends will not take a permanent back seat to their work. For example, one young lawyer stated:

> *There is a perception that senior attorneys worked 16-hour days for years, so younger attorneys are expected to do the same. I am not willing to do that. . . . Work is important, but so are family, friends, and social activities.*

Drawing Lines, Respecting Boundaries

Respondents continually stated their view: work has boundaries. Many seemed dramatically impacted by the way in which Boomers and Gen Xers threw themselves into work in a manner that seemed to lack limitations. A college student observed:

> *I watched both of my parents give up all aspects of their personal lives to get ahead in their careers, and I have come to the conclusion that money just isn't worth that sacrifice.*

Another respondent spoke of avoiding the mistakes other generations made, for example:

> . . . *Previous generations were told that if they just buckle down and toil at the same job for 30 years, there is a pot of gold at the end of the rainbow. Gen Y'ers are more wary of this particular fantasy and more motivated to look for personal fulfillment.*

These observations solidified the decision to forge a different path and seek a more well-rounded life, as this respondent described:

> *We want to enjoy life now rather than making sacrifices so we can enjoy it later. . . . That type of sacrifice didn't pay off for my parents and many of their peers because of the ways in which companies have changed their practices in recent years. My generation has watched our parents sacrifice only to be told they will not have retirement benefits, good health care, or an early retirement. For me, that makes it more important to enjoy life now—there's no guarantee that all that sacrifice will pay off.*

Respondents generally expressed a willingness to devote extra time if they felt passion about their work, but still drew boundaries, as this graduate student who worked part-time noted:

> *To me, it depends on the job. As to my current job, I would rather not give them more of my time. But I also have an internship about which I am passionate, and I am willing to give them more time, even though I don't get compensated for that time, because I enjoy that work more and am passionate about it. For a really good job, I might be willing to give up more personal/family time than a not-so-good job.*
>
> *In my opinion, Gen Y is not willing to compromise. If they love the work they do, they may be more willing to go the extra mile on some projects. But they want it all, and they'd rather have more family time than be working like a crazy person.*

Respondents also questioned how they will reconcile their expectations in an environment that may not be paying attention to their concerns. For example:

> *In previous jobs, work-life balance is very important. That also includes social opportunities through work, which can help soften the blow of long and hard working hours. Compared to my mother's experience, which I feel was a "I can have everything; I can do everything; have a career, have a family . . . " I think many of my friends and I feel like "I can have everything, but maybe or maybe not at the same time" and in addition, we are keen on having a LIFE outside of work, not letting work be the only thing that defines us. We are a very demanding generation—we want the best, but we don't want to compromise lifestyle. It's a very tough battle. And I'm not sure that the current workplace can really offer that, so it might lead to dissatisfaction in a lot of people. I've already seen that happen with friends, and we're only 25! Running back to school because we are completely unprepared for the "real world"!*

Laying the Groundwork, Setting an Example

Many respondents described investing time in developing a career path that will provide needed flexibility when they have children. Some have even helped create an environment conducive for others, as this respondent stated:

> *I am currently a doctoral candidate, and a big part of why I have gone through the hard work of 1) getting this degree and 2) helping to start a non-profit, is so that I have more control over my own work/ life balance. Both myself and my husband are in very high impact jobs, but are in small organizations with a fair amount of flexibility, or at the very least, autonomy. So for us, a work/life balance is very important, and part of it is working a lot now so that we'll be financially/flexibly secure when we're ready to have children. I already have built a job that gives me the flexibility to take time when I need it and create my*

own workload. That often means I put in a lot of long hours, but I control my work and I love what I do. I also can set hours that work for me, identify work locations that are appealing, and work to create a space that respects the lives of all of our employees so that everyone has the same opportunities as the Directors here. I think it's important that people get paid a wage that enables them the financial stability to spend time with their family. I also think that a workplace should be a community that respects people's time, abilities and talents as much as the bottom line.

Several described how they were motivated to choose their professions by the opportunity for work-family integration. For example:

Teaching high school science, at an independent school, with summers off, gives me lots of family time, which is why this is the career of choice (though not what I originally planned and went to school for).

As the survey responses demonstrated, Millennials have learned the lesson well: if they do not change the workplace, they will forever be relegated to stealing moments with their own family. They reject the concept that work must be all encompassing and that their children will be better off for it. Noted one post-graduate student:

I saw my parents work hard, and I plan to work hard. And like my parents, I want better for my children than what I had, and that means my children will have quality time with their parents.

The Opportunity That Should Come From Crisis

If anything positive emerges from the prolonged impacts of the economic crisis, it should be a recognition that it is time to redesign the workplace. Smart leadership sees crisis as an opportunity for creativity. Leaders grappling with the continuing impacts of a weak economy can benefit by experimenting with ways to reduce expenses for the organization and its employees. One significant way to accomplish this is through flexible work arrangements. Respondents did not miss this point:

> *You would think that the recession would cause companies and firms to be open to creative ways to reduce expenses by encouraging flexible work schedules, office sharing, work sharing, more part-time programs, but they are not. They continue to address the problem in the "traditional sense" by trying to fix the problem with money alone. It doesn't work.*

The Bottom Line

Even as respondents consistently expressed their expectation that they will blend work, family and personal responsibilities and interests, they also recognized that these priorities come with trade-offs, particularly with respect to money. The majority made clear that they are unwilling to pay the price of a career that both demands constant sacrifice and expects the deferral of happiness until retirement.

One respondent described the impact of a change of jobs that provided for a saner blend of work and family responsibilities and a job with greater meaning:

> *I DID change my job to have more time. I was working 80+ hours a week ... I loved my job but hated what it was doing to my life. Traveling so much I went to amazing countries but only saw the airport and a board room, making money but no time to spend it, feeling I was contributing nothing to society, single at 27 because I had no time to date etc. . . . so I quit my job, became a preschool teacher and am now back in school getting my Masters in teaching. I no longer have to worry about choosing a career or my family/future kids, I get to see my friends, have personal time to spend how I choose and get to travel and really enjoy myself ... I couldn't be happier. I contribute to society which feels good. Granted I make much less now, but I think I got the best deal of all!*

For Millennials, it is precisely this steadfast commitment to their own clearly defined priorities that may result in a complete redesign of where, when, and how work is conducted.

PART THREE

Chapter 13

Adapting the Workplace to Develop Tomorrow's Leaders

Many Millennials are straddling two economic worlds as they leave the more comfortable environment of home and begin their journey on the road to economic independence. It is a journey complicated by the way they have internalized those earlier messages to expect opportunities and success, as compared to the starker realties they must confront in a depressed economy.

Within the confines of this new economic reality, Millennials are struggling to understand how to adjust their life goals and maintain high expectations for their future. Many do so while remaining close to their parents and grateful for a safety net. But challenges arise as a result of their upbringing that warrant focused attention from Millennials and the workplace. For example, on their road to independence, Millennials will need to be better equipped to manage their own finances.[170] Moreover, workplace leaders will need to invest their time and devote resources to training and developing their future talent pool.

Building Resilience; Retaining Optimism

The workplace is faced with welcoming a generation that, accustomed to having a voice in decisions that impact their lives, brings a different view of hierarchy and an expectation that their opinions matter. As will be discussed, workplaces that open lines of communication and develop more transparent practices will be well-situated for developing their future leaders.

Millennials need support from senior generations who understand the challenges they face as they enter the workforce. Author Jenny Blake highlighted the upheaval that can follow graduation: "There is no manual for the real world. In high school and college we have teachers, guidance counselors, and course requirements. But the minute we graduate it seems we are immediately expected to understand where to go, what to do, and how to get wherever we're going next—even when we have no clue where 'next' is. For the first time in many of our lives, we feel paralyzed without a defined road map—or without any clue how to create one."[171]

Senior generations can best help Millennials adapt to the workplace by reframing their own perspective. For example, they can refrain from judging the Millennials because they ask too many questions ("they don't know how to do an assignment without hand-holding") or request too much feedback ("they always want to hear how they are doing").

Instead, they should understand that what they are likely seeing are the manifestations of a protected upbringing. Younger employees may simply be looking for the reassurances they grew accustomed to as they begin to venture into unknown territory at work, seek out stretch assignments, and otherwise anticipate the workplace version of a report card through direct feedback.

Notwithstanding the difficult economic climate they have been facing, Millennials still have hopes and expectations for success at work. To retain that self-confidence, however, Millennials will require a sufficient reservoir of resilience to face and overcome the challenges that inevitably exist in any job. And they will best meet those challenges in a workplace committed to talent management.

Seeing past "entitlement" to appreciate self-confidence

The elimination of the label of "entitlement" as a defining quality of Millennials would have a powerful impact on how the generations relate to one another in the future. Millennials have been raised to believe in themselves and, in doing so, exhibit a resolute strength. This strength is not entitlement. Millennials seem fundamentally programmed to believe in their future success, which is fortunate, since the economy serves as a sobering backdrop to their positive expectations. As Professor Arnett reported in his research: "Despite the difficulties that come along with managing their own lives, most emerging adults look forward to a future they believe is filled with promise."[172]

This optimism guides their choices in significant ways. Millennials already have an innate sense of what they need to have a fulfilling life, and will continue to pursue that, as this respondent indicated:

> *It can be seen as a sense of entitlement or just that we are less willing to settle.*

This optimism is also likely to get them through a perilous economy. As one survey reported: "The global financial economic downturn has done little to dent the optimism of the millennial generation. The majority (67%) expect to be better off than their parents' generation and 32% expect to be considerably better off."[173]

Once Boomers and Gen Xers learn to recognize the Millennials' self-confidence as a positive building block of future leadership, they should feel more comfortable investing time and resources in developing their next generation of leaders, rather than focusing on a misperception of arrogant or disrespectful behaviors.

Developing Navigational Skills

A challenge that arises from having grown up with a large safety net is learning how to thrive in an environment that encourages risk-taking through reach assignments and problem-solving without clear direction. There is, after all, a difference between being pushed by parents along the path to success, and knowing what to do when that path must be traveled alone.

Workplace navigation skills are critical to career success and advancement, but it should not be assumed that all young workers arrive adept at steering their way forward. The politics of work can be treacherous. Determining who the people are who can help one's career and who should be avoided is as important as learning the substance of the job.

But these may not necessarily be skills that Millennials have had to learn, at least in any depth. If one's childhood environment was open, welcoming, and supportive, adapting to a "sink or swim" atmosphere requires skills that may not yet be fully developed.

The challenge for senior leaders at work is to decide how much time and effort they are willing to invest in helping to integrate new employees. Employers can make a tremendous difference by creating a comprehensive employee integration process.

This can begin with extended orientation and training programs that are integrated into the culture of the workplace and offer new employees an opportunity to better understand the work environment and the employer's goals and objectives. Topics can cover a range of issues, from the substantive job requirements to more strategic career support. Employers who make a meaningful investment in training can use it as an effective recruitment tool as well. Some businesses provide details on their websites about the extensive training that new employees can receive.

Organizations should consider coaching opportunities to help Millennials adjust to uncertainty in the workplace and to learn how to seek difficult assignments and otherwise take risks. A workplace which has support mechanisms in place to help Millennials learn from their negative experiences is more likely to retain skilled employees than a workplace which takes a hands-off approach.

Survey respondents understood that, by focusing on a stereotypical notion of its generation as entitled, senior generations can more easily avoid providing the support Millennials need as they try to navigate today's complex workplace. As one respondent stated:

> I don't think generalizations such as [entitled] are helpful in describing an entire generation or solving the problems that some people in my age-range face becoming accustomed to the workplace.

Repeatedly, respondents made clear that they valued transparency and that they wanted to work in a place where the rules were clear and applied equally. This would be consistent with a generation raised in a structured environment with scheduled activities. The politics of a workplace can seem particularly obscure to someone used to clear instructions and expectations. One respondent offered a common example of how Millennials can feel thwarted by workplaces that are not transparent:

> *It is always a challenge because I have seen people being offered more money or more flexibility when they try to leave an organization—but, why weren't they given that offer before? It makes people feel less valued when they feel they have to leave or threaten to leave to get what they want.*

A strategic process to provide systematic and regular feedback will result in a more effective and loyal workforce. Such a process will help all generations address Millennials' need for clearer instructions and less ambiguity, and will help Boomers and Gen Xers move beyond a style of limited transparency.

Workplace leaders sacrifice employee satisfaction and motivation by neglecting to respond to what their Millennial employees value. For example, working in teams can make a positive difference as workplace experts regularly note that group projects and team-building activities build upon the tendency of Millennials to be more social and group-focused.[174] Organizations which understand and respond to Millennials' values will benefit as they obtain optimal performance from their employees.

Replacing Clout with Mutual Respect

In a survey conducted between 2000 and 2005, the Center for Creative Leadership identified the concept of clout as the source of most intergenerational conflict: " . . . generational conflict and comments about unacceptable behavior on the part of another generation often stem from a particular group's notion that it gets to make the rules and that the other group has to follow these rules. . . . Thus the generation gap enters the workplace, getting blamed for conflicts that really have nothing to do with fundamental generational differences . . . and everything to do with the natural desire of older people to maintain their clout and the desire of younger people to increase their clout."[175]

Communication skills have long been associated with strong management and an effective work environment. It is, therefore, somewhat ironic that Millennials can be criticized for asking too many questions and even seen as disrespectful for doing so. Getting past this reaction, however, is critical to bridging generational differences at work.

A free and open exchange of ideas and questions invariably leads to a better result. As reported in the Center for Creative Leadership's study: "There is an almost endless amount of research demonstrating that better decisions (of all types) are made when people feel free to ask questions." [176] Accordingly, the senior leader who is able to respond to a question with acceptance and a willingness to provide a clear response will help build much stronger ties to younger workers.

Respondents frequently spoke of their desire to be respected in the workplace. Whether they felt they received that respect impacted the enthusiasm they brought to their job, as this response demonstrated:

> *If I feel like I'm respected and valued, I'll do more. But if not, then I will do what is required and don't want to do more.*

A respondent optimistically spoke of her continued efforts to make positive changes, notwithstanding the unsolicited cautionary advice others offer:

> *Older generation male colleagues accept the system as poor and encourage that I not try to change the system (losing battle). At the same time, they remind me that I have been hired because I am young and dynamic and creative, and am there to propose improvements. Over the past year I have watched these same naysayers lose footing in the organization with a new, more dynamic one put in place.*

The Value of Inefficiency

Millennials may occasionally need to distinguish between efficiency and an opportunity to build relationships at work. Although many respondents perceived that they lost productivity due to the inefficient communication styles of older colleagues, they can turn this to their advantage by capitalizing on the opportunities that arise from direct communications.

The convenience of technology can make it easy to miss the relationships that are built as an outgrowth of more personal, albeit slower, communication alternatives. This comment from a respondent in the public relations field demonstrates this point:

> *My managers often come up to me during the day and begin random conversations about clients. These conversations are not organized and end up wasting my time. I recommended that if you have a quick question, send an email or an IM and I will understand the task and get the work done. I don't need a half hour conversation in order to complete my tasks at hand.*

That lost half-hour may, to the contrary, be the basis for a relationship that can prove helpful when this Millennial is looking for advice from a senior colleague or a connection to another individual that might assist career advancement. Some perceived inefficiencies are not inefficient at all, but rather a way of communicating with and getting to know co-workers.

This point was not lost on some respondents who saw how that extra time can create a new loyal colleague. For example:

> *I share an office space with a woman in her 70s, and fairly frequently spend time setting up files on her computer, reformatting her documents, etc. I don't really mind, but this isn't part of my job description and does take time away from my central duties. On the other hand, helping her with basic tech issues has helped in developing a good working relationship.*

Building Relationships Through Expertise

There is significant opportunity in being viewed, at a young age, as an expert in an area of importance to the office. The positive side of being so proficient in an area critical to workplace effectiveness is learning to seize on the opportunities it provides to develop relationships and add value. Several respondents, for example, wisely saw the collateral benefits that derive from serving as the office technology guru. For example, a respondent noted:

> I work at a high-tech PR agency, so it is a requirement to have an understanding of technology. However, my supervisors are not as familiar with new media, so I find myself relaying what I have learned to them. For once, they are learning from younger generations.

Particularly in a troubled economy, such value can add to one's own sense of economic stability, as one marketing professional noted:

> Knowledge is power in the work place. So if I know how to use a particular program or operate the computer, the more job security I have.

Similar wisdom was expressed by another respondent in the design field:

> I have found that working to teach others new technology is a great way to work. While it may take more time, it will be more helpful in the future. Sometimes, people are unwilling to learn new technology until they see why they should learn it ('Why do I need to know this? X works just as well.') I think the first step is showing why there is a need and then showing how to use new tech to meet those needs in a better way.

A Millennial lawyer revealed a dual role as tutor and cheerleader:

> It's imperative to show the benefit of the technology to the non-savvy person before they will try it on their own. It's also crucial

to be able to answer questions. I see a lot of people becoming frustrated because a certain 'new technology' does not work for them. In most situations, I have accepted the fact that I will hit many road bumps when learning new technology. It seems that when people from older generations hit road bumps, they revert back to the 'old way' of doing things. Don't give up earlier generations!

Responding to Technology Barriers

The data demonstrating that IT restrictions in the workplace are widely ignored poses daunting challenges for employers. There may be many reasons why a workplace would want to limit the use of technology. Some of those reasons may be to protect intellectual property or because of a fear that employees will be tempted to stray from their assigned work. If the reasons are either not clear or seem illogical, then noncompliance is a likely outcome. Communication, therefore, is critical. An Accenture survey noted: "The key to finding the right balance is education focused on the business imperatives behind technology restrictions, and communicated in ways that appeal to Millennials."[177]

Technology provides tremendous opportunities to improve written work products. Tools that promote efficiency by lessening the likelihood of errors should also be embraced—and taught to all generations. As the respondents noted, Millennials may already be reliant on some of these tools, so their accessibility at work can be important to the quality of the work product.

Workplaces should also pay greater attention to the dynamics that occur around technology issues. Power struggles emerge in a variety of ways. As technology becomes increasingly ubiquitous, the frequency of technological changes can be overwhelming, leaving less skilled workers feeling vulnerable. Particularly for more senior workers, the fear of becoming obsolete can lead to counter-productive behaviors. Perceived power imbalances can result in behaviors that undermine efficiency, productivity, and morale, warranting prompt intervention by workplace leaders.

Organizations that ignore suggestions offered by younger employees about ways to use technology to take advantage of marketing trends and opportunities do so at their peril. Millennials have a tremendous vantage point, and their ideas can provide an important perspective that would otherwise be missed by senior workers less facile with social media's role in marketing and branding.

Similarly, workplaces should establish procedures to encourage employees to share ideas and suggestions. Such steps can include the development of a forum to discuss the pros and cons of ideas presented, appointment of a task force to further investigate suggested technological improvements, or other programs that demonstrate attention to and an interest in new ideas. By being proactive, the organization sends a strong signal to its employees that new ways of solving problems are always welcome.

People of all generations who offer suggestions are invested in the organization. Accordingly, all ideas should be encouraged. Having been encouraged to speak up throughout their lives, Millennials expect their ideas will be taken seriously when they speak up at work. This does not mean that every recommendation warrants implementation. It does, however, warrant a response. Failure to do so can result in lost opportunities to implement improvements and harm morale.

By bridging the technology divide, workplaces can provide an opportunity for Millennials to shine and for senior workers to learn and grow. Millennials may be uniquely situated to translate technological complexities and to help demonstrate the ways that pushing past discomfort can result in greater ease and efficiency.

Assessing Skills, Recognizing Value, and Reverse Mentoring

By teaching more senior workers needed skills, Millennials are developing important relationships through their role as reverse mentors. This role can however, prove burdensome if unrecognized. When workplaces do not monitor the extra time spent by Millennials in undertaking additional tech support responsibilities, the result can be unfinished assignments and increased attrition.

The older generations' discomfort with technology, over-reliance on the technical support of younger workers, and, in some cases, outright refusal to incorporate available efficiencies into workplace interactions can drive Millennials to distraction (literally). Survey responses offer a number of important lessons for implementing effective strategies that can facilitate stronger intergenerational communications and more effective use of technology.

To begin the process of traversing the technology divide, employers should assess the capacities of both senior and junior workers, and identify functional areas where the divide is impeding efficiency. For example, who has the expertise that can best improve workplace communications? Who needs to be taught and who should be asked to do the teaching? The expectation that youth is always correlated with knowledge of the latest technology creates false expectations among more senior workers.

In this assessment, it is also necessary to analyze how each proposed fix to identified technology gaps impacts the responsibilities of all employees. Every profession has its own challenges and impediments to the effective use of technology. Even those professions that think of themselves as proficient may be missing opportunities or, in some instances, may not be requiring enough of their employees to understand how to optimally use the technology available to them. By understanding its own specific challenges, each workplace can then develop a plan to implement short- and long-term measures to bridge the technology gap.

For Millennials, often impatient with the pace of change at their workplace, it is important that the assessment be transparent and provide information that explains any constraints on progress. For example, does the workplace have limited financial resources which are impacting the purchase of newer technology and training programs? Are fellow workers uncomfortable with and resistant to learning new technologies? If the latter, are there opportunities for enterprising Millennials to make useful suggestions and assist with a more constructive role in implementing change?

Workplaces should consider implementing ways to provide Millennials with some form of internal credit for their role as technology teacher. The informal role of tutor more likely interferes with or otherwise unfairly impacts an employee's ability to do the job for which he or she was hired—and for which he or she is being paid. The assumption that younger workers should be available throughout the day to teach their less proficient colleagues imposes an unfair burden on these employees and impedes work-place productivity.

If technology tutoring is more than an incidental part of an employee's day, then greater structure needs to be created around the role. For example, personalized IT instruction could formally be included in job descriptions and be properly compensated or otherwise recognized. Alternatively, employers could dedicate resources to retain professional IT support to train workers and to be available to answer questions, lessening the burden on those who are informally filling that role.

In addition, reverse mentoring programs can be implemented and structured to help Millennials develop stronger relationships with the more senior colleagues they mentor. An effective reverse mentoring program will recognize Millennials for their specific contributions and benefit from the efficiencies they can help create. As one large employer reports about the positive impacts of its reverse mentoring program: "Reverse mentoring provides corporate leaders with a valuable generational perspective on topics not typically engaged at that level in an organizational hierarchy.

The opportunities for learning and open discussion that reverse mentoring provides are fluid and countless. The new relationships formed by mentors and mentees can be inspiring and genuine. Perhaps the most important gift of reverse mentoring, regardless of the specific business issues the strategy can be used to address, is the affirmation in all sectors of a company and across generations that the next big idea can come from anywhere."[178]

The Dual Benefits of Feedback and Transparency

If the hallmark of a healthy work environment is open and frequent communication, perhaps the "everyone gets a trophy" stereotype can be replaced by systems which help senior generations become more adept at providing feedback to young workers eager to improve their skills. The Millennials' desire for ongoing feedback could have a positive impact on the workplace if it results in the adoption of a comprehensive performance appraisal process that includes regular feedback on assignments.

Direct workplace benefits result from leaders who demonstrate an interest in their employees. People are more engaged at work when they feel that their supervisors care about their professional development, as this respondent noted:

> *The best work experience I had was with a non-profit that had an Executive Director who promoted professional development and teamwork. For example, performance reviews included self-assessments with questions like 'where do you see yourself in 1 year, 3 years, and 5 years?' and 'what skills do you wish you could develop?' When reviewing the self-assessment, managers were instructed to think about ways to meet those professional goals — and if the organization could not — to think of outside opportunities where employees could develop those skills. As a result, employees felt rewarded, mentored, and part of a community.*

Another respondent, who described herself as highly motivated and always available to do more, equated lack of communication with attrition at her former workplace:

> *I worked for a small firm that has very little employee loyalty. As a result, almost everyone there has their eye on job openings. When I left, one of the owners didn't even acknowledge that I was leaving even though all 25 employees worked in one studio. I feel like the community aspect of a workplace is important. Not everyone will get along, but when you're with people for 40+ hours a week, there needs to be a sense of loyalty and community at some level.*

For feedback to be fully meaningful, however, Millennials themselves need to engage in honest self-reflection. As has been highlighted in prior chapters, the survey respondents frequently demonstrated a pattern of recognizing potentially challenging behaviors in their Millennial colleagues that they did not see in themselves. This trend appears in other data as well. For example, Bentley University's survey of Millennials reported: "While Millennials give their peers mixed reviews when it comes to work, they offer mostly positive assessments of their own personality traits and skills. These positive self-evaluations carry across subgroups of this population, including by gender."[179]

Feedback can only be optimally effective as a learning tool if one can be open to and learn from the negative comments as well as the positive. Developing receptivity to criticism is difficult and requires a clear mirror.

Feedback and transparency in the workplace are related tools that are relevant to the retention of Millennials. Author and human resources expert W. Stanton Smith observed the importance of transparency to Millennials as a generation that rejects "traditional business models" built on "hierarchies of privileged information." Rather, Millennials seek to understand: "1) what leaders are doing; 2) what the future could look like for them if they stay with a particular business; and 3) what challenges and opportunities the business faces."[180]

Working Smarter, and Hoping You Will As Well

The business imperative to develop Millennials as leaders is clear and compelling. As stated in an Executive Briefing issued by the Boston College Center for Work & Family: "The Millennial generation is continuing to impact the workplace through its size and diverse range of talents. Moreover, as Baby Boomers retire or scale back, the leadership roles they have occupied for so long will need to be filled. Because Generation X is too small to completely fill the void, Millennials will quickly need to undertake many of these leadership roles. Accordingly, there is a clear workplace imperative for business organizations to support the Millennials in their growth and development as future leaders. By identifying and cultivating leadership talent early, employers can best position their workplaces for smooth leadership transitions and a stronger future."[181]

Today's newest entrants to the workplace believe they work hard and smart—and they would like to see their workplaces similarly do so. When they feel valued, their devotion can be limitless, as this respondent's comments demonstrate:

My employers have accepted me into their family literally. Since interning my senior year of college, I have helped them build their company. I have been with them through thick and thin. When I first started working full-time, I knew there would be weeks where paychecks wouldn't come in but they have always made up the difference later. No matter how rocky things get, I am willing to stick with them.

The task ahead is clear: transform work into an environment that takes into account the needs of the 21st century worker. This can best be accomplished if workplace leaders understand that what Millennials seek from the workplace is in complete harmony with an effective, well-run organization.

In fact, what Millennials seek is consistent with what all generations want from their work environment. When working adults in all age groups were asked about the importance of particular job attributes, the top two identified by the respondents as "essential" or "very important" were (1) work-life balance and a (2) positive work environment/culture.[182] When respondents in the study by the Center for Creative Leadership were asked to identify what their organization could do to retain them as a committed employee, the results were consistent. Employees of all generations identified: (1) good compensation; (2) learning and development; (3) opportunities for advancement; (4) respect and recognition; and (5) good quality of life outside work.[183]

Ironically, as a result of their own upbringing, Millennials instinctively understand what those who raised them need to be taught: the best way to keep employees loyal and engaged is through meaningful training and professional development opportunities, effective communication, strong leadership and guidance, efficient time management, and a culture that supports all workers in meeting their professional challenges, their family responsibilities, and their personal needs.

Chapter 14

The Future Thanks You for Your Sanity—How Millennials Have Redefined Success and What It Means for the Future

Millennials are well-acquainted with the workplace ethos: no one works as hard as Baby Boomers (at least according to most Baby Boomers), and their Gen X protégés. The Millennials have also learned from watching their parents do almost everything full-throttle that these workplace successes came with a price. They frequently purchased as many services for their children as they could afford and turned the concept of "quality time" into a generational slogan. And with constant advances in technology, their brief moments together as a family have become increasingly encumbered by distracting devices.

The lessons were not lost on the younger generation. They recognize that even as Boomers and Gen Xers gave their all to work, they were not immune to the economics of their times. Many Millennials, during the recession years of their own childhood, watched their parents struggle through enormous changes in the corporate sector. Loyalty was often met with layoffs, and "do more with less" became the verbal mascot of corporate, non-profit, and government sectors during various parts of the 1980s and 1990s. As a result, Millennials saw their parents respond to severe workplace challenges by working harder and conforming more.

The Millennials learned from their parents' experiences. The world in which they grew up profoundly impacted their views about their relationship to work. They have seen the effects of a hard-driving workplace culture where loyalty often went unrecognized, and they now seek to find their own path to greater satisfaction. A 2013 study stated: "unlike their boomer parents, Millennials are not workaholics. They believe in a clearly defined work/life balance, and they expect companies to have policies in place to help them achieve this. Though goal-oriented, Millennials are not as long-sighted as their predecessors. They are less willing to pay dues, and are unlikely to pursue the delayed gratification of a gradual promotion track."[184]

Millennials offer a perspective that starts with the belief that one's work ethic should not be judged by outdated views of "face-time" or other ineffective ways of measuring whether someone is working hard. As we have seen, these judgments often result in incorrect assumptions about how Millennials work.

Taken together, survey responses offer a vision of a workplace where technology serves not as a tether, but as a component of an overall redesign of work—a redesign that allows for greater attention to family and personal commitments without sacrificing productivity. Millennials reject the notion of work as an all-consuming endeavor and loyalty on the job as an unreciprocated arrangement. Moreover, they see loyalty as a word that has boundaries; they do not intend to mistake loyalty and commitment for being consumed by work. They are astute observers who well understand that workplace demands for commitment can often be code for expectations of loyalty without reciprocity.

Instead, Millennials seek a workplace where they can use their skills wisely, without sacrificing personal and family time to satisfy someone else's definitions of hard work and commitment. These views evolved from their childhood observations and personal experiences. As Millennials begin to achieve critical mass in the workplace, they bring an unprecedented opportunity to reconsider how we work, where we work, and how to bring new ways of thinking to our jobs.

The Power of Joined Forces

The need for a workplace response to changing demographics is clear, compelling, and overdue. As Professor Gerson wrote: "The tensions between changing lives and resistant institutions have created dilemmas for everyone."[185]

Enduring change will require the focused intent of women and men who, as Gerson notes, pursue gender flexibility in caretaking and bread-winning roles and a stable family structure: "In the place of fixed, rigid behavioral strategies and mental categories demarcating separate spheres for women and men, gender flexibility involves more equal sharing and more fluid boundaries for organizing and apportioning emotional, social, and economic care."[186]

Through their size and determination, Millennials are in a position to redefine success for themselves and for others. Repeatedly, the respondents offered an upbeat assessment of their view of life as multi-dimensional and made clear that they are not willing to sacrifice one dimension for another. Respondents expressed their intent to shape a future that reframes the work-life debate away from the elusive concept of balance and towards flexibility for everyone. The benefits extend to the workplace: "Access to the flexibility needed to fulfill work and family responsibilities is one factor that is associated with higher levels of engagement among Gen Y employees . . . ".[187]

The Work Benefits of Happiness

Many respondents drew a link between increased happiness and greater productivity at work—comments that were consistent with research on happiness. A respondent described this connection:

> I do not have kids (I do plan to one day), however I still have a family (boyfriend, cat, parents, sisters, etc.) who I want to spend time with. I think in order to be happy at work you really do need to have a work/life balance. You need time to take care of yourself and take care of personal things, and have fun . . . I really think employers

need to start to embrace the idea of work/life issues much more than they currently do.

The responses made clear that a well-rounded life is critically important and worth striving towards:

> *When there is an extra push to get something accomplished I will put in extra time but I won't stay late every day because I know not everything is going to be accomplished in a day because of the amount of work assigned. Having time to volunteer, spend time with family, exercise, and religious activities are also very important to me. When I feel balanced I get more done during the hours I am at work.*

One study encourages employers to be proactive by positioning their workforce to recruit talented Millennials and to engage them throughout the hiring process as well as during their employment with the company. Strategies include "passive engagement," which may consist of "communications that leverage existing vehicles like intranet, newsletters and messages from senior leadership," and "active engagement," which encompasses "participation in structured volunteer events . . . These experiences are life changing for participants and have great impact on morale, pride and loyalty."[188]

Redefining Success

The survey results as well as other research demonstrate that Millennials reject the notion that success is measured by income and long hours. Millennials see a much broader meaning to the word. They see success as including the opportunity to participate fully in the lives of their families. And they are not embarrassed to include among their key priorities the need to exercise and maintain friendships. Further, they will seek workplaces where the growth and development of employees are a strategic focus and where a culture of inclusion and respect is a priority.

Millennials may have been a generation raised by parents who hovered closely, but they are now poised to take their own flight, soaring beyond the protective world they knew into uncharted territories where they can leave their own positive mark on the world. The survey results and other research offer a clear indication that Millennials can be expected to respond to challenging economic circumstances without sacrificing their core principles. They are bringing into the workplace extraordinary energy and significant resolve to shape the type of workplace they are seeking as they build their careers.

This young generation, however, cannot succeed without both organizational and societal support. For example, Clark University Professor Jeffrey Arnett calls for the expansion of programs that provide opportunities for Millennials to tap into their desire to serve others. He also urges that: "The other step that can be taken for the benefit of emerging adults is to stop promoting negative stereotypes about them, that they are selfish, lazy, and worse than ever. These false claims are harmful, not only because they are false and therefore unfair but because they discourage adult society from supporting the programs that would give emerging adults a broader range of opportunities for education, work, and service. It is time to retire the damaging and false stereotypes and instead celebrate today's emerging adults for the extraordinary generation they are."[189]

If their collective voice is heard, Millennials will be a force for positive change in the workplace and thrive as future leaders. Based on what they have demonstrated to date, there is every reason to believe they will succeed.

Millennials' Legacy

As is the case whenever significant differences among age groups are observed, the question arises: are we seeing these differences because the Millennials are, in fact, different from their Boomer and Gen X predecessors, or is the workplace simply feeling the effects of a large number of young people making their presence known?

This is a question that can only be answered in retrospect, after the full impact of the Millennials in the workplace has been felt, years from now. With each study and detailed analysis of the Millennials, however, the image is emerging of a generation that has the potential to make a tremendous positive difference—at work and in the world. The final answer, however, remains to be determined: it is up to Millennials to choose the ultimate impact of their generational legacy.

If their path so far proves to be guidance for the future, post-Millennial generations are likely to enter a workplace that is far more flexible, transparent, and respectful of work-family challenges than the workplace of today. And they will have the Millennials to thank for it.

Notes

Introduction

1. According to a report from the Corporate Leadership Council, "Thirty-six percent of employees are effective at peer interaction, and only 7% of organizations focus engagement initiatives on improving these interactions. . . . When employees are effective at critical peer interactions, average engagement capital can improve by 66%." See: Corporate Leadership Council, *The Power of Peers: Building Engagement Capital through Peer Interaction* (Web, The Corporate Executive Board Company, 2011), 8. http://greatmanager.ucsf.edu/files/CLC_The _Power_of_Peers_Building_Engagement_Capital_Through_Peer_Interaction.pdf.

Data also confirms that the multi-generational workplace may be decreasing employee engagement. A study of over 3,200 U.S. employers discovered that "after controlling for characteristics such as age, position type, company size and tenure, the researchers found that the greater the variation of age groups within a company, the lower the overall engagement for all generations." The founder of the consulting firm that conducted the study remarked, "for organizations with low engagement scores, we find a 'we vs. they' conflict between the generations. Increased diversity of generations affects the scores negatively much more than diversity of sex or race." The research shows that if an employer has twice the age diversity of a national average, it is six times more likely to have an overall employee engagement score in the bottom quartile." See: Adrienne Fox, "Mixing it Up: With four—almost five—generations in the workplace, tensions can arise through misunderstandings and miscommunication," *HR Magazine*, May 2011, 2.

2. Earlier books on generational issues included as the fourth generation in the workplace the Traditionalists, born between approximately 1900 and 1945. While their impact on establishing workplace norms and cultures continues,

their physical presence is now dwarfed by the three generations that have succeeded them. Most Traditionalists have fully retired from the workplace. For a more detailed discussion of the Traditionalists and their characteristics, see, e.g., Lynne C. Lancaster and David Stillman, *When Generations Collide: Who They Are. Why They Clash. How to Solve the Generational Puzzle at Work* (New York: HarperCollins Publishers Inc., 2002), 13.

3. The survey data was collected through the "snowball" methodology. That is, the survey was originally distributed via the author's networks, with the request that participants then widely disburse the survey through their own networks. Additional respondents were sought via a request through the web site HARO ("Help A Reporter Out"), a popular site where reporters, journalists and authors can seek interview sources.

4. The Sloan Center on Aging & Work, Boston College, Through a Different Looking Glass: The Prism of Age (Web: The Sloan Center on Aging & Work, 2012). http://www.bc.edu/content/dam/files/research_sites/agingandwork/pdf/publications/RB03_PrismofAge.pdf.

5. Calvin Hennick, "Fresh Approach to Career Path," *The Boston Globe*, January 3, 2013, 6 (quoting Rachel Reiser, author of *Millennials on Board: The Impact of the Rising Generation on the Workplace* (Acton, MA: First Printing Inc., 2010)).

6. Nathan Heller, "Semi-Charmed Life," *The New Yorker Magazine*, January 14, 2013, 67. One author described how technology has altered the lens through which younger generations view discriminatory behaviors: "Technology has exposed the racism, sexism, and other types of discrimination that our parents suspected in their workplaces and society. We grew up watching proof of discriminatory conduct. Television cameras, recording devices, and the internet gave us access to what happens behind the closed doors of the old boys' club. Once upon a time, the hard-working little guy was only able to speculate that he was continuously denied a promotion because of his race, ethnicity, or any other characteristic that the majority determined made him different and subsequently less qualified. . . . Thanks to the videos on YouTube and Google, today

we often know who the man is and what he looks like." Natalie Holder-Winfield, *Recruiting and Retaining a Diverse Workforce: New Rules for a New Generation* (Portland, OR: First Books, 2007), xxiii-xxiv.

7. Keli Goff, Party Crashing: How the Hip-Hop Generation Declared Political Independence (New York: Basic Civitas Books, 2008), 16.

8. An interesting blog posting by an older Millennial who taught younger Millennials noted: "After all, when I graduated college in 2002, we had cell phones, but we used them just to call people. We had email, but no social media personas." Laurie Edwards, "Teaching the 'Me Me Me' Generation," *WUBUR*, June 2013, 1–2. http://cognoscenti.wbur.org/2013/06/18/ millennials-in-the-classroom-laurie-edwards.

9. One article which focused on the naming of the post-Millennial generation included a suggestion that 10 years may be a more appropriate time-span for future generations. With respect to the names in contention for the next generation, this author's personal preference is a twist on the "iGen" references, which would be IGen for "the Involved Generation" as a hopeful testament to the existing—and growing—acceptance of diversity and inclusion among younger people. See: Bruce Horovitz, *After Gen X, Millennials, What Should Next Generation Be?* (Web: USA Today, May 4, 2012). http://usatoday30.usatoday.com/ money/advertising/story/2012–05–03/naming-the-next-generation/54737518/1.

Chapter 2

10. See, e.g., Stephen Ohlemacher, "Many Baby Boomers Plan to Retire Late," *CBS News*, February 11, 2009. http://www.cbsnews.com/2100-201 _162-2917476.html. For an interesting article on the delayed retirement of Boomer-aged college professors, see Colleen Flaherty, "Working Way Past 65," *Inside Higher Ed*, June 17, 2013, 2–3. http://www.insidehighered.com/news /2013/06/17/data-suggest-baby-boomer-faculty-are-putting-retirement.

11. See, e.g., Adrienne Fox, "Mixing it Up: With four—almost five—generations in the workplace, tensions can arise through misunderstandings and

miscommunication," *HR Magazine*, May 2011, 25 (citing research from the Center for Work-Life Policy). See also: Gad Levanon, and Ben Cheng, *Trapped on the Worker Treadmill?* (Web: The Conference Board, Feb 1, 2013). http://www.conference-board.org/press/pressdetail.cfm?pressid=4716.

See also: Sylvia Ann Hewlett, Laura Sherbin, and Karen Sumberg, "How Gen Y & Boomers Will Reshape Your Agenda," *HBR* (July-August 2009): 121–126, "The combination of Generation Y eagerly advancing up the professional ranks and Baby Boomers often refusing to retire has, over the course of a few short years, dramatically shifted the composition of the workforce . . . ", at 121.

12. First Command Financial Services, "7 Reasons to Keep Working During Retirement," Journey Magazine, 2011, 2–3. http://fcjourney.com/seven-reasons-keep-working-during-retirement. On a related note, a 2011 study by AARP found that while 43% of working Boomers were looking forward to retirement, 41% reported that they did not want to stop working. See: AARP and GFK Custom Research North America, *Baby Boomers Envision What's Next?* (Web: AARP, 2011), 4. http://assets.aarp.org/rgcenter/general/boomers-envision-retirement-2011.pdf. See also: Associated Press, "More Baby Boomers Delay Retirement," *The Fiscal Times*, November 10, 2011. http://www.thefiscaltimes.com/Articles/2011/11/10/More-Baby-Boomers-Delay-Retirement.

13. Leonard Steinhorn, *The Greater Generation: In Defense of the Baby Boom Legacy* (New York: Thomas Dunne Books, 2006), xiv.

14. Richard Washington, "Baby Boomers Beware: Millennials Are Coming," *Market Research Blog*, April 17, 2013, 1. http://blog.marketresearch.com/blog-home-page/bid/264242/Baby-Boomers-Beware-Millennials-Are-Coming-MarketResearch-com.

15. In a review of Touré Neblett's book about the pop icon Prince and his impact on Gen X, the reviewer references the book's " . . . potpourri of supposed Gen X traits: 'cynicism, skepticism, sarcasm, and irony.'" Siddhartha Mitter, "Prince: a Gen X icon?", *The Boston Globe*, March 22, 2013, 25.

16. Arthur J. Norton, and Louisa F. Miller, "Marriage, Divorce, and Remarriage in the 1990's," *U.S. Department of Commerce* (October, 1992), 1.

17. See, e.g., Lynne C. Lancaster and David Stillman, *When Generations Collide: Who They Are. Why They Clash. How to Solve the Generational Puzzle at Work* (New York: HarperCollins Publishers Inc., 2002), 25–26. For a detailed analysis of divorce statistics, see: http://www.census.gov/hhes/socdemo/marriage /data/cps/p23–180/p23–180.pdf.

18. AARP, *Leading a Multigenerational Workforce* (Web: AARP, 2007), 12. http://assets.aarp.org/www.aarp.org_/cs/misc/leading_a_multigenerational_ workforce.pdf.

19. Radcliffe Public Policy Center, *Life's Work: Generational Attitudes toward Work and Life Integration* (2000), 2.

20. Gayla Schaefer, "Workplace Challenges Coming," *Florida Today*, April 9, 2007, 2. http://www.floridatoday.com/article/20070409/BUSINESS/704090316 /Workplace-challenges-coming.

21. Jacqueline Doherty, "On the Rise," *Barron's Cover,* April 29, 2013. http://online.barrons.com/article/SB50001424052748703889404578440972 842742076.html#articleTabs_article%3D1.

22. Jacqueline Doherty, "On the Rise," *Barron's Cover,* April 29, 2013. http://online.barrons.com/article/SB50001424052748703889404578440972 842742076.html#articleTabs_article%3D1.

23. Christian Kurz, "The Next Normal: An Unprecedented Look at Millennials Worldwide," *Viacom*, November 15, 2012. http://blog.viacom.com/2012 /11/the-next-normal-an-unprecedented-look-at-millennials-worldwide/.

24. Consumerlab, "Young Professions at Work," *Ericsson Consumer Insight*, April 2013, 3. http://www.slideshare.net/EricssonSlides/ young-professionals-at-work.

25. Erica Dhawan, "Gen-Y Workforce and Workplace Are Out of Sync," *Forbes,* January 23, 2012. http://www.forbes.com/sites/85broads/2012/01/23/gen-y-workforce-and-workplace-are-out-of-sync/.

26. Neil Howe and William Strauss, *Millennials Rising: The Next Great Generation* (New York: Vintage Books, 2000), 4. A PEW study reported: "Millennials . . . are more ethnically and racially diverse than older generations, more educated, less likely to be working and slower to settle down." Paul Taylor and Scott Keeter, *Millennials: Confident. Connected. Open to Change* (Web: PEW Research Center, 2010), 9. http://www.pewsocialtrends.org/files/2010/10/millennials-confident-connected-open-to-change.pdf.

Chapter 3

27. PricewaterhouseCoopers, *Millennials at Work: Reshaping the Workplace* (Web: PwC, 2011). http://www.pwc.com/en_M1/m1/services/consulting/documents/millennials-at-work.pdf.

28. Paul Taylor and Scott Keeter, *Millennials: Confident. Connected. Open to Change* (Web: PEW Research Center, 2010), 10. http://www.pewsocialtrends.org/files/2010/10/millennials-confident-connected-open-to-change.pdf.

29. Emily Douglas, "A Quick Look at our Nation's Education Data," *Education Week Blog*, May 21, 2013, 1–3. http://blogs.edweek.org/topschooljobs/k-12_talent_manager/2013/05/nations_education_data.html?utm_medium=twitter&utm_source=twitterfeed.

30. Neil Howe and William Strauss, *Millennials Rising: The Next Great Generation* (New York: Vintage Books, 2000), 281.

31. One author responded to the criticism senior women express about young women who do not exhibit the same spirit of activism to important causes such as reproductive rights: "When older pro-choice groups begin treating young women not as ungrateful, unschooled whippersnappers but as powerful women who were raised with different sets of expectations, with

new modes of communication and protest, and who face a different set of obstacles, perhaps then they will begin to really see them. Perhaps when these leaders stop demanding that young women acknowledge *their* history, *their* priorities, *their* forms of resistance, and start instead to acknowledge the new kinds of activism that young people, not their elders, have succeeded in creating online, perhaps they will start to be able to make out these phantom young women." Young women, she suggests, turned to social media and away from the more traditional measures as a way to have a voice with each other, rather than feel overwhelmed by older activists: "Many of the young women who formed and populate the feminist blogosphere will tell you that they took to the Internet because they found no welcome in institutional women's organizations and decided not to work within a system designed and run by leaders who did not trust them, take them seriously, or show any interest in their opinions." Rebecca Traister, "Where Did all the Angry Young Women Go?" *Salon*, April 20, 2010. http://www.salon.com/2010/04/20/next _generation_abortion/.

32. Bentley University Center for Women and Business, *Millennials in the Workplace* (Web: Bentley University, 2012), 32. http://www.bentley.edu/centers /sites/www.bentley.edu.centers/files/centers/cwb/millennials-report.pdf.

33. Sibson Consulting, *Millennials in the Sales Force: It's Time to Get to Know This Generation* (Web: The Segal Group, April 2009), 16. http://www .sibson.com/services/sales-force-effectiveness/Millennials-in-the-Sales-Force-Survey-Results.pdf.

34. PricewaterhouseCoopers, University of Southern California and London Business School, *PwC's NextGen: A Global Generational Study* (Web: PwC, 2013), 8. http://www.pwc.com/en_GX/gx/hr-management-services/pdf/pwc-nextgen-study-2013.pdf.

Chapter 4

35. Jean M. Twenge, *Generation Me: Why Today's Young Americans Are More Confident, Assertive, Entitled—and More Miserable Than Ever Before*

(New York, NY: Free Press, 2006), 4. Twenge's research focused on those born in the 1970s through the 1990s.

36. Neil Howe and William Strauss, *Millennials Rising: The Next Great Generation* (New York: Vintage Books, 2000), 81.

37. Over the years, the methods used to question the child witnesses in these cases have come under significant scrutiny and many have been discredited, resulting in several overturned convictions. For an interesting study analyzing interview techniques of children see: Sena Garven, James Wood, Roy Malpass, and John Shaw, "More Than Suggestion: The Effect of Interviewing Techniques From the McMartin Preschool Case," *Journal of Applied Psychology* 83(3): 347–359.

38. Paula Fass, *Child Kidnapping in America* (Web: Ohio State University, January 2010), 1–5. http://origins.osu.edu/article/child-kidnapping-america. These fears have not ebbed with time, as parents remain vigilantly on guard. One columnist observed, "to give a child permission to go to the corner store or to play freely with her friends in the woods without supervision is now considered a borderline risky decision, one fraught with anxiety and which necessitates that parents engage in an extensive cost-benefit analysis. Parents who allow their kids to venture out and about freely face intense scrutiny." Meredith O'Brien, "Letting Kids Roam Alone: Parents who give Kids Independence face Intense Scrutiny," *MetroWest Daily News*, July 12, 2009, Sunday Opinion E1.

39. Peter Gray, "Freedom to Learn: The Decline of Play and Rise in Children's Mental Disorders," *Psychology Today*, January 26, 2010. http://www.psychologytoday.com/blog/freedom-learn/201001/the-decline-play-and-rise-in-childrens-mental-disorders. Peter Gray, "Why Have Trustful Parenting & Children's Freedom Declined," *Psychology Today*, July 29, 2009. http://www.psychologytoday.com/blog/freedom-learn/200907/why-have-trustful-parenting-children-s-freedom-declined. Peter Gray, "As Children's Freedom Has Declined, So Has Their Creativity," *Psychology Today*, September 17, 2012. http://www.psychologytoday.com/blog/freedom-learn/201209/children-s-freedom-has-declined-so-has-their-creativity. See also: David Pimentel, "Criminal Child

Neglect and the 'Free Range Kid': Is Overprotective Parenting the New Standard of Care," *Utah Law Review* 2012 (at 947).

40. Neil Howe and William Strauss, *Millennials Rising: The Next Great Generation* (New York: Vintage Books, 2000), 86.

41. Robin Marantz Henig, "What Is It About 20-Somethings?", *New York Times Magazine*, August 22, 2010, 37.

42. Neil Howe and William Strauss, *Millennials Rising: The Next Great Generation* (New York: Vintage Books, 2000), 123.

43. Neil Howe and William Strauss, *Millennials Rising: The Next Great Generation* (New York: Vintage Books, 2000), 187.

44. Paul Taylor and Scott Keeter, *Millennials: Confident. Connected. Open to Change* (Web: PEW Research Center, 2010), 17. http://www.pewsocialtrends.org/files/2010/10/millennials-confident-connected-open-to-change.pdf.

45. Jeffrey Jensen Arnett, PhD., Joseph Schwab, "The Clark University Poll of Emerging Adults: Thriving, Struggling & Hopeful", December, 2012, 9. http://www.clarku.edu/clark-poll-emerging-adults/pdfs/clark-university-poll-emerging-adults-findings.pdf. The study reports interesting ethnic differences, noting: "more African American (39%) and Latino (41%) emerging adults saying their parents are more involved than they would like, compared to 24% of Whites." At 10.

46. Stephanie Rosenbloom, "Mommy and Daddy's Little Life Coach," *New York Times*, April 5, 2007. http://www.nytimes.com/2007/04/05/fashion/05advice.html?pagewanted=all&_r=0.

47. See, e.g., Eric Hoover, "College Confidential: a Field Guide," *Chronicle of Higher Education*, April 29, 2013. http://chronicle.com/article/College-Confidential-A-Field/138865/. Hoover describes the popular website College Confidential, which hosts forums and message boards, evaluates colleges and

provides advice on the application process and which has received hundreds of millions of page views. In describing how parents exhibit their role as co-shoppers, he writes: "It's common for parents to use 'we' often, as in 'We applied to five colleges' or 'We liked William & Mary.'"

A Boston Globe article titled "The Myth of the Frankenstudent," noted that "the pressure to have kids who are 'outstanding' and 'well-rounded' is intense, and it starts earlier and earlier." In one anecdote, the parents of a kindergartener who discovered their little girl sitting at the table drooping over her packet of vacation homework were "appalled to hear themselves saying, 'Hey! Wake up! *Color*." The article further observed that "the climate of parental anxiety [surrounding the college admissions process] is nuts. The way kids are being packaged for college is cynical and fake [. . .] but opting out of it is nerve-wrecking too. If everyone else is playing the game, can your child afford not to?" The author questioned: "But are we really seeing better kids, or just slicker packaging? We think our children need to be academically brilliant; musically and athletically gifted; and dedicated to serving, if not downright saving, humanity. Are there really a lot of people like this? Or are we creating Frankenstudents—artificial monsters, impossible composites of skills and achievements that rarely co-exist in real life?" Joan Wickersham, "The Myth of the Frankenstudent," *Boston Globe*, April 15, 2010. http://www.boston.com/bostonglobe/editorial_opinion/oped/articles/2010/04/15/the_myth_of_the_frankenstudent/.

The continued pressure that parents feel to facilitate an environment that helps their children succeed was captured by this writer: "So in the run-up to the tryouts I became frenzied. I suggested we hire a (Division 1) college player for a quickie brush-up. I contemplated going behind his back to explain to the basketball coach that he would miss part of tryouts because of play practice—not for lack of interest." Beth Teitell, "In Season of Resolutions, Parents Line Up to Fess Up," *Boston Globe*, December 28, 2012. http://www.bostonglobe.com/lifestyle/2012/12/28/did-care-more-than-son-did-made-middle-school-basketball-team/b5uAngPtYfIj258H3V4C2J/story.html.

48. See, e.g., Ariel Kaminer, "On a College Waiting List? Sending Cookies Isn't Going to Help," *New York Times*, May 11, 2013. http://www.nytimes.com/2013/05/12/education/on-the-waiting-list-some-college-applicants-try-a-little-dazzle.html?pagewanted=all&_r=0. Kaminer quotes the director of admissions at

Union College, who described the high level of parental involvement: "There's a mother who e-mails me every third day—they must have timers on these things . . . [T]here's one parent who calls up and yells at me: 'I can't believe this happened! This is a horrible thing!' And then he calls 10 minutes later and says, 'I'm sorry.' Then he calls and says, 'I know you don't like me. I'm being a complete pest.'"

49. Phil Gardner, *Parent Involvement in the College Recruiting Process: To What Extent?* (Web: Collegiate Employment Research Institute, 2007), 2. http://ceri.msu.edu/publications/pdf/ceri2–07.pdf. See also: Julie Halpert, *11 Ways Parents Can Hurt Their Child's Job Chances* (Web: The Fiscal Times, June 18, 2013), 1. http://www.thefiscaltimes.com/Articles/2013/06/18/10-Ways-Parents-Can-Hurt-Their-Childs-Job-Chances.aspx#page1.

50. Kelly Wallace, "Bring Your Parents to Work Day: Positive Trend or Helicopter Parenting?", CNN Living. http://www.cnn.com/2013/11/07/living/linkedin-bring-your-parents-work-day/.

Chapter 5

51. Eugene Steuerle, Signe-Mary McKernan, Caroline Radcliffe and Sisi Zhang, *Lost Generations? Wealth Building among Young Americans* (Web: Urban Institute, March 2013), 1. http://www.urban.org/UploadedPDF /412766-Lost-Generations-Wealth-Building-Among-Young-Americans.pdf. The slow recovery from the economic crisis continues to threaten the economic independence of Millennials as they enter their adult years. One commentator harshly criticized the senior generations whose practices contributed to the economic circumstances: "Today's youth, both here and abroad, have been screwed by their parents' fiscal profligacy and economic mismanagement . . . No generation has suffered more from the Great Recession than the young. Median net worth of people under 35, according to the U.S. Census, fell 37 percent between 2005 and 2010; those over 65 took only a 13 percent hit." Joel Kotkin, "Generation Screwed," *Newsweek* (July 23 & 30, 2012), 42.

The impact on spending is significant: "The Millennials' relationship with money seems quite simple. They do not have a lot of it, and what they do have, they seem reluctant to spend. Millennials are buying fewer cars and houses, and despite their immersion in consumer culture, particularly electronics, they are not really spending beyond their limited means." Annie Lowrey, "Do Millennials Stand a Chance in the Real World?", *New York Times,* March 26, 2013. http://www.nytimes.com /2013/03/31/magazine/do-millennials-stand-a-chance-in-the-real-world.html.

52. Blaire Briody, "How Clinging to Mommy and Daddy is Ruining a Generation," *Fiscal Times,* February 8, 2012, 2. http://www.thefiscaltimes.com/Articles /2012/02/08/How-Clinging-to-Mommy-and-Daddy-is-Ruining-a-Generation .aspx#page1.

53. Paul Taylor and Scott Keeter, *Millennials: Confident. Connected. Open to Change* (Web: PEW Research Center, 2010), 12. http://www.pewsocialtrends .org/files/2010/10/millennials-confident-connected-open-to-change.pdf.

54. Paul Taylor and Scott Keeter, *Millennials: Confident. Connected. Open to Change* (Web: PEW Research Center, 2010), 39. http://www.pewsocialtrends.org /files/2010/10/millennials-confident-connected-open-to-change.pdf. Of interest, the data showed that, of those who reported that they rely on their families for financial support, 38% were white, 33% were black, and 28% were Hispanic.

55. Lawrence Mishel, "Entry-Level Workers' Wages Fell in Last Decade," Economic Policy Institute, March 7, 2012. http://www.epi.org/publication/ ib327-young-workers-wages/.

56. Paul Taylor and Rich Morin, *Home for the Holidays . . . and Every Other Day: Recession Brings Many Young People Back to the Nest* (Web: PEW Research Center, November 24, 2009), 2. http://www.pewsocialtrends.org/files /2010/10/millennials-confident-connected-open-to-change.pdf.

57. The Center for Information and Research on Civic Learning and Engagement, The National Conference on Citizenship, Mobalize.org, and Harvard University Institute of Politics, *Millennials Civic Health Index* (Web: Harvard University, February, 2013), 5. http://www.iopnewsletter.com/news/02052013 _NCC_Millennial.pdf.

58. "Generation Jobless," *The Economist*, April 27, 2013, 58–60.

59. Jay Fitzgerald, "It's Tough Out There: Graduates Entering the Work-force are Finding More Opportunities—if they Look Hard Enough," *Boston Sunday Globe*, April 28, 2013, 1–2. http://www.bostonglobe.com/business /2013/04/27/thaw-job-market-for-new-college-grads-but-still-cold-out-there/ nA2oN2t5UIB6kPxjxJO5VM/story.html. The article further reported that the outlook for liberal arts graduates was particularly challenging as compared to graduates with computer science and technical degrees such as electrical and chemical engineering who were more likely to obtain professional jobs and at significantly higher starting salaries than those with "classic liberal arts degrees . . . assuming they can even find a professional position within their chosen field."

60. PricewaterhouseCoopers, *Millennials at Work: Reshaping the Workplace* (Web: PwC, 2011), 8. http://www.pwc.com/en_M1/m1/services/consulting/ documents/millennials-at-work.pdf.

61. Joseph P. Khan, "The Broke Generation," *Boston Globe*, May 29, 2012, G11. Commenting on the significant wealth gap between Millennials and older Boomers, a Boston Globe editorial noted the critical importance of a college degree for those entering the job market: "Even as the cost of a college degree rises, it's increasingly become more of a minimum qualification than a guaran-teed pass to the middle class. And unlike those who came of age during a period of extended prosperity, today's young people are facing the worst job market in decades." *The Kids Aren't All Right*," *Boston Globe*, November 16, 2011.
For an interesting article showing how college students are deferring their plans in order to address their debt, see: Gail Waterhouse, "A Higher Degree of Debt," *Boston Sunday Globe*, August 25, 2013, G-1.
Notwithstanding the significant burden that these levels of debt impose, it is important to note that, for some, the barriers to achieving an education through loans are still too high. A Clark University Poll reported: "Ethnic and socioeconomic backgrounds play a major role in opportunities for higher edu-cation. One half (50%) of African American emerging adults have not been able to find enough financial support for their educational goals, as compared

to 37% of Latino emerging adults and 32% of Whites. With regard to socio-economic status (SES), nearly half (45%) of emerging adults from a lower SES have not had enough financial support to reach their educational goals, while 34% from a middle SES and 28% from a higher SES have had the same struggle." Jeffrey Jensen Arnett, PhD., Joseph Schwab, "The Clark University Poll of Emerging Adults: Thriving, Struggling & Hopeful", December, 2012, 12. http://www.clarku.edu/clark-poll-emerging-adults/pdfs/clark-university-poll-emerging-adults-findings.pdf.

62. Richard Washington, "Baby Boomers Beware: Millennials are Coming," *Market Research Blog*, April 17, 2013, 2. http://blog.marketresearch.com/blog-home-page/bid/264242/Baby-Boomers-Beware-Millennials-Are-Coming-MarketResearch-com. The student debt crisis, however, does not alter the importance of a college degree. "Over the past 40 years, wages for college graduates have risen, whereas wages for those with only a high school diploma have steadily declined." Jeffrey Jensen Arnett, PhD., Joseph Schwab, "The Clark University Poll of Emerging Adults: Thriving, Struggling & Hopeful", December, 2012, 13. http://www.clarku.edu/clark-poll-emerging-adults/pdfs/clark-university-poll-emerging-adults-findings.pdf.

63. Richard Settersten and Barbara E. Ray, *Not Quite Adults: Why 20-Somethings are Choosing a Slower Path to Adulthood and Why It's Good for Everyone* (New York, NY: Random House Inc., 2010), 35. The authors further noted: "In a country that increasingly demands education to get ahead, not getting an education locks in disadvantage for generations." At 28. See also: Jay Fitzgerald, "A College Degree is Costly, But It Pays Off Over Time" *Boston Sunday Globe*, October 12, 2012, G-1.

64. An interesting example of this collaborative/competitive tension can be found in these comments about the future economy: " . . . the economy may end up looking a little like the *World of Warcraft*. Part of the game involves bands of fighters raiding each other. The other part . . . is the collaborative work that goes into preparing their weapons and strategies. Independent groups of online warriors post as many as 12,000 new ideas every day preparing for the next raid..." See: "Net Gains or Net Losses: Is the Internet Changing Human

Nature?" *ParisTech Review,* Jun. 24, 2010. http://www.paristechreview.com
/2010/06/24/gains-losses-is-the-internet-changing-human-nature/.

65. Alexandra Robbins, *The Overachievers: The Secret Lives of Driven Kids*
(New York, NY: Hyperion, 2006), 14. In describing a culture pushing children to overachieve, Robbins further stated: "The high school environment is
no longer about a student's pre-adult exploration with the goal of narrowing
down likes and dislikes so that he or she ultimately can choose a college cur-
riculum, vocational school, or career path that fits. Instead, it has become a
hotbed for Machiavellian strategy in which students (and parents) pile on AP
after AP, activity after activity, acclaim after acclaim, with the goal of tailoring
high school resumes for what they often feel will be the defining moment of
their lives: the college admission process." At 14.

Of interest, when SAT scores and college graduation rates of Millennials are compared to Gen Xers and Boomers, Millennials generally shine. For
example, Millennials who took the SATs in 2005 (born in 1988) achieved
a higher combined score than any teens born since 1956. Neil Howe, "The
Kids Are Alright, But Their Parents . . . " *Washington Post,* December 8,
2008. http://articles.washingtonpost.com/2008–12–07/opinions/36778799_1
_generation-jones-generation-xers-dumbest-generation.

66. Richard Washington, "Baby Boomers Beware: Millennials are Coming," *Market Research Blog,* April 17, 2013, 2. http://blog.marketresearch.com
/blog-home-page/bid/264242/Baby-Boomers-Beware-Millennials-Are-Coming-
MarketResearch-com.

67. Dan Schawbel, *Me 2.0: 4 Steps to Building your Future Revised and
Updated Edition* (New York, NY: Kaplan Publishing, 2010), 23. See also: Dan
Schawbel, *Promote Yourself: The New Rules for Career Success* (New York,
NY: St. Martin's Press, 2013).

Chapter 6

68. Ron Alsop, *The Trophy Kids Grow Up* (San Francisco: Jossey-Bass,
2008), 27.

69. McCullough stated, for example: "You are not special. You are not exceptional . . . Yes, you've been pampered, cosseted, doted upon, helmeted, bubble-wrapped. Yes, capable adults with other things to do have held you, kissed you, fed you, wiped your mouth, wiped your bottom, trained you, taught you, tutored you, coached you, listened to you, counseled you, encouraged you, consoled you and encouraged you again. You've been nudged, cajoled, wheedled and implored. You've been feted and fawned over and called sweetie pie. [. . .] But do not get the idea you're anything special. Because you're not. [. . .] 'But, Dave,' you cry, 'Walt Whitman tells me I'm my own version of perfection! Epictetus tells me I have the spark of Zeus!' And I don't disagree. So that makes 6.8 billion examples of perfection, 6.8 billion sparks of Zeus. You see, if everyone is special, then no one is. If everyone gets a trophy, trophies become meaningless." David McCullough Jr., "You're Not Special," *Swellesley Report*, June 5, 2012, 1–3. http://theswellesleyreport .com/2012/06/wellesley-high-grads-told-youre-not-special/.

70. Chelsea Lowe, "For Millennials, Salary is not All," *Boston Business Journal*, June 15, 2012 (quoting a senior vice president at The Futures Co.). http://www.bizjournals.com/boston/print-edition/2012/06/15/for-millennials-salary-is-not-all.html?page=all.

71. For an interesting perspective regarding the influence of celebrity behavior on teenage girls, see: Kathleen Deveny and Raina Kelley, "Girls Gone Bad?" *Newsweek*, February 12, 2007, 41–47. In a book about Millennials and American politics, the authors chronicle the impact of television comedies and the way in which the favorite shows of Baby Boomers, Gen X, and Millennials mirror popular culture of the times. See: Morley Winograd and Michael D. Hais, *Millennial Makeover: MySpace, YouTube & the Future of American Politics* (Piscataway, NJ: Fourth Printing, 2008), 72–78.

72. Neil Swidey, "When you Wish Upon A Star," *Boston Globe*, May 27, 2012, 19.

73. Elspeth Reeve, "Every Every Every Generation Has Been The Me Me Me Generation," *Atlantic Wire*, May 9, 2013. http://www.theatlanticwire.com /national/2013/05/me-generation-time/65054/.

74. Harvard Institute of Politics, *Solid Majority of Young Adults Concerned About Meeting Their Bills and Obligations* (Web: Harvard Institute, March 9, 2010), 1. http://www.iop.harvard.edu/march-9-2010-majority-young-adults-concerned-about-meeting-their-bills-and-obligations-harvard-poll.

75. PricewaterhouseCoopers, *Millennials at Work: Reshaping the Workplace* (Web: PwC, 2011), 4. http://www.pwc.com/en_M1/m1/services/consulting/documents/millennials-at-work.pdf. The survey provided interesting global data: Graduates in the US, UK, and Republic of Ireland and Hong Kong were the most willing to make compromises, and those in Japan, Turkey, South Africa and Belgium were the least willing. At 12.

76. Accenture, *U.S. Workers Under Pressure to Improve Skills, But Need More Support from Employers* (Web: Accenture, 2011), 1. http://newsroom.accenture.com/article_display.cfm?article_id=5343.

Chapter 7

77. Whether growing up digital is more beneficial or harmful for Millennials is a source of great debate. The December 2010 issue of *Philadelphia* Magazine featured an article suggesting that the brains of technology-addicted children are fundamentally different from those of their parents, a cause of major concern. The article notes: "when you sat at a school desk and recited your times tables over and over, when you wrote out the periodic table of elements, when you practiced cursive penmanship, you were reinforcing memories, creating familiar paths for synapses, literally rewiring your brain for top-down attention. Your children's neural networks are very different. Thanks to their Internet exposure, in place of steady repetition, they're confronted, daily, by a barrage of novelty. There's no pattern, no order, in either the input or the pathways it carves [. . .] So the tech stuff isn't benign, though kids think it is. And it's been deliberately developed to make it hard for them to turn away." Sandy Hingston, "Is It Just Us, Or Are Kids Getting Really Stupid?", *Philadelphia Magazine*, November 26, 2010. http://www.phillymag.com/articles/feature-is-it-just-us-or-are-kids-getting-really-stupid/.

78. Rachel Reiser, *Millennials on Board: The Impact of the Rising Generation on the Workplace* (Acton, MA: First Printing Inc., 2010), 76. Reiser further states: "One consequence of being constantly tapped into media is that one is **always** hooked in, never just sitting and reflecting. I could ask any psychologist or child development specialist if taking time to reflect on one's day is important for personal development and the ability to develop key life skills like coping and resiliency, and they would resoundingly argue that it is beyond important, and is in fact imperative. Millennials are the first to tell us, and I have heard it many times, that they really do not allow themselves this time or activity." At 82.

79. John Palfry and Urs Gasser, *Born Digital: Understanding the First Generation of Digital Native* (New York: Basic Books, 2008), 287. Research by Sodexo observed that Millennials are driving new ways to develop collaborative communication and learning: "A growing contingent in the workforce, this generation has a preference for connecting and learning digitally. They want to have access to people from throughout their organizations and have the freedom to choose who they seek knowledge from or share insights with." Sodexo, *Workplace Trends 2013* (Web: Sodexo, 2013), 26. http://viewer.zmags.com/publication/f045b66f#/f045b66f/2.

80. Paul Taylor and Scott Keeter, *Millennials: Confident. Connected. Open to Change* (Web: PEW Research Center, 2010), 25. http://www.pewsocialtrends.org/files/2010/10/millennials-confident-connected-open-to-change.pdf.

81. Christine Barton, Jeff Fromm, and Chris Egan, *The Millennial Consumer: Debunking Stereotypes* (Web: The Boston Consulting Group, April 16, 2012), 4. http://www.brandchannel.com/images/papers/536_BCG_The_Millennial_Consumer_Apr_2012%20(3)_tcm80–103894.pdf.

82. Amy Goldwasser, *Red: Teenage Girls in America Write on What Fires Up Their Lives Today* (New York, NY: Penguin Publishing, 2007), xv.

83. Jean M. Twenge, *Generation Me: Why Today's Young Americans Are More Confident, Assertive, Entitled—and More Miserable Than Ever Before* (New York, NY: Free Press, 2006), 36.

One article noted: "We interrupt conversations for documentation all the time. A selfie like any photograph interrupts experience to mark the moment. . . . Technology doesn't just do things for us. It does things to us, changing not just what we do but who we are." Sherry Turkle, "The Documented Life," *The New York Times*, December 15, 2013. http://www.nytimes.com/2013/12/16/opinion/the-documented-life .html?_r=0. A version of this op-ed appears in print on December 16, 2013, on page A25 of the New York edition with the headline: The Documented Life.

84. Alyssa Rosenberg, "Why Time Magazine Put A Woman On The Cover Of Its Issue Complaining About Millennials," *Think Progress,* May 9, 2013. http://thinkprogress.org/alyssa/2013/05/09/1987901/why-time-magazine-put-a -woman-on-the-cover-of-its-issue-complaining-about-millenials/.

85. John K. Mullen, "Digital Natives Are Slow To Pick Up Nonverbal Cues," *HBR Blog Network,* Mar. 16, 2012. http://blogs.hbr.org/2012/03/digital- natives-are-slow-to-pi/. Another article reviewing a series of studies reported: "[Technology] may also be having a bad effect on life communication skills. . . . One recent study of 200 18 to 23-year-olds . . . found that younger people who spend a lot of time online aren't as good at reading facial expressions as people who spend less time online." See: "Net Gains or Net Losses: Is the Internet Changing Human Nature?", *ParisTech Review,* Jun. 24, 2010. http://www.paristechreview .com/2010/06/24/gains-losses-is-the-internet-changing-human-nature/.

86. PricewaterhouseCoopers, *Millennials at Work: Reshaping the Workplace* (Web: PwC, 2011), 4. http://www.pwc.com/en_M1/m1/services/consulting/ documents/millennials-at-work.pdf.

87. Dennis McCafferty, "Some CEOs Disregard Social-Media Reputation," *CIO Insight Blog,* December 31, 2012, slides 1, 6. http://www.cioinsight .com/it-strategy/business-intelligence/slideshows/some-ceos-disregard-social- media-reputation which references the following infographic: http://zenogroup .com/content/sites/default/files/Zeno%20Group%20Digital%20Readiness %20Survey%20infographic_with%20links.pdf.

88. Adrienne Fox, "Mixing it Up: With four—almost five—generations in

the workplace, tensions can arise through misunderstandings and miscommunication," *HR Magazine*, May 2011, 25.

89. Accenture Management Consulting, Technology and Outsourcing, *Jumping the Boundaries of Corporate IT: Accenture Global Research on Millennials' Use of Technology* (Web: Accenture, 2010), 4. http://nstore.accenture.com/technology/millennials/global_millennial_generation_research.pdf.

90. Accenture Management Consulting, Technology and Outsourcing, *Jumping the Boundaries of Corporate IT: Accenture Global Research on Millennials' Use of Technology* (Web: Accenture, 2010), 6. http://nstore.accenture.com/technology/millennials/global_millennial_generation_research.pdf.

91. PricewaterhouseCoopers, *Millennials at Work: Reshaping the Workplace* (Web: PwC, 2011), 9. http://www.pwc.com/en_M1/m1/services/consulting/documents/millennials-at-work.pdf. As an added point of interest, "Millennials in Africa were the most likely to feel this way (75% versus 65% worldwide)".

92. Accenture Management Consulting, Technology and Outsourcing, *Jumping the Boundaries of Corporate IT: Accenture Global Research on Millennials' Use of Technology* (Web: Accenture, 2010), 7. http://nstore.accenture.com/technology/millennials/global_millennial_generation_research.pdf. The study noted that although the majority of young Millennials do use email for school activities, they "spend significantly more time texting . . . instant messaging . . . and on social network sites." At 7.

93. Accenture Management Consulting, Technology and Outsourcing, *Jumping the Boundaries of Corporate IT: Accenture Global Research on Millennials' Use of Technology* (Web: Accenture, 2010), 9. http://nstore.accenture.com/technology/millennials/global_millennial_generation_research.pdf.

94. Accenture Management Consulting, Technology and Outsourcing, *Jumping the Boundaries of Corporate IT: Accenture Global Research on Millennials' Use of Technology* (Web: Accenture, 2010), 4. http://nstore.accenture.com/technology/millennials/global_millennial_generation_research.pdf.

95. Consumerlab, "Young Professions at Work," *Ericsson Consumer Insight*, April 2013, 5. http://www.slideshare.net/EricssonSlides/young-professionals-at-work. The study further found that over 40% of young respondents used their personal networks of friends and contacts (as opposed to their colleagues) to solve work-related issues several times a week, compared with approximately a third of Gen X respondents and a quarter of Boomer respondents.

96. Accenture Management Consulting, Technology and Outsourcing, *Jumping the Boundaries of Corporate IT: Accenture Global Research on Millennials' Use of Technology* (Web: Accenture, 2010) 6–7. http://nstore.accenture.com/technology/millennials/global_millennial_generation_research.pdf.

97. Judith Finer Freedman, Ed.D, *Cracking the Code: Unlocking the Potential of Future Leaders in the Legal Profession* (West, 2010), 34.

98. Dan Berrett, *Students May Be Reading Plenty, but Not for Class* (Web: The Chronicle of Higher Education, May 1, 2013), 1–5. http://chronicle.com/article/Students-May-Be-Reading/138911/. The article quoted SuHua Huang, the author of a study of reading habits of US college students and an assistant professor of reading education at Midwestern State University: " . . . students seemed to have difficulty putting away their Internet-capable cellphones during class, often keeping them on their laps or in their hands. Some students explained that they needed to do so to keep from missing a message from family members or friends or to pick up extra hours at their jobs." She also described cell phone usage that "reached the point of obsession" and reported that few seemed to follow instructions, take notes, or even bring their textbooks to class yet: "Some students completed their assignments and sent them to their instructors in the middle of class."

99. Dan Berrett, *Students May Be Reading Plenty, but Not for Class* (Web: The Chronicle of Higher Education, May 1, 2013). http://chronicle.com/article/Students-May-Be-Reading/138911/. One of the comments following the article stated: "They might . . . be social media natives but they don't know anything about organizing files on either their hard drive or in the cloud. Many have a hard time simply downloading and uploading files. They don't know the difference between an MS Word file and a Google Doc."

Chapter 8

100. "Before you rest secure in the knowledge that at least you have a whole 1/10 of a second to make that great first impression at your next job interview, the authors acknowledge that future research may well close that window even smaller." Eric Wargo, "How Many Seconds to a First Impression?" *Association for Psychological Science Observer* 19.7, July, 2006, 1. http://www.psychologicalscience.org/index.php/publications/observer/2006/july-06/how-many-seconds-to-a-first-impression.html.

See also: "Judgments made after a 100-ms exposure correlated highly with judgments made in the absence of time constraints, suggesting that this exposure time was sufficient for participants to form an impression." Janine Willis and Alexander Todorov, "First Impressions: Making up your Mind After a 100-Ms Exposure to a Face," *Princeton University Department of Psychological Science* 17.7, July 2006, 1. http://psych.princeton.edu/psychology/research/todorov/pdf/Willis&Todorov-PsychScience.pdf.

Another article noted: "According to 2011 research by Harvard Medical School and Massachusetts General Hospital, people assess your competence and trustworthiness in a quarter of a second (250 milliseconds)—based solely on how you look." Jenna Goudreau, "The Seven Ways Your Boss is Judging Your Appearance," *Forbes Magazine*, November 30, 2012, 3. http://www.forbes.com/sites/jennagoudreau/2012/11/30/the-seven-ways-your-boss-is-judging-your-appearance/.

101. Piper Jaffray Companies, *Taking Stock With Teens Survey Summary: 2013* (Web: Piper Jaffray, 2013), 1. http://www.piperjaffray.com/2col.aspx?id=287&releaseid=1805593.

102. "Teenage Consumer Spending Statistics," *Statistic Brain*, September 8, 2013, 1. http://www.statisticbrain.com/teenage-consumer-spending-statistics/. One article reported that children influence approximately $600 billion in adult spending a year. See Stephanie Rosenbloom, "Mommy and Daddy's Little Life Coach," *New York Times*, April 5, 2007. http://www.nytimes.com/2007/04/05/fashion/05advice.html?pagewanted=all&_r=0.

103. See Associated Press, "White House Footwear Fans Flip-Flop Kerfuffle,"

NBC News, July 2005, 1–2. http://www.nbcnews.com/id/8670164/ns/us_
news/t/white-house-footwear-fans-flip-flop-kerfuffle/#.Ud7yYT7wJpt; David
Bohrer, "NU's Lacrosse Team Sparks Flip-Flop Flap at White House," *USA
Today*, July 2005, 1. http://usatoday30.usatoday.com/news/offbeat/2005–07
–19-flip-flops_x.htm.

104. Jenna Goudreau, "The Seven Ways Your Boss is Judging Your
Appearance," *Forbes Magazine*, November 30, 2012, 3. http://www.forbes
.com/sites/jennagoudreau/2012/11/30/the-seven-ways-your-boss-is-judging-
your-appearance/.

105. Paul Taylor and Scott Keeter, *Millennials: Confident. Connected. Open to
Change* (Web: PEW Research Center, 2010), 57, 58. http://www.pewsocialtrends
.org/files/2010/10/millennials-confident-connected-open-to-change.pdf.

106. Lynne Marek, "Frivolous Suits: Judges Wonder, 'Who Dressed You,
Counselor'?", *The National Law Journal*, May 21, 2009. http://www.law.com
/jsp/article.jsp?id=1202484611544&slreturn=20130918162428.

107. Jenny Blake, *Life After College* (Philadelphia: Running Press Book
Publishers, 2011), 53.

Chapter 9

108. Jeffrey Jensen Arnett, PhD., *Emerging Adulthood: The Winding Road
from the Late Teens through the Twenties* (New York: Oxford University Press,
2004), 3–4.

109. Jeffrey Jensen Arnett, PhD., *Emerging Adulthood: The Winding Road
from the Late Teens through the Twenties* (New York: Oxford University Press,
2004), 21. Arnett notes that: " . . . emerging adulthood exists today mainly in
the industrialized or 'postindustrial' countries of the West, along with Asian
countries such as Japan and South Korea."

110. Paul Taylor and Scott Keeter, *Millennials: Confident. Connected. Open*

to Change (Web: PEW Research Center, 2010), 18. http://www.pewsocialtrends
.org/files/2010/10/millennials-confident-connected-open-to-change.pdf.

111. Bruce Tulgan, Not Everyone Gets A Trophy: How to Manage Generation Y (San Francisco: Jossey-Bass, 2009), 8.

112. Meg Jay, The Defining Decade: Why your Twenties Matter—and how to
Make the Most of them Now (New York, NY: Hatchette Book Group, 2012), 7.

113. Jeffrey Jensen Arnett, PhD., Emerging Adulthood: The Winding Road
from the Late Teens through the Twenties (New York: Oxford University Press,
2004), 22–23.

114. Simon Waxman, "In Defense of my Generation," Cognoscenti, September
26, 2012. http://cognoscenti.wbur.org/2012/09/26/millennial-media-simon-waxman.
Waxman further stated: "Where some journalists see worrisome delay, we see life
unfolding in real-time, at a pace we don't really control. Where they seem to believe
that non-conjugal love, advanced degrees, traveling, and rented apartments are bar-
ricades against adult life, we can't help but shrug. I don't know a single person my
age who cares whether our parents' generation classifies us as adults. When I share
these stories with friends—usually via Facebook, where our covens of adolescence
gather—I get nothing but eye rolling in response. Are we the only ones who appreciate that immaturity happens at every age and stage of life?"

115. Chip Espinoza, Mick Ukleja and Craig Rusch, Managing the Millennials:
Discover the Core Competencies for Managing Today's Workforce (Hoboken,
NJ: Jon Wiley & Sons, Inc., 2010), 135.
For an article describing the way Millennials may have responded to ambig-
uous messages in the classroom, see: Lauren Stiller Rikleen, *Cheating and
the Millennial Generation* (Web: The Podium, Boston Globe On-Line, Sept.
14, 2012). http://www.bostonglobe.com/opinion/2012/09/14/cheating-and-
millennial-generation/imgghIcKXbdBAGuFKmZQaN/story.html.

116. Alexandra Robbins & Abby Wilner, *Quarterlife Crisis: The Unique
Challenges of Life in your Twenties* (New York, NY: Penguin Inc., 2001), 3.

117. Dan Schawbel, *Millennial Branding Student Employment Gap Study Summary Report* (Web: Millennial Branding, May 14, 2012), 1. http://millennialbranding.com/2012/05/millennial-branding-student-employment-gap-study/. See also: Hannah Seligson, "The Age of the Permanent Intern," *Washingtonian Magazine*, February 6, 2013, 2. http://www.washingtonian.com/articles/people/the-age-of-the-permanent-intern/.

118. Hannah Seligson, "The Age of the Permanent Intern," *Washingtonian Magazine*, February 6, 2013, 2. http://www.washingtonian.com/articles/people/the-age-of-the-permanent-intern/. Seligson interviewed a 25 year-old Ivy League graduate who moonlighted as a waitress while undertaking various internships in the hope of finding full-time employment: "After all, who wants to still be an intern at an age when you should have a 401(k) and a modicum of job security, or at least be earning more than you did at your summer job during high school? 'People my age expect to start at the bottom . . . but in this economy the bottom keeps getting lower and lower.'"

119. See, e.g. Keenan Mayo, "Why Interns are Suing 'Saturday Night Live,' Hollywood, and Other Dream Employers," *Business Week,* July 12, 2013. http://www.businessweek.com/articles/2013–07–12/why-interns-are-suing-saturday-night-live-hollywood-and-other-dream-employers.

120. The case is *Glatt v. Fox Searchlight Pictures, Inc.*, US District Court for the Southern District of New York (decision dated June 11, 2013). The decision was widely covered in the media and in blogs; see e.g. Martha J. Zackin, "Unpaid Internships May Be More Costly Than You May Think," *Employment Matters Blog,* June 11, 2013. http://www.employmentmattersblog.com/2013/06/unpaid-internships-may-be-more-costly-than-you-may-think/.

121. Steven Greenhouse, "Charlie Rose Show Agrees to Pay Up to $250,000 to Settle Interns Lawsuit," *The New York Times*, December 20, 2013. http://mediadecoder.blogs.nytimes.com/2012/12/20/charlie-rose-show-agrees-to-pay-up-to-250000-to-settle-interns-lawsuit/?smid=tw-mediadecodernyt&seid=auto&_r=0.

Chapter 10

122. Sibson Consulting, *Millennials in the Sales Force: It's Time to Get to Know This Generation* (Web: The Segal Group, April 2009), 15. http://www .sibson.com/services/sales-force-effectiveness/Millennials-in-the-Sales-Force-Survey-Results.pdf.

123. PricewaterhouseCoopers, University of Southern California and London Business School, *PwC's NextGen: A Global Generational Study* (Web: PwC, 2013), 6. http://www.pwc.com/en_GX/gx/hr-management-services/pdf/ pwc-nextgen-study-2013.pdf.

124. Mary Nestor-Harper, *Infographic Shows What HR Pros Think of Millennials* (Web: TheCareerNetwork, June 2013), 1–2. http://www.beyond.com/ articles/infographic-shows-what-hr-pros-think-of-12625-article.html.

125. Adrienne Fox, "Mixing it Up: With four—almost five—generations in the workplace, tensions can arise through misunderstandings and miscommunication," *HR Magazine*, May 2011, 24. (Citing to research from the Center for Work-Life Policy.)

126. For an apt analogy, see Praveen Purushotham's comment in The Boston Globe's article, Hennick, Calvin, *Fresh Approach to Career Path* (January 3, 2013): "Millennials view employers as 'service providers,' not much different from a cellphone carrier. You can't say, 'this is my service, take it or leave it,' because they will leave it." Praveen Purushotham is the global head of marketing at Virtusa Corp., an information technology services company.

127. Sibson Consulting, *Millennials in the Sales Force: It's Time to Get to Know This Generation* (Web: The Segal Group, April 2009), 20. http://www .sibson.com/services/sales-force-effectiveness/Millennials-in-the-Sales-Force-Survey-Results.pdf.

128. PricewaterhouseCoopers, University of Southern California and London Business School, *PwC's NextGen: A Global Generational Study* (Web:

PwC, 2013), 13. http://www.pwc.com/en_GX/gx/hr-management-services/pdf/pwc-nextgen-study-2013.pdf.

129. PricewaterhouseCoopers, *Millennials at Work: Reshaping the Workplace* (Web: PwC, 2011), 7. http://www.pwc.com/en_M1/m1/services/consulting/documents/millennials-at-work.pdf.

130. Dalton Conley, "Welcome to Elsewhere," *Newsweek*, January 16, 2009, 60.

131. See, e.g., Ann Trieger Kurland, "Her Teenage Invention Flowers into Food Spoilage Prevention," *Boston Globe,* March 14, 2012. One article described the trend of college students pursuing their entrepreneurial dreams: "But like a growing number of his peers from MIT, and scores of other new graduates at top universities, he's eschewing corporate America for the unpredictable world of scrappy Internet start-ups." The article further noted that, in 2012, investors provided seed funding to 1,749 early-stage tech companies, up 64% from the year before. Michael B. Farrell, "New Grads Drawn to New Business," *Boston Globe,* June 7, 2013.

For an interesting example of a Millennial using elective office to be a change agent, see: Martine Powers, *Hard-Charging Start for Youngest Mayor*, Boston Globe (July 24, 2012), 1.

For an interesting article on earning and spending patterns of today's young millionaires, see: Reuters, "Make Way for the Millennial Millionaires," *Fiscal Times*, August 5, 2013. http://www.thefiscaltimes.com/Articles/2013/08/05/Make-Way-for-the-Millennial-Millionaires. See also: Alex Hampl, "Twenty-Five Under 25," *Sports Illustrated*, October 30, 2013. http://sportsillustrated.cnn.com/specials/25under25/index.html.

More than ever, opportunities abound for young people to develop their leadership skills and work on behalf of social and economic causes, making a tremendous difference in the world. For an article describing the contributions made by a group of young women leaders, see: *Girls20Summit*, accessed Oct. 4, 2013. http://www.girls20summit.com/about/. See also Bea Fields, Scott Wilder, Jim Bunch and Rob Newbold, *Millennial Leaders: Success Stories From Today's Most Brilliant Generation Y Leaders* (Buffalo Grove, IL: Writers of the Round Table Press, 2008).

132. Hannah Seligson, "No Jobs? Young Graduates Make Their Own," *New York Times*, December 11, 2010. http://www.nytimes.com/2010/12/12/business /12yec.html?pagewanted=all.

133. PricewaterhouseCoopers, *Millennials at Work: Reshaping the Workplace* (Web: PwC, 2011), 5. http://www.pwc.com/en_M1/m1/services/consulting /documents/millennials-at-work.pdf. Other research by PwC highlighted these shifting centers of growth: "Many traditional business hubs such as Paris, London, and Moscow, will be dwarfed in population size by Mumbai, Delhi, and Dhaka. Of the 30 most highly populated cities in 1950, only 19 remained among the top 30 as of 2007. In addition, 11 new cities that had never before registered as large enough populations have hit the top 30. By 2025, only 16 cities that ranked among the top 30 most populated in 1950 will remain on the list. Of these, only three are located in the United States, representing a significant shift from 75 years earlier. London and Lima will come out of the top 30, and three new cities that were not even ranked in 2007 will emerge: Lahore, Shenzhen, and Chennai." PricewaterhouseCoopers, *Talent Mobility 2020: The Next Generation of International Assignments* (Web: PwC, 2010), 8. http://www.pwc.com/gx/en/managing-tomorrows-people/future-of-work/pdf /talent-mobility-2020.pdf.

134. Cliff Zukin, Mark Szeltner, *Talent Report: What Workers Want in 2012* (Web: Net Impact and Rutgers University, May 2012), 10. http://www.heldrich .rutgers.edu/sites/default/files/content/Net_Impact_Talent_Report_0.pdf.

Of interest, one article describes both Boomers and Millennials as "bookend generations" because of, among other characteristics, their shared "journey in search of meaning". See Sylvia Hewlett, "The 'Me' Generation Gives Way to the 'We' Generation," *Financial Times*, June 19, 2009. http://www.ft.com/cms /s/0/f8b0aca4–5c69–11de-aea3–00144feabdc0.html#axzz2i6l6tvzf.

135. Jeffrey Jensen Arnett, PhD., Joseph Schwab, "The Clark University Poll of Emerging Adults: Thriving, Struggling & Hopeful", December, 2012, 14. http://www.clarku.edu/clark-poll-emerging-adults/pdfs/clark-university-poll-emerging-adults-findings.pdf.

For an interesting article describing research on the health benefits of meaning, as compared to happiness, see: Emily Esfahani Smith, "Meaning is Healthier Than Happiness," *The Atlantic*, August 1, 2013. http://www.theatlantic.com/ health/archive/2013/08/meaning-is-healthier-than-happiness/278250/.

136. Sodexo, *Workplace Trends 2013* (Web: Sodexo, 2013), 18. http://viewer .zmags.com/publication/f045b66f#/f045b66f/2.

137. Courtney E. Martin, *Do It Anyway: The New Generation of Activists* (Boston, MA: Beacon Press, 2010), xiv, xviii.

138. Christine Barton, Jeff Fromm, and Chris Egan, *The Millennial Consumer: Debunking Stereotypes* (Web: The Boston Consulting Group, April 16, 2012), 9. http://www.brandchannel.com/images/papers/536_BCG_The_Millennial _Consumer_Apr_2012%20(3)_tcm80–103894.pdf. The study further stated that Millennials are receptive to cause marketing and more likely than other generations to purchase items that are associated with a cause.

139. In describing the effect Millennials are already having in the workplace on changing corporate behavior, a Boston Globe columnist wrote: "Rather than wiling away days on Facebook and marching into corner offices to demand raises every five minutes, younger workers—armed with that extra self-confidence— are pushing companies to do more good in the community. Young job seekers lucky enough to be in demand are choosing employers based partly on whether they're good citizens." Yvonne Abraham, "Youthful Take on Business," *Boston Globe,* October 30, 2011, B1.

140. Joanne G. Sujansky and Jan Ferri-Reed, *Keeping The Millennials: Why Companies Are Losing Billions In Turnover To This Generation—And What To Do About It* (Hoboken, NJ: John Wiley & Sons, 2009), 44. The authors note the link between the Millennials' engagement in charitable causes in the workplace and their experiences as students: "Remember, most of these children were raised in an environment in which they were required to contribute service to the community. This wasn't just a casual expectation. In some places, student community service was considered an essential factor in receiving the credentials necessary to graduate from secondary school." At 45.

141. See: Alexandra Levit and Sanja Licina, *How the Recession Shaped Millennial and Hiring Manager Attitudes about Millennials' Future Careers* (Web: Career Advisory Board, 2012). http://newsroom.devry.edu/images/20004/Future%20of%20Millennial%20Careers%20Report.pdf.

An interesting example of how deep the roots of engagement run can be found in a longitudinal study of graduates of a suburban Massachusetts high school from the class of 2009 which reported significant engagement in their college community: the study reported that 68% were involved in community service/volunteer activities, 76% participated in clubs or activities, and 48% worked in paid employment. See Judith Martin, *Pathways After Graduation Study: Year Two for the Class of 2009; Year One for the Class of 2010* (Pathways, July 2013), 5.

Chapter 11

142. Adrienne Fox, "Mixing it Up: With four—almost five—generations in the workplace, tensions can arise through misunderstandings and miscommunication," *HR Magazine*, May 2011, 25.

143. Razor Suleman and Bob Nelson, "Motivating the Millennials: Tapping into the Potential of the Youngest Generation", *Leader to Leader Journal*, No. 62, Fall 2011 (Web: Frances Hesselbein Leadership Institute, 2011). http://www.hesselbeininstitute.org/knowledgecenter/journal.aspx?ArticleID=889. The authors further stated: "Managers need to take the time to help coach millennial employees and in the process show them how they can make a positive, meaningful impact at work. Redefine the time frame for this generation's focus and show them how the things they are doing now can lead to things they want to be doing later."

144. Richard Halicks, "Teens of Means: Some affluent parents give their kids everything—except the ability to connect with other people," Atlanta Journal-Constitution, July 23, 2006, 2–3.

145. PricewaterhouseCoopers, University of Southern California and London Business School, PwC's NextGen: A Global Generational Study (Web:

PwC, 2013), 9. http://www.pwc.com/en_GX/gx/hr-management-services/pdf/
pwc-nextgen-study-2013.pdf.

Chapter 12

146. American Psychological Association, Stress by Generation (Web:
APA.org, February, 2013), 1–3. http://www.apa.org/news/press/releases/
stress/2012/generations.aspx. See also: American Psychological Association, Health Care System Falls Short on Stress Management (Web: APA.
org, February 7, 2013), 1–2. http://www.apa.org/news/press/releases/2013
/02/stress-management.aspx.

Also of interest: A survey conducted at a Massachusetts high school in 2002
discovered that 47% of middle school students and 76% of high school students
described their lives as stressful. Peak stress occurred during junior year when
84% of students characterized themselves as stressed, which likely correlates
with the college application process. See: Social Science Research and Evaluation, Inc., *Data from the 2001–2002 Wayland Adolescent Behavior Survey*
(Print: Wayland High School, 2002), 13.

147. Kathleen Gerson, *The Unfinished Revolution: How a New Generation
is Reshaping Family, Work, and Gender in America* (New York: Oxford University Press, 2010), 5.

148. Marcie Pitt-Catsouphes and Christina Matz-Costa, *Engaging the 21st
Century Multi-Generational Workforce: Findings from the Age & Generations Study* (Web: The Sloan Center on Aging and Work at Boston College,
2009), 25. http://www.bc.edu/content/dam/files/research_sites/agingandwork/
pdf/publications/IB20_Engagement.pdf.

149. Jerry Krueger and Emily Killham, "Why Dilbert Is Right," *Gallup Business Journal*, March 9, 2006, 1. http://businessjournal.gallup.com/content/21802
/why-dilbert-right.aspx.

150. Tamara Erickson, *Plugged In: The Generation Y Guide to Thriving at
Work* (Boston, MA: Harvard Business Press, 2008), 77.

151. Paul Taylor and Scott Keeter, *Millennials: Confident. Connected. Open to Change.* (Web: PEW Research Center, 2010), 24. http://www.pewsocialtrends .org/files/2010/10/millennials-confident-connected-open-to-change.pdf.

152. Cliff Zukin, Mark Szeltner, *Talent Report: What Workers Want in 2012* (Web: Net Impact and Rutgers University, May 2012), 3. http://www.heldrich .rutgers.edu/sites/default/files/content/Net_Impact_Talent_Report_0.pdf.

153. Cliff Zukin, Mark Szeltner, *Talent Report: What Workers Want in 2012* (Web: Net Impact and Rutgers University, May 2012), 8. http://www.heldrich .rutgers.edu/sites/default/files/content/Net_Impact_Talent_Report_0.pdf.

154. Boston College Center for Work & Family in the Carroll School of Management, The New Dad: Caring, Committed, and Conflicted (Web: BC CWF, 2011). http://www.thenewdad.org/the_new_dad_research/the_new_dad _caring_committed_and_conflicted_2011. Other important studies on the changing roles of fathers in the workplace from the Boston College Center for Work & Family include: The New Dad: Exploring Fatherhood within a Career Context (2010), http://www.thenewdad.org/the_new_dad_research /the_new_dad_exploring_fatherhood_within_a_career_context_2010; The New Dad: Right at Home (2012), http://www.thenewdad.org/the_new_dad _research/the_new_dad_right_at_home_2012; and The New Dad: A Work (and Life) in Progress (2013), http://www.thenewdad.org/the_new_dad_a _work_life_in_progress.

155. Jeffrey Jensen Arnett, PhD., Joseph Schwab, "The Clark University Poll of Emerging Adults: Thriving, Struggling & Hopeful", December, 2012, 16. http://www.clarku.edu/clark-poll-emerging-adults/pdfs/clark-university-poll-emerging-adults-findings.pdf.

156. Cliff Zukin, Mark Szeltner, *Talent Report: What Workers Want in 2012* (Web: Net Impact and Rutgers University, May 2012), 12. http://www.heldrich .rutgers.edu/sites/default/files/content/Net_Impact_Talent_Report_0.pdf.

157. Bentley University Center for Women and Business, *Millennials in the*

Workplace (Web: Bentley University, 2012), 13. http://www.bentley.edu/centers/sites/www.bentley.edu.centers/files/centers/cwb/millennials-report.pdf.

158. Families and Work Institute, *Generation and Gender in the Workplace* (Web: The American Business Collaboration, 2002), 3. http://familiesandwork.org/site/research/reports/genandgender.pdf.

159. PricewaterhouseCoopers, University of Southern California and London Business School, *PwC's NextGen: A Global Generational Study* (Web: PwC, 2013), 8. http://www.pwc.com/en_GX/gx/hr-management-services/pdf/pwc-nextgen-study-2013.pdf. The study also mentions that slightly more women than men were concerned about striking a better work-life balance: 15% of males and 21% of females indicated that they would give up some of their pay and slow the pace of promotion in exchange for working fewer hours.

160. PricewaterhouseCoopers, University of Southern California and London Business School, *PwC's NextGen: A Global Generational Study* (Web: PwC, 2013), 9. http://www.pwc.com/en_GX/gx/hr-management-services/pdf/pwc-nextgen-study-2013.pdf.

161. Marcie Pitt-Catsouphes, Christina Matz-Costa, and Elyssa Besen, *Workplace Flexibility: Findings from the Age & Generations Study* (Web: The Sloan Center on Aging and Work at Boston College, 2009), 8. http://www.bc.edu/content/dam/files/research_sites/agingandwork/pdf/publications/IB19_WorkFlex.pdf.

162. See, e.g., Donna Wagner, "The Broken System of Long-Term Care in America," *The Sloan Center on Aging & Work at Boston College*, September 18, 2013. http://agingandwork.bc.edu/blog/the-broken-system-of-long-term-care-in-america/.

163. Kathleen Gerson, *The Unfinished Revolution: How a New Generation is Reshaping Family, Work, and Gender in America* (New York: Oxford University Press, 2010), 12.

164. Studies of the leadership and compensation gender pay gap exist in every profession. For a recent study of the gender gap in compensation in the legal profession, see: Lauren Stiller Rikleen, *Closing the Gap: A Road Map for Achieving Gender Pay Equity in Law Firm Partner Compensation* (Web: American Bar Association, 2013). http://www.americanbar.org/content/dam/aba/administrative/women/closing_the_gap.authcheckdam.pdf.

See also: Evelyn Murphy with E.J. Graff, Getting Even: Why Women Don't Get Paid Like Men and What to Do About It (New York, NY: Touchstone, 2005).

165. Marcie Pitt-Catsouphes, Christina Matz-Costa and Elyssa Besen, *Workplace Flexibility: Findings from the Age and Generations Study* (Web: The Sloan Center on Aging & Work, January 2009), 6. http://www.bc.edu/content/dam/files/research_sites/agingandwork/pdf/publications/IB19_WorkFlex.pdf.

166. Toon Taris, and Paul Schreurs, Well-Being and Organizational Performance: An Organizational-Level Test of the Happy-Productive Worker Hypothesis, *Work & Stress* 23:2 (2009): 120–136.

167. Ans De Vos and Sara De Hauw, *Do Different Times Call for Different Measures? The Psychological Contract of the Millennial Generation in Times of Economic Recession.* Vlerick Leuven Gent Working Paper Series (2010), 3.

168. PricewaterhouseCoopers, *Millennials at Work: Reshaping the Workplace* (Web: PwC, 2011). http://www.pwc.com/en_M1/m1/services/consulting/documents/millennials-at-work.pdf.

169. PricewaterhouseCoopers, *Millennials at Work: Reshaping the Workplace* (Web: PwC, 2011), 12. http://www.pwc.com/en_M1/m1/services/consulting/documents/millennials-at-work.pdf.

Chapter 13

170. One article summarized data showing a decline in economic literacy among young people. For example, joint studies from the Treasury Department and the Department of Education revealed declining financial literacy scores

among high school students. Similarly, data from an ongoing survey conducted by the Jumpstart Coalition for Personal Financial Literacy demonstrated that: "In 1997, the average score on a 31-question financial literacy exam given as part of the survey was 57.3%. In 2008, the average score was at its lowest ever, 48.3%." Hadley Malcolm, "Millennials Struggle with Financial Literacy," *USA Today*, April 24, 2012. http://usatoday30.usatoday.com/money/perfi/basics/story /2012–04–23/millenials-financial-knowledge/54494856/1.

171. Jenny Blake, *Life After College* (Philadelphia: Running Press Book Publishers, 2011), 7.
Another book that provides helpful advice for Millennials in the job search process is: Lindsey Pollack, *Getting from College to Career: Your Essential Guide to Succeeding in the Real World* (New York, NY: HarperBusiness, 2012).

172. Jeffrey Jensen Arnett, PhD., *Emerging Adulthood: The Winding Road from the Late Teens through the Twenties* (New York: Oxford University Press, 2004), 228.

173. PricewaterhouseCoopers, *Millennials at Work: Reshaping the Workplace* (Web: PwC, 2011), 9. http://www.pwc.com/en_M1/m1/services/consulting /documents/millennials-at-work.pdf. The survey provided the following global data: "Generally, millennials in Western Europe are less optimistic, with 54% believing they'll be better off than their parents' generation and 26% believing they'll be worse off. North American millennials are among the most optimistic, with just 13% expecting to be worse off than their parents and 67% expecting to be better off." At 9.

174. See, e.g. Razor Suleman and Bob Nelson, *Motivating the Millennials: Tapping into the Potential of the Youngest Generation*, Leader to Leader Journal, No. 62, Fall 2011 (Web: Frances Hesselbein Leadership Institute, 2011). http://www.hesselbeininstitute.org/knowledgecenter/journal.aspx?ArticleID=889 . Suleman and Nelson note that: "Millennials are a very social generation, so allow them to work together on projects and set up frequent social situations such as team-building activities and celebrations outside work. If they tend to work best with others and the way they get into a project is to talk it through

with coworkers—great, let them do that [. . .] You may not need to have your job be fun to get it done, but don't fault them if that's their preference." They further note that: "The days of 'one size fits all' when it comes to employee motivation are long gone. What thrills and delights one employee may be boring and insulting to another. Avoid this problem by allowing employees to choose what best motivates them—be it the latest electronic merchandise, an experience, or a charity donation—when they have the opportunity to be thanked for having done a great job."

175. Jennifer J. Deal, Retiring the Generation Gap: How Employees Young & Old Can Find Common Ground (San Francisco: Jossey-Bass, 2007), 11, 13.

176. Jennifer J. Deal, Retiring the Generation Gap: How Employees Young & Old Can Find Common Ground (San Francisco: Jossey-Bass, 2007), 46.

177. Accenture Management Consulting, Technology and Outsourcing, Jumping the Boundaries of Corporate IT: Accenture Global Research on Millennials' Use of Technology (Web: Accenture, 2010), 10. http://nstore.accenture.com/ technology/millennials/global_millennial_generation_research.pdf.

178. Kim Lee DeAngelis, Reverse Mentoring at the Hartford: Cross Generational Transfer of Knowledge About Social Media (Web: Boston College Center for Work and Family, 2013), 16. http://www.bc.edu/content/dam/files/ research_sites/agingandwork/pdf/publications/hartford.pdf.
An additional interesting discussion of intergenerational mentoring can be found at: Sylvia Ann Hewlett, Laura Sherbin, and Karen Sumberg, "How Gen Y & Boomers Will Reshape Your Agenda," HBR (July-August 2009): 121–126.

179. Bentley University Center for Women and Business, Millennials in the Workplace (Web: Bentley University, 2012), 16. http://www.bentley.edu/centers /sites/www.bentley.edu.centers/files/centers/cwb/millennials-report.pdf.

180. W. Stanton Smith, *Decoding Generational Differences: Changing your Mindset . . . Without Losing your Mind* (Greenville, SC: W. Stanton Smith LLC, 2010), 40. Smith further stated: "A best practice regarding transparency is as

follows: be clear about what you as a leader have decided not to be transparent about. This straightforwardness is highly preferable to appearing to be open when there is no intention of being open or when circumstances dictate that you as a leader cannot be transparent." At 41. F. Brittany Hite, *Employers Rethink How They Give Feedback* (Web: Wall Street Journal, October 13, 2008). http://online.wsj.com/news/articles/SB122385967800027549.

181. Lauren Stiller Rikleen, *Creating Tomorrow's Leaders: The Expanding Roles of Millennials in the Workplace* (Boston College Center for Work & Family), 8. https://www.bc.edu/content/dam/files/centers/cwf/pdf/BCCWF%20EBS-Millennials%20FINAL.pdf.

182. Cliff Zukin, Mark Szeltner, *Talent Report: What Workers Want in 2012* (Web: Net Impact and Rutgers University, May 2012), 22. http://www.heldrich.rutgers.edu/sites/default/files/content/Net_Impact_Talent_Report_0.pdf.

183. Jennifer J. Deal, *Retiring the Generation Gap: How Employees Young & Old Can Find Common Ground* (San Francisco: Jossey-Bass, 2007), 171.

Chapter 14

184. Consumerlab, "Young Professions at Work," *Ericsson Consumer Insight*, April 2013, 4. http://www.slideshare.net/EricssonSlides/young-professionals-at-work.

185. Kathleen Gerson, *The Unfinished Revolution: How a New Generation is Reshaping Family, Work, and Gender in America* (New York: Oxford University Press, 2010), 6.

186. Kathleen Gerson, The Unfinished Revolution: How a New Generation is Reshaping Family, Work, and Gender in America (New York: Oxford University Press, 2010), 10.

187. Marcie Pitt-Catsouphes and Christina Matz-Costa, Engaging the 21st Century Multi-Generational Workforce: Findings from the Age & Generations

Study (Web: The Sloan Center on Aging and Work at Boston College, 2009), 3. http://www.bc.edu/content/dam/files/research_sites/agingandwork/pdf/publications/IB20_Engagement.pdf.

188. Cone Inc. in collaboration with AMP Agency, 2006 Millennial Cause Study: The Millennial Generation: Pro-social and Empowered to Change the World (Web: Gateway Center for Giving: 2006), 18–19. http://www.centerforgiving.org/LinkClick.aspx?fileticket=9cKyEls7NXg%3D&tabid=86&mid=471.

189. Arnett, Jeffrey Jensen, PhD., "The Evidence for Generation We and Against Generation Me," *Emerging Adulthood* 1.1, 2013, 9. http://cofc-01.wpengine.netdna-cdn.com/writing/files/2012/08/Arnett-Twenge.pdf.

Bibliography

AARP, Leading a Multigenerational Workforce (Web: AARP, 2007). http://assets.aarp.org/www.aarp.org_/cs/misc/leading_a_multigenerational_workforce.pdf. Endnote 18

AARP and GFK Custom Research North America, Baby Boomers Envision What's Next? (Web: AARP, 2011). http://assets.aarp.org/rgcenter/general/boomers-envision-retirement-2011.pdf. Endnote 12.

Abraham, Yvonne, "Youthful Take on Business," Boston Globe, October 30, 2011. Endnote 139.

Accenture, U.S. Workers Under Pressure to Improve Skills, But Need More Support from Employers (Web: Accenture, 2011). http://newsroom.accenture.com/article_display.cfm?article_id=5343. Endnote 76.

Accenture Management Consulting, Technology and Outsourcing, Jumping the Boundaries of Corporate IT: Accenture Global Research on Millennials' Use of Technology (Web: Accenture, 2010). http://nstore.accenture.com/technology/millennials/global_millennial_generation_research.pdf. Endnotes 89, 90, 92, 93, 94, 96, 177.

Alsop, Ron, The Trophy Kids Grow Up (San Francisco: Jossey-Bass, 2008). Endnote 68.

American Psychological Association, Health Care System Falls Short on Stress Management (Web: APA.org, February 7, 2013). http://www.apa.org/news/press/releases/2013/02/stress-management.aspx. Endnote 146.

American Psychological Association, Stress by Generation (Web: APA.org, February, 2013). http://www.apa.org/news/press/releases/stress/2012/generations.aspx. Endnote 146.

Arnett, Jeffrey Jensen, PhD., Emerging Adulthood: The Winding

Road from the Late Teens through the Twenties (New York: Oxford University Press, 2004). Endnotes 108, 109, 113, 172.

Arnett, Jeffrey Jensen, PhD., "The Evidence for Generation We and Against Generation Me," Emerging Adulthood 1.1, 2013. http://cofc-01.wpengine.netdna-cdn.com/writing/files/2012/08/Arnett-Twenge.pdf. Endnote 189.

Arnett, Jeffrey Jensen, PhD. and Schwab, Joseph, "The Clark University Poll of Emerging Adults: Thriving, Struggling & Hopeful", December, 2012. http://www.clarku.edu/clark-poll-emerging-adults/pdfs/clark-university-poll-emerging-adults-findings.pdf. Endnotes 45, 61, 62, 135, 155.

Associated Press, "More Baby Boomers Delay Retirement," The Fiscal Times, November 10, 2011. http://www.thefiscaltimes.com/Articles/2011/11/10/More-Baby-Boomers-Delay-Retirement. Endnote 12.

Associated Press, "White House Footwear Fans Flip-Flop Kerfuffle," NBC News, July 2005. http://www.nbcnews.com/id/8670164/ns/us_news/t/white-house-footwear-fans-flip-flop-kerfuffle/#.Ud7yYT7wJpt. Endnote 103.

Barton, Christine, Fromm, Jeff and Egan, Chris, The Millennial Consumer: Debunking Stereotypes (Web: The Boston Consulting Group, April 16, 2012). http://www.brandchannel.com/images/papers/536_BCG_The_Millennial_Consumer_Apr_2012%20(3)_tcm80-103894.pdf. Endnotes 81, 138.

Bentley University Center for Women and Business, Millennials in the Workplace (Web: Bentley University, 2012). http://www.bentley.edu/centers/sites/www.bentley.edu.centers/files/centers/cwb/millennials-report.pdf. Endnotes 32, 157, 179.

Berrett, Dan, Students May Be Reading Plenty, but Not for Class (Web: The Chronicle of Higher Education, May 1, 2013). http://chronicle.com/article/Students-May-Be-Reading/138911/. Endnotes 98, 99.

Blake, Jenny, Life After College (Philadelphia: Running Press Book Publishers, 2011). Endnotes 107, 171.

Bohrer, David, "NU's Lacrosse Team Sparks Flip-Flop Flap at White

House," USA Today, July 2005. http://usatoday30.usatoday
.com/news/offbeat/2005-07-19-flip-flops_x.htm. Endnote 103.

Boston College Center for Work & Family in the Carroll
School of Management, The New Dad: A Work (and
Life) in Progress (2013). http://www.thenewdad.org/
the_new_dad_a_work_life_in_progress. Endnote 154.

Boston College Center for Work & Family in the Carroll School
of Management, The New Dad: Caring, Committed,
and Conflicted (Web: BC CWF, 2011). http://www
.thenewdad.org/the_new_dad_research/the_new_dad_
caring_committed_and_conflicted_2011. Endnote 154.

Boston College Center for Work & Family in the Carroll School
of Management, The New Dad: Exploring Fatherhood
within a Career Context (2010). http://www.thenewdad
.org/the_new_dad_research/the_new_dad_exploring_
fatherhood_within_a_career_context_2010. Endnote 154.

Boston College Center for Work & Family in the Carroll
School of Management, The New Dad: Right at Home
(2012). http://www.thenewdad.org/the_new_dad_research
/the_new_dad_right_at_home_2012. Endnote 154.

Briody, Blaire, "How Clinging to Mommy and Daddy is
Ruining a Generation," Fiscal Times, February 8,
2012. http://www.thefiscaltimes.com/Articles/2012
/02/08/How-Clinging-to-Mommy-and-Daddy-is-
Ruining-a-Generation.aspx#page1. Endnote 52.

Center for Information and Research on Civic Learning and
Engagement, The National Conference on Citizenship,
Mobalize.org, and Harvard University Institute of
Politics, Millennials Civic Health Index (Web: Harvard
University, February, 2013). http://www.iopnewsletter.com
/news/02052013_NCC_Millennial.pdf. Endnote 57.

Cone Inc. in collaboration with AMP Agency, 2006 Millennial
Cause Study: The Millennial Generation: Pro-social
and Empowered to Change the World (Web: Gateway
Center for Giving: 2006). http://www.centerforgiving

.org/LinkClick.aspx?fileticket=9cKyEls7NXg
%3D&tabid=86&mid=471. Endnote 188.

Conley, Dalton, "Welcome to Elsewhere," Newsweek,
January 16, 2009. Endnote 130.

Consumerlab, "Young Professions at Work," Ericsson Consumer
Insight, April 2013. http://www.slideshare.net/EricssonSlides
/young-professionals-at-work. Endnotes 24, 95, 184.

Corporate Leadership Council, The Power of Peers:
Building Engagement Capital through Peer Interaction
(Web, The Corporate Executive Board Company,
2011). http://greatmanager.ucsf.edu/files/CLC
_The_Power_of_Peers_Building_Engagement_Capital
_Through_Peer_Interaction.pdf. Endnote 1.

Deal, Jennifer J., Retiring the Generation Gap: How Employees
Young & Old Can Find Common Ground (San Francisco:
Jossey-Bass, 2007). Endnotes 175, 176, 183.

DeAngelis, Kim Lee, Reverse Mentoring at the Hartford: Cross
Generational Transfer of Knowledge About Social Media
(Web: Boston College Center for Work and Family, 2013).
http://www.bc.edu/content/dam/files/research_sites/
agingandwork/pdf/publications/hartford.pdf. Endnote 178.

Deveny, Kathleen and Raina Kelley, Raina, "Girls Gone
Bad?" Newsweek, February 12, 2007. Endnote 71.

De Vos, Ans and De Hauw, Sara, Do Different Times Call for
Different Measures? The Psychological Contract of the
Millennial Generation in Times of Economic Recession. Vlerick
Leuven Gent Working Paper Series (2010). Endnote 167.

Dhawan, Erica, "Gen-Y Workforce and Workplace Are Out
of Sync," Forbes, January 23, 2012. http://www.forbes
.com/sites/85broads/2012/01/23/gen-y-workforce-
and-workplace-are-out-of-sync/. Endnote 25.

Divorce statistics: http://www.census.gov/hhes/socdemo/
marriage/data/cps/p23-180/p23-180.pdf. Endnote 17.

Doherty, Jacqueline, "On the Rise," Barron's Cover, April
29, 2013. http://online.barrons.com/article/SB50001

42405274870388940457844097284274 2076.html #articleTabs_article%3D1. Endnotes 21, 22.

Douglas, Emily, "A Quick Look at our Nation's Education Data," Education Week Blog, May 21, 2013. http://blogs .edweek.org/topschooljobs/k-12_talent_manager/2013 /05/nations_education_data.html?utm_medium=twitter &utm_source=twitterfeed. Endnote 29.

Edwards, Laurie, "Teaching the 'Me Me Me' Generation," WUBUR, June 2013. http://cognoscenti.wbur.org/2013/06/18 /millennials-in-the-classroom-laurie-edwards. Endnote 8.

Erickson, Tamara, Plugged In: The Generation Y Guide to Thriving at Work (Boston, MA: Harvard Business Press, 2008). Endnote 150.

Espinoza, Chip, Ukleja, Mick and Rusch, Craig, Managing the Millennials: Discover the Core Competencies for Managing Today's Workforce (Hoboken, NJ: Jon Wiley & Sons, Inc., 2010). Endnote 115.

Families and Work Institute, Generation and Gender in the Workplace (Web: The American Business Collaboration, 2002). http://familiesandwork.org/site /research/reports/genandgender.pdf. Endnote 158

Farrell, Michael B., "New Grads Drawn to New Business," Boston Globe, June 7, 2013. Endnote 131.

Fass, Paula, Child Kidnapping in America (Web: Ohio State University, January 2010). http://origins.osu.edu /article/child-kidnapping-america. Endnote 38.

Fields, Bea, Wilder, Scott, Bunch, Jim and Newbold, Rob, Millennial Leaders: Success Stories From Today's Most Brilliant Generation Y Leaders (Buffalo Grove, IL: Writers of the Round Table Press, 2008). Endnote 131.

First Command Financial Services, "7 Reasons to Keep Working During Retirement," Journey Magazine, 2011. http://fcjourney .com/seven-reasons-keep-working-during-retirement. Endnote 12.

Fitzgerald, Jay, "A College Degree is Costly, But It Pays Off Over Time", Boston Sunday Globe, October 12, 2012. Endnote 63.

Fitzgerald, Jay, "It's Tough Out There: Graduates Entering the

Workforce are Finding More Opportunities—if they Look Hard Enough," Boston Sunday Globe, April 28, 2013. http://www.bostonglobe.com/business/2013/04/27/thaw-job-market-for-new-college-grads-but-still-cold-out-there/nA2oN2t5UIB6kPxjxJO5VM/story.html. Endnote 59.

Flaherty, Colleen, "Working Way Past 65," Inside Higher Ed, June 17, 2013. http://www.insidehighered.com/news/2013/06/17/data-suggest-baby-boomer-faculty-are-putting-retirement. Endnote 10.

Fox, Adrienne, "Mixing it Up: With four—almost five—generations in the workplace, tensions can arise through misunderstandings and miscommunication," HR Magazine, May 2011. Endnotes 1, 11, 88, 125, 142.

Freedman, Judith Finer, Ed.D, Cracking the Code: Unlocking the Potential of Future Leaders in the Legal Profession (West, 2010). Endnote 97.

Gardner, Phil, Parent Involvement in the College Recruiting Process: To What Extent? (Web: Collegiate Employment Research Institute, 2007). http://ceri.msu.edu/publications/pdf/ceri2-07.pdf. Endnote 49.

Garven, Sena, Wood, James, Malpass, Roy and Shaw, John, "More Than Suggestion: The Effect of Interviewing Techniques From the McMartin Preschool Case," Journal of Applied Psychology 83(3). Endnote 37.

"Generation Jobless," The Economist, April 27, 2013. Endnote 58.

Gerson, Kathleen, The Unfinished Revolution: How a New Generation is Reshaping Family, Work, and Gender in America (New York: Oxford University Press, 2010). Endnotes 147, 163, 185, 186.

Girls20Summit, accessed Oct. 4, 2013. http://www.girls20summit.com/about/. Endnote 131.

Glatt v. Fox Searchlight Pictures, Inc., US District Court for the Southern District of New York (decision dated June 11, 2013). Endnote 120.

Goff, Keli, Party Crashing: How the Hip-Hop Generation Declared Political Independence (New York: Basic Civitas Books, 2008). Endnote 7.

Goldwasser, Amy, Red: Teenage Girls in America Write on What Fires Up Their Lives Today (New York, NY: Penguin Publishing, 2007). Endnote 82.

Goudreau, Jenna, "The Seven Ways Your Boss is Judging Your Appearance," Forbes Magazine, November 30, 2012. http://www.forbes.com/sites/jennagoudreau /2012/11/30/the-seven-ways-your-boss-is-judging-your-appearance/. Endnotes 100, 104.

Gray, Peter, "As Children's Freedom Has Declined, So Has Their Creativity," Psychology Today, September 17, 2012. http://www .psychologytoday.com/blog/freedom-learn/201209/children-s -freedom-has-declined-so-has-their-creativity. Endnote 39.

Gray, Peter, "Freedom to Learn: The Decline of Play and Rise in Children's Mental Disorders," Psychology Today, January 26, 2010. http://www.psychologytoday.com /blog/freedom-learn/201001/the-decline-play-and-rise-in-childrens-mental-disorders. Endnote 39.

Gray, Peter, "Why Have Trustful Parenting & Children's Freedom Declined," Psychology Today, July 29, 2009. http://www .psychologytoday.com/blog/freedom-learn/200907/why-have-trustful-parenting-children-s-freedom-declined. Endnote 39.

Greenhouse, Steven, "Charlie Rose Show Agrees to Pay Up to $250,000 to Settle Interns Lawsuit," The New York Times, December 20, 2013. http://mediadecoder .blogs.nytimes.com/2012/12/20/charlie-rose-show-agrees-to-pay-up-to-250000-to-settle-interns-lawsuit/ ?smid=tw-mediadecodernyt&seid=auto&_r=0. Endnote 121.

Halicks, Richard, "Teens of Means: Some affluent parents give their kids everything—except the ability to connect with other people," Atlanta Journal-Constitution, July 23, 2006. Endnote 144.

Halpert, Julie, 11 Ways Parents Can Hurt Their Child's Job Chances (Web: The Fiscal Times, June 18, 2013). http://www .thefiscaltimes.com/Articles/2013/06/18/10-Ways-Parents-Can-Hurt-Their-Childs-Job-Chances.aspx#page1. Endnote 49.

Hampl, Alex, "Twenty-Five Under 25," Sports Illustrated,

October 30, 2013. http://sportsillustrated.cnn.com
/specials/25under25/index.html. Endnote 131.

Harvard Institute of Politics, Solid Majority of Young Adults
Concerned About Meeting Their Bills and Obligations (Web:
Harvard Institute, March 9, 2010). http://www.iop.harvard
.edu/march-9-2010-majority-young-adults-concerned-about-
meeting-their-bills-and-obligations-harvard-poll. Endnote 74.

Heller, Nathan, "Semi-Charmed Life," The New Yorker
Magazine, January 14, 2013. Endnote 6.

Henig, Robin Marantz, "What Is It About 20-Somethings?", New
York Times Magazine, August 22, 2010. Endnote 41.

Hennick, Calvin, "Fresh Approach to Career Path," The
Boston Globe, January 3, 2013. Endnotes 5, 126.

Hewlett, Sylvia, "The 'Me' Generation Gives Way to the
'We' Generation," Financial Times, June 19, 2009.
http://www.ft.com/cms/s/0/f8b0aca4-5c69-11de-aea3-
00144feabdc0.html#axzz2i6l6tvzf. Endnote 134.

Hewlett, Sylvia Ann, Sherbin, Laura and Sumberg, Karen,
"How Gen Y & Boomers Will Reshape Your Agenda,"
HBR (July-August 2009). Endnotes 11, 178.

Hingston, Sandy, "Is It Just Us, Or Are Kids Getting Really
Stupid?", Philadelphia Magazine, November 26, 2010.
http://www.phillymag.com/articles/feature-is-it-just-
us-or-are-kids-getting-really-stupid/. Endnote 77.

Hite, F. Brittany, Employers Rethink How They Give Feedback
(Web: Wall Street Journal, October 13, 2008). http://online.wsj
.com/news/articles/SB122385967800027549. Endnote 180.

Holder-Winfield, Natalie, Recruiting and Retaining a
Diverse Workforce: New Rules for a New Generation
(Portland, OR: First Books, 2007). Endnote 6.

Hoover, Eric, "College Confidential: a Field Guide," Chronicle
of Higher Education, April 29, 2013. http://chronicle.com/
article/College-Confidential-A-Field/138865/. Endnote 47.

Horovitz, Bruce, After Gen X, Millennials, What
Should Next Generation Be? (Web: USA Today,

May 4, 2012). http://usatoday30.usatoday.com
/money/advertising/story/2012-05-03/naming-the-
next-generation/54737518/1. Endnote 9.

Howe, Neil, "The Kids Are Alright, But Their
Parents …", Washington Post, December 8, 2008.
http://articles.washingtonpost.com/2008-12-07/
opinions/36778799_1_generation-jones-generation-
xers-dumbest-generation. Endnote 65.

Howe, Neil and Strauss, William, Millennials Rising:
The Next Great Generation (New York: Vintage
Books, 2000). Endnotes 26, 30, 36, 40, 42, 43.

Jay, Meg, The Defining Decade: Why your Twenties Matter—
and how to Make the Most of them Now (New York,
NY: Hatchette Book Group, 2012). Endnote 112.

Kaminer, Ariel, "On a College Waiting List? Sending Cookies
Isn't Going to Help," New York Times, May 11, 2013.
http://www.nytimes.com/2013/05/12/education/on-the-
waiting-list-some-college-applicants-try-a-little-dazzle
.html?pagewanted=all&_r=0. Endnote 48.

Khan, Joseph P., "The Broke Generation," Boston
Globe, May 29, 2012. Endnote 61.

Kotkin, Joel, "Generation Screwed," Newsweek
(July 23 & 30, 2012), 42. Endnote 51.

Krueger, Jerry and Killham, Emily, "Why Dilbert Is Right," Gallup
Business Journal, March 9, 2006. http://businessjournal.gallup
.com/content/21802/why-dilbert-right.aspx. Endnote 149.

Kurland, Ann Trieger, "Her Teenage Invention
Flowers into Food Spoilage Prevention," Boston
Globe, March 14, 2012. Endnote 131.

Kurz, Christian, "The Next Normal: An Unprecedented Look
at Millennials Worldwide," Viacom, November 15, 2012.
http://blog.viacom.com/2012/11/the-next-normal-an-
unprecedented-look-at-millennials-worldwide/. Endnote 23.

Lancaster, Lynne C. and Stillman, David, When Generations
Collide: Who They Are. Why They Clash. How to

Solve the Generational Puzzle at Work (New York: HarperCollins Publishers Inc., 2002). Endnotes 2, 17.

Levanon, Gad, and Cheng, Ben, Trapped on the Worker Treadmill? (Web: The Conference Board, Feb 1, 2013). http://www.conference-board.org/press /pressdetail.cfm?pressid=4716. Endnote 11.

Levit, Alexandra and Licina, Sanja, How the Recession Shaped Millennial and Hiring Manager Attitudes about Millennials' Future Careers (Web: Career Advisory Board, 2012). http://newsroom.devry.edu/images/20004/Future%20of %20Millennial%20Careers%20Report.pdf. Endnote 141.

Lowe, Chelsea, "For Millennials, Salary is not All," Boston Business Journal, June 15, 2012. http://www.bizjournals .com/boston/print-edition/2012/06/15/for-millennials-salary-is-not-all.html?page=all. Endnote 70.

Lowrey, Annie, "Do Millennials Stand a Chance in the Real World?", New York Times, March 26, 2013. http://www .nytimes.com/2013/03/31/magazine/do-millennials-stand-a -chance-in-the-real-world.html. Endnote 51.

Malcolm, Hadley, "Millennials Struggle with Financial Literacy," USA Today, April 24, 2012. http://usatoday30.usatoday .com/money/perfi/basics/story/2012-04-23/millenials-financial-knowledge/54494856/1. Endnote 170.

Marek, Lynne, "Frivolous Suits: Judges Wonder, 'Who Dressed You, Counselor'?", The National Law Journal, May 21, 2009. http://www.law.com/jsp/article.jsp?id=1202484611544 &slreturn=20130918162428. Endnote 106.

Martin, Courtney E., Do It Anyway: The New Generation of Activists (Boston, MA: Beacon Press, 2010). Endnote 137.

Martin, Judith, Pathways After Graduation Study: Year Two for the Class of 2009; Year One for the Class of 2010 (Pathways, July 2013). Endnote 141.

Mayo, Keenan, "Why Interns are Suing 'Saturday Night Live,' Hollywood, and Other Dream Employers," Business Week, July 12, 2013. http://www.businessweek.com/articles

/2013-07-12/why-interns-are-suing-saturday-night-live-hollywood-and-other-dream-employers. Endnote 119.

McCafferty, Dennis, "Some CEOs Disregard Social-Media Reputation," CIO Insight Blog, December 31, 2012. http://www.cioinsight .com/it-strategy/business-intelligence/slideshows/some-ceos-disregard-social-media-reputation, which references the following infographic: http://zenogroup.com/content/sites /default/files/Zeno%20Group%20Digital%20Readiness %20Survey%20infographic_with%20links.pdf. Endnote 87.

McCullough, David, Jr., "You're Not Special," Swellesley Report, June 5, 2012. http://theswellesleyreport.com/2012/06/ wellesley-high-grads-told-youre-not-special/. Endnote 69.

Mishel, Lawrence, "Entry-Level Workers' Wages Fell in Last Decade," Economic Policy Institute, March 7, 2012. http://www.epi .org/publication/ib327-young-workers-wages/. Endnote 55.

Mitter, Siddhartha, "Prince: a Gen X icon?", The Boston Globe, March 22, 2013. Endnote 15.

Mullen, John K., "Digital Natives Are Slow To Pick Up Nonverbal Cues," HBR Blog Network, Mar. 16, 2012. http://blogs.hbr .org/2012/03/digital-natives-are-slow-to-pi/. Endnote 85.

Murphy, Evelyn with Graff, E.J., Getting Even: Why Women Don't Get Paid Like Men and What to Do About It (New York, NY: Touchstone, 2005). Endnote 164.

Nestor-Harper, Mary, Infographic Shows What HR Pros Think of Millennials (Web: TheCareerNetwork, June 2013). http://www.beyond.com/articles/infographic-shows-what-hr-pros-think-of-12625-article.html. Endnote 124.

"Net Gains or Net Losses: Is the Internet Changing Human Nature?", ParisTech Review, Jun. 24, 2010. http://www .paristechreview.com/2010/06/24/gains-losses-is-the-internet-changing-human-nature/. Endnotes 64, 85.

Norton, Arthur J. and Miller, Louisa F., "Marriage, Divorce, and Remarriage in the 1990's," U.S. Department of Commerce (October, 1992). Endnote 16.

O'Brien, Meredith, "Letting Kids Roam Alone: Parents who

give Kids Independence face Intense Scrutiny," MetroWest Daily News, July 12, 2009, Sunday Opinion. Endnote 38.

Ohlemacher, Stephen, "Many Baby Boomers Plan to Retire Late," CBS News, February 11, 2009. http://www.cbsnews .com/2100-201_162-2917476.html. Endnote 10.

Palfry, John and Gasser, Urs, Born Digital: Understanding the First Generation of Digital Native (New York: Basic Books, 2008). Endnote 79.

Pimentel, David, "Criminal Child Neglect and the 'Free Range Kid': Is Overprotective Parenting the New Standard of Care," Utah Law Review 2012 (at 947). Endnote 39.

Piper Jaffray Companies, Taking Stock With Teens Survey Summary: 2013 (Web: Piper Jaffray, 2013). http://www.piperjaffray.com /2col.aspx?id=287&releaseid=1805593. Endnote 101.

Pitt-Catsouphes, Marcie and Matz-Costa, Christina, Engaging the 21st Century Multi-Generational Workforce: Findings from the Age & Generations Study (Web: The Sloan Center on Aging and Work at Boston College, 2009). http://www .bc.edu/content/dam/files/research_sites/agingandwork/pdf /publications/IB20_Engagement.pdf. Endnotes 148, 187.

Pitt-Catsouphes, Marcie, Matz-Costa, Christina and Besen, Elyssa, Workplace Flexibility: Findings from the Age & Generations Study (Web: The Sloan Center on Aging and Work at Boston College, 2009). http://www.bc.edu /content/dam/files/research_sites/agingandwork/pdf/ publications/IB19_WorkFlex.pdf. Endnotes 161, 165

Pollack, Lindsey, Getting from College to Career: Your Essential Guide to Succeeding in the Real World (New York, NY: HarperBusiness, 2012). Endnote 171.

Powers, Martine, Hard-Charging Start for Youngest Mayor, Boston Globe (July 24, 2012). Endnote 131.

PricewaterhouseCoopers, Millennials at Work: Reshaping the Workplace (Web: PwC, 2011). http://www.pwc.com/en_M1/ m1/services/consulting/documents/millennials-at-work.pdf. Endnotes 27, 60, 75, 86, 91, 129, 133, 168, 169, 173.

PricewaterhouseCoopers, Talent Mobility 2020: The Next
    Generation of International Assignments (Web: PwC, 2010).
    http://www.pwc.com/gx/en/managing-tomorrows-people/
    future-of-work/pdf/talent-mobility-2020.pdf. Endnote 133.
PricewaterhouseCoopers, University of Southern California
    and London Business School, PwC's NextGen: A Global
    Generational Study (Web: PwC, 2013). http://www.pwc
    .com/en_GX/gx/hr-management-services/pdf/pwc-nextgen-
    study-2013.pdf. Endnotes 34, 123, 128, 145, 159, 160.
Radcliffe Public Policy Center, Life's Work: Generational Attitudes
    toward Work and Life Integration (2000). Endnote 19.
Reeve, Elspeth, "Every Every Every Generation Has Been
    The Me Me Me Generation," Atlantic Wire, May 9,
    2013. http://www.theatlanticwire.com/national/2013
    /05/me-generation-time/65054/. Endnote 73.
Reiser, Rachel, Millennials on Board: The Impact of the
    Rising Generation on the Workplace (Acton, MA:
    First Printing Inc., 2010). Endnotes 5, 78.
Reuters, "Make Way for the Millennial Millionaires," Fiscal
    Times, August 5, 2013. http://www.thefiscaltimes
    .com/Articles/2013/08/05/Make-Way-for-the-
    Millennial-Millionaires. Endnote 131.
Rikleen, Lauren Stiller, Cheating and the Millennial
    Generation (Web: The Podium, Boston Globe On-Line,
    Sept. 14, 2012). http://www.bostonglobe.com/opinion
    /2012/09/14/cheating-and-millennial-generation/
    imgghIcKXbdBAGuFKmZQaN/story.html. Endnote 115.
Rikleen, Lauren Stiller, Closing the Gap: A Road Map for Achieving
    Gender Pay Equity in Law Firm Partner Compensation
    (Web: American Bar Association, 2013). http://www
    .americanbar.org/content/dam/aba/administrative/women
    /closing_the_gap.authcheckdam.pdf. Endnote 164.
Rikleen, Lauren Stiller, Creating Tomorrow's Leaders: The
    Expanding Roles of Millennials in the Workplace
    (Boston College Center for Work & Family).

https://www.bc.edu/content/dam/files/centers/cwf/pdf/BCCWF
%20EBS-Millennials%20FINAL.pdf. Endnote 181.

Robbins, Alexandra, The Overachievers: The Secret Lives of Driven
Kids (New York, NY: Hyperion, 2006). Endnote 65.

Robbins, Alexandra and Wilner, Abby, Quarterlife Crisis:
The Unique Challenges of Life in your Twenties (New
York, NY: Penguin Inc., 2001). Endnote 116.

Rosenberg, Alyssa, "Why Time Magazine Put A Woman On The
Cover Of Its Issue Complaining About Millennials," Think
Progress, May 9, 2013. http://thinkprogress.org/alyssa/2013
/05/09/1987901/why-time-magazine-put-a-woman-on-the-
cover-of-its-issue-complaining-about-millenials/. Endnote 84.

Rosenbloom, Stephanie, "Mommy and Daddy's Little
Life Coach," New York Times, April 5, 2007.
http://www.nytimes.com/2007/04/05/fashion/05advice
.html?pagewanted=all&_r=0. Endnotes 46, 102.

Schaefer, Gayla, "Workplace Challenges Coming," Florida
Today, April 9, 2007. http://www.floridatoday
.com/article/20070409/BUSINESS/704090316
/Workplace-challenges-coming. Endnote 20.

Schawbel, Dan, Me 2.0: 4 Steps to Building your Future
Revised and Updated Edition (New York, NY:
Kaplan Publishing, 2010). Endnote 67.

Schawbel, Dan, Millennial Branding Student Employment Gap
Study Summary Report (Web: Millennial Branding, May 14,
2012). http://millennialbranding.com/2012/05/millennial-
branding-student-employment-gap-study/. Endnote 117.

Schawbel, Dan, Promote Yourself: The New Rules for Career Success
(New York, NY: St. Martin's Press, 2013). Endnote 67.

Seligson, Hannah, "No Jobs? Young Graduates Make
Their Own," New York Times, December 11, 2010.
http://www.nytimes.com/2010/12/12/business
/12yec.html?pagewanted=all. Endnote 132.

Seligson, Hannah, "The Age of the Permanent Intern,"
Washingtonian Magazine, February 6, 2013.

http://www.washingtonian.com/articles/people/the-age-of-the-permanent-intern/. Endnotes 117, 118.

Settersten, Richard and Ray, Barbara E., Not Quite Adults: Why 20-Somethings are Choosing a Slower Path to Adulthood and Why It's Good for Everyone (New York, NY: Random House Inc., 2010). Endnote 63.

Sibson Consulting, Millennials in the Sales Force: It's Time to Get to Know This Generation (Web: The Segal Group, April 2009). http://www.sibson.com/services /sales-force-effectiveness/Millennials-in-the-Sales-Force-Survey-Results.pdf. Endnotes 33, 122, 127.

Sloan Center on Aging & Work, Boston College, Through a Different Looking Glass: The Prism of Age, (Web: The Sloan Center on Aging & Work, 2012). http://www.bc .edu/content/dam/files/research_sites/agingandwork/pdf /publications/RB03_PrismofAge.pdf. Endnote 4.

Smith, Emily Esfahani, "Meaning is Healthier Than Happiness," The Atlantic, August 1, 2013. http://www.theatlantic .com/health/archive/2013/08/meaning-is-healthier-than-happiness/278250/. Endnote 135.

Smith, W. Stanton, Decoding Generational Differences: Changing your Mindset … Without Losing your Mind (Greenville, SC: W. Stanton Smith LLC, 2010). Endnote 180.

Social Science Research and Evaluation, Inc., Data from the 2001-2002 Wayland Adolescent Behavior Survey (Print: Wayland High School, 2002). Endnote 146.

Sodexo, Workplace Trends 2013 (Web: Sodexo, 2013). http://viewer .zmags.com/publication/f045b66f#/f045b66f/2. Endnotes 79, 136.

Steinhorn, Leonard, The Greater Generation: In Defense of the Baby Boom Legacy (New York: Thomas Dunne Books, 2006). Endnote 13.

Steuerle, Eugene, McKernan, Signe-Mary, Radcliffe, Caroline and Zhang, Sisi, Lost Generations? Wealth Building among Young Americans (Web: Urban Institute, March 2013). http://www.urban.org/UploadedPDF

/412766-Lost-Generations-Wealth-Building-
  Among-Young-Americans.pdf. Endnote 51.
Sujansky, Joanne G. and Ferri-Reed, Jan, Keeping The
  Millennials: Why Companies Are Losing Billions In
  Turnover To This Generation—And What To Do About It
  (Hoboken, NJ: John Wiley & Sons, 2009). Endnote 140.
Suleman, Razor and Nelson, Bob, "Motivating the Millennials:
  Tapping into the Potential of the Youngest Generation",
  Leader to Leader Journal, No. 62, Fall 2011 (Web:
  Frances Hesselbein Leadership Institute, 2011).
  http://www.hesselbeininstitute.org/knowledgecenter/
  journal.aspx?ArticleID=889. Endnotes 143, 174.
Swidey, Neil, "When you Wish Upon A Star," Boston
  Globe, May 27, 2012. Endnote 72.
Taris, Toon and Schreurs, Paul, Well-Being and
  Organizational Performance: An Organizational-Level
  Test of the Happy-Productive Worker Hypothesis,
  Work & Stress 23:2 (2009). Endnote 166.
Taylor, Paul and Keeter, Scott, Millennials: Confident.
  Connected. Open to Change (Web: PEW Research
  Center, 2010). http://www.pewsocialtrends.org/files/2010
  /10/millennials-confident-connected-open-to-change
  .pdf. Endnotes 26, 28, 44, 53, 54, 80, 105, 110, 151.
Taylor, Paul and Morin, Rich, Home for the Holidays ... and
  Every Other Day: Recession Brings Many Young People
  Back to the Nest (Web: PEW Research Center,
  November 24, 2009). http://www.pewsocialtrends
  .org/files/2010/10/millennials-confident-
  connected-open-to-change.pdf. Endnote 56.
"Teenage Consumer Spending Statistics," Statistic Brain,
  September 8, 2013. http://www.statisticbrain.com/
  teenage-consumer-spending-statistics/. Endnote 102.
Teitell, Beth, "In Season of Resolutions, Parents Line Up
  to Fess Up," Boston Globe, December 28, 2012.
  http://www.bostonglobe.com/lifestyle/2012/12/28/

did-care-more-than-son-did-made-middle-school-basketball-team
/b5uAngPtYfIj258H3V4C2J/story.html. Endnote 47.

"The Kids Aren't All Right," Boston Globe,
November 16, 2011. Endnote 61.

Traister, Rebecca, "Where Did all the Angry Young Women
Go?", Salon, April 20, 2010. http://www.salon.com
/2010/04/20/next_generation_abortion/. Endnote 31.

Tulgan, Bruce, Not Everyone Gets A Trophy: How to Manage
Generation Y (San Francisco: Jossey-Bass, 2009). Endnote 111.

Turkle, Sherry, "The Documented Life," The New York
Times, December 15, 2013. http://www.nytimes.com
/2013/12/16/opinion/the-documented-life.html?_r=0.
A version of this op-ed appears in print on December
16, 2013, on page A25 of the New York edition with
the headline: The Documented Life. Endnote 83.

Twenge, Jean M., Generation Me: Why Today's Young Americans Are
More Confident, Assertive, Entitled—and More Miserable Than
Ever Before (New York, NY: Free Press, 2006). Endnotes 35, 83.

Wagner, Donna, "The Broken System of Long-Term Care in America,"
The Sloan Center on Aging & Work at Boston College,
September 18, 2013. http://agingandwork.bc.edu/blog/the-
broken-system-of-long-term-care-in-america/. Endnote 162.

Wallace, Kelly, "Bring Your Parents to Work Day: Positive Trend or
Helicopter Parenting?", CNN Living. http://www.cnn.com/2013
/11/07/living/linkedin-bring-your-parents-work-day/. Endnote 50.

Wargo, Eric, "How Many Seconds to a First Impression?",
Association for Psychological Science Observer 19.7,
July, 2006. http://www.psychologicalscience.org/index
.php/publications/observer/2006/july-06/how-many-
seconds-to-a-first-impression.html. Endnote 100.

Washington, Richard, "Baby Boomers Beware: Millennials
are Coming," Market Research Blog, April 17, 2013.
http://blog.marketresearch.com/blog-home-page
/bid/264242/Baby-Boomers-Beware-Millennials-Are-
Coming-MarketResearch-com. Endnotes 14, 62, 66.

Waterhouse, Gail, "A Higher Degree of Debt," Boston
    Sunday Globe, August 25, 2013. Endnote 61.

Waxman, Simon, "In Defense of my Generation," Cognoscenti,
    September 26, 2012. http://cognoscenti.wbur.org/2012/09
    /26/millennial-media-simon-waxman. Endnote 114.

Wickersham, Joan, "The Myth of the Frankenstudent,"
    Boston Globe, April 15, 2010. http://www.boston.com
    /bostonglobe/editorial_opinion/oped/articles/2010/04
    /15/the_myth_of_the_frankenstudent/. Endnote 47.

Willis, Janine and Todorov, Alexander, "First Impressions: Making
    up your Mind After a 100-Ms Exposure to a Face," Princeton
    University Department of Psychological Science 17.7, July
    2006. http://psych.princeton.edu/psychology/research/todorov
    /pdf/Willis&Todorov-PsychScience.pdf. Endnote 100.

Winograd, Morley and Hais, Michael D., Millennial Makeover:
    MySpace, YouTube & the Future of American Politics
    (Piscataway, NJ: Fourth Printing, 2008). Endnote 71.

Zackin, Martha J., "Unpaid Internships May Be More Costly
    Than You May Think," Employment Matters Blog,
    June 11, 2013. http://www.employmentmattersblog
    .com/2013/06/unpaid-internships-may-be-more-
    costly-than-you-may-think/. Endnote 120.

Zukin, Cliff, Szeltner, Mark, Talent Report: What Workers Want in
    2012 (Web: Net Impact and Rutgers University, May 2012).
    http://www.heldrich.rutgers.edu/sites/default/files/content/Net
    _Impact_Talent_Report_0.pdf. Endnotes 134, 152, 153, 156, 182.